Enforcement Instruments for Social Human Rights
along Supply Chains

Labor and Globalization

Volume 9
Edited by Christoph Scherrer

Christoph Scherrer
(Ed.)

Enforcement Instruments for Social Human Rights along Supply Chains

Rainer Hampp Verlag	Augsburg, München 2017

Bibliographic information published by the Deutsche Nationalbibliothek

Deutsche Nationalbibliothek lists this publication in the Deutsche Nationalbibliografie; detailed bibliographic data are available in the Internet at http://dnb.d-nb.de.

ISBN 978-3-86618-894-5
Labor and globalization: ISSN 2196-5382
First published 2017

Cover photo: A garment worker in the Dharavi locality of Mumbai, 2016, by Christoph Scherrer.

© 2017   Rainer Hampp Verlag   Augsburg, München
         Vorderer Lech 35   86150 Augsburg, Germany
         www.Hampp-Verlag.de

All rights reserved. No part of this publication may be reprinted or reproduced or utilized in any form or by any electronic, mechanical, or other means, now known or hereafter invented, including photocopying and recording, or in any information storage or retrieval system, without permission in writing from the publisher.

In case of complaints please contact Rainer Hampp Verlag.

Contents

List of Figures and Tables iv

Acknowledgments v

Notes on Contributors vi

1. Introduction 1
    Christoph Scherrer
2. Economic Arguments for International Workers' Rights 6
    Christoph Scherrer
3. Overview of Enforcement Instruments for Workers' Rights along
    Supply Chains 18
    Stefan Beck / Christoph Scherrer
4. Instruments of German Foreign Economic Policy for Promoting
    Co-Determination along Supply Chains 50
    Alison Schulz
5. The Enforcement of Workers' Rights through Conditional or Promotional
    Trade Agreements: A Comparison of US and EU Social Chapters 155
    Madelaine Moore
6. Corporate Due Diligence: A Contribution to the Enforcement of
    Human Rights? 186
    Christian Scheper

List of Figures and Tables

Figures

Figure 3.1: ILO member countries with trade agreements including labor provisions by region, 2013 21

Figure 3.2: Increase in number of labor provisions in bilateral and regional trade agreements, 1990 – 2013 22

Figure 4.1: Review Process of KfW Bank's Export Financing 77

Figure 4.2: The different evaluation standards 79

Figure 4.3: Due Diligence Procedure for Export Credit Guarantees, Investment Guarantees and Untied Loan Guarantees 85

Tables

Table 3.1: Labor Provisions in US PTAs 23

Table 3.2: Different types of labor provisions in EU trade agreements 25

Table 3.3: Comparison of Basic Elements for a Labor Chapter 29

Acknowledgments

This volume brings together a few very recent studies on the enforcement issue of social human rights. While each of them is offering valuable insights in its own right, together they provide a fuller picture of the current debates on the instruments necessary for improving the working conditions of workers in global supply chains. Therefore, I asked the authors of these studies whether they would be interested in contributing an updated version of their studies to a volume on enforcement instruments for social human rights along supply chains. I am pleased that the authors responded positively and also got permission from the organizations that previously published their studies as working papers.

The contribution of Stefan Beck and me is taken from a longer study commissioned by ACTRAV of the International Labor Organization. It was published as a Global Labour University working paper in October 2016 ("Trade regulation and global production networks"). The contribution of Alison Schultz is a translation of a study published in German (Schultz und Scherrer, 2017: Mitbestimmung in Zulieferketten. Instrumente der deutschen Außenwirtschaftspolitik, Hans-Böckler-Stiftung, Working Paper Forschungsförderung Nr. 033) with the financial support of the Hans-Böckler-Foundation. The contribution of Madelaine Moore builds on a study commissioned by the Friedrich-Ebert-Foundation for its project on "Core Labour Standards Plus". The chapter by Christian Scheper is a modified and updated version of Part I of the study "Corporate Obligations with Regard to Human Rights Due Diligence", published by the Friedrich-Ebert-Foundation in 2015 (and co-authored with R. Grabosch). My own brief chapter on the economic arguments for international workers' rights builds on a number of previous publications.

I thank Kosmas Kota for translating the long study by Alison Schultz and the Hans-Böckler-Stiftung for funding the English language translation. I like to express my thanks to Nicole Magura for formatting the manuscripts.

Many thanks also to Rainer Hampp at Hampp Verlag who was enthusiastic about the book project from the very beginning. Financial support was granted by the International Center for Development and Decent Work which is one of the five Centers of Excellence for Exchange and Development program managed by the German Academic Exchange Service (DAAD) using funds from the German Federal Ministry for Economic Cooperation and Development (BMZ).

Christoph Scherrer   Berlin, May 2017

Notes on Contributors

Stefan Beck is an adjunct lecturer at the University of Kassel, focused on political economy and comparative research on capitalism. He holds a PhD in political science from Kassel University. He published on the export surpluses of Germany ("Vom fordistischen zum kompetitiven Merkantilismus", Metropolis) and issues of international trade in general.

Madelaine Moore is an associate PhD fellow at the International Center for Development and Decent Work (ICDD) at the University of Kassel. She received her MA in Labor Policies and Globalization from the Berlin School of Economics and Law and the University of Kassel as part of the Global Labour University. The PhD thesis is about struggles over access to water from a Social Reproduction Feminist perspective. Her areas of interest include social movements, Social Reproduction Feminism, Labour Rights and Global Value Networks.

Christian Scheper is a postdoctoral researcher at the Institute for Development and Peace at the University of Duisburg-Essen. His work focuses on human rights, transnational corporations and the politics of global production. He holds a PhD in political science from the University of Kassel. In his dissertation he analyzed the discourse on corporate responsibility for human rights in the context of global production networks.

Christoph Scherrer is director of the International Center for Development and Decent Work at Kassel University. He works on issues of the international political economy and labor. His most recent books are: Public Banks in the Age of Financialization: A Comparative Perspective (Edward Elgar; forthcoming), Combating Inequality: The Global North and South (co-edited with A.Gallas/H. Herr/F. Hoffer, Routledge, 2015), Financial Cultures and Crisis Dynamics (co-edited with B. Jessop/B. Young, Routledge, 2014)

Alison Schultz is a master student of Global Political Economy at the University of Kassel. She has published on the Latin American debt crisis (with L. Rama Iglesias "What Kind of Challenges does a Debtors' Cartel Face? An Analysis of the Latin American Debt Crisis", New Research in Global Political Economy 2015/2) and is currently working on fossil fuel divestment.

1. Introduction

Christoph Scherrer

Dire working conditions are prevalent in the labor-intensive segments of global value chains. Suicides, such as those that occurred at the some of the Foxconn consumer electronics assembly plants in China, and accidents such as the collapse of the Rana Plaza garment factory in Bangladesh, have made consumers more attentive to the plight of workers. For many years, trade unions and human rights nongovernmental organizations have called on corporations and governments to take responsibility for ensuring the human rights of the workers in sweatshops around the world. In response, corporations have developed internal codes of conduct and have hired corporate social responsibility staff and consultants to certify their suppliers' labor relations. By signing on to the United Nations Covenant on Economic, Social and Cultural Rights and membership to the International Labor Organization, governments have committed themselves to respect social and human rights, encompassing freedom of association and the right to organize and bargain collectively. Economically advanced countries have also written OECD guidelines for businesses outside their home countries. And recently all member countries of the United Nations have underlined their commitments to the human rights of workers by including the goal to "Promote sustained, inclusive and sustainable economic growth, full and productive employment and decent work for all" in the Sustainable Development Goals for 2030.

The rising awareness of the plight of workers in supply chains and the pronouncements of governments and corporations has not, however, resulted in improved working conditions for most of these workers. For example, the infamous Rana Plaza building had been inspected shortly before it collapsed. After this tragedy, efforts were mounted to prevent another disaster from occurring, but despite the great attention the tragedy gained, the preventative measures implemented fall far short from what is necessary (Khan/Wichterich 2015). Some governments have even committed themselves in trade agreements to uphold labor standards. Yet, the most famous and elaborate labor chapter in a trade agreement, the labor side agreement to the North American Free Trade Agreement (NAFTA) has not protected workers against labor rights violations (Greven 2012). In sum, corporations and governments have yet to take the step from pronouncements to the actual enforcement of their commitments.

The lack of enforcement of labor rights is the unresolved key issue in the world of work. It therefore deserves our attention. This volume takes up the challenge and explores the effectiveness and feasibility of the enforcement instruments under discussion. It starts with a general overview of the currently considered instruments for ensuring better working conditions and respect for the human rights of workers. Using the example of Germany, it then goes a step further and explores governmental instruments that although have the potential, are yet to be employed in favor of workers' rights. After these overviews the following two chapters deal with specific instruments. The first remains in the hands of governments; the instrument of a labor rights clause or social chapter in an international trade agreement. The second shifts the responsibility of safeguarding workers' rights along the supply chain to corporations by means of the concept of due diligence as espoused in the United Nations Guiding Principles on Business and Human Rights.

This volume uses the term "supply chain" for the complex national borders crossing production networks because it is the term the ILO has adopted. Within these "chains" the focus of this volume is on those segments which capture the least of the end value of the product in relationship to the human effort expended on it.

Summary of Chapters

The volume starts with a brief economic argument in favor of international workers' rights. Of course, international core labor rights are human rights and as such need to be respected. However, given the dominance of economic justifications for public policies, it is quite obvious that proponents of human rights stand a better chance to be heard if they can buttress their legal and normative reasoning with economic arguments. In his contribution *Christoph Scherrer* points out that the arguments of those advocating internationally binding workers' rights are based on a neo-institutional view of the market mechanism, while those of their critics stem from a neo-classical approach. A close reading of the core premises of the neoclassical approach, however, reveals that core workers' rights can also be justified within the neoclassical paradigm. Workers' rights are constitutive for markets (since the market is defined as an exchange of goods among free persons) and they can address market failures such as power imbalances or barriers to market exit. Workers' rights are an important precondition for the development of "human capital" and therefore contribute to economic efficiency.

If standards are beneficial from the neo-institutional as well as the neo-classical perspective, Scherrer asks, why then are they not voluntarily adopted? Besides political motives, he identifies economic reasons. Although the "high road" promises long-term benefits, it may incur short-term costs. While attempts to assess the cost impact of adherence to ILO conventions have not delivered reliable results thus far, even small differences in production costs can be expected to be decisive for market success. Most export goods from developing countries are sold to wholesalers or transnational corporations, which command a strong market position vis-à-vis the producers. This competitive situation, however, is the very reason why social standards have to be negotiated internationally. As long as it is possible for an economic region to gain a competitive advantage by undercutting the social standards in other regions, these other regions are in danger of losing their market share and hence employment opportunities. The greater the similarity between the competing regions with regard to factor endowment and market position, the more acute is this danger. It will be particularly high if market success depends on a single factor, namely low-skilled labor. In such a case, the danger from lower standards cannot be offset by other factors. This situation is particularly true of developing countries, which face the constant risk that new regions with an even larger reservoir of low skilled labor will break into the world market. For these reasons, Scherrer argues, developing countries cannot raise their social standards in isolation but only in conjunction with other countries by multilateral agreement.

The next chapter by *Stefan Beck* and *Christoph Scherrer* provides an overview of some of the recent initiatives to protect workers in supply chains and assesses their effectiveness. They cover labor chapters in bilateral trade agreements, the use of public procurement for the promotion of products made under "fair" conditions, Global Framework Agreements between global union federations and transnational corporations concerning workers' rights at subsidiaries, codes of conduct of companies, the United Nation's Guiding Principles on Business and Human Rights, and the stakeholder action of the German government. They conclude their overview with the rather discouraging insight that so far none of the many initiatives seem to be particularly effective. Global Framework Agreements seem to be quite effective as long as local actors are involved right from the start. The United Nations Guiding Principles hold some promise, so long as governments are willing to support and pressure companies to implement them. The same holds true for the social conditionality of public procurement. Most promising remains trade conditionality. However, if only a rather weak social chapter in a trade agreement is politically achievable, it risks justifying trade liberalization measures and the strengthening of investors' rights which will undercut the bargaining strength of labor. Therefore, Beck and Scherrer conclude that it is not sufficient to discuss specific instruments for the promotion of labor rights along value chains; one also needs to address the general governance of international trade and investments.

In her chapter *Alison Schultz* assesses the various initiatives the German government has undertaken to promote co-determination along global supply chains. Co-determination is a peculiar German labor market institution. At the plant level it provides for works councils and at the level of a company's board for the representation of workers. Its core underlying principles are, however, universal, i.e. the right of association, the right to trade union freedom and collective bargaining. As an instrument of social dialogue it also belongs to one of the four pillars of the ILO's decent work agenda. Schultz starts out with an overview of the German co-determination system and the current state of the research on co-determination in Germany. This is followed by an analysis of different policies of the federal government of Germany that are relevant to foreign economic policy, and have the potential to promote codetermination. She analyzes the instruments of the federal ministries of economics, finance, economic cooperation and development, and of foreign affairs and the Reconstruction Credit Institute. In addition, she explores the likely impact of the Comprehensive Economic and Trade Agreement (CETA) on labor rights.

The most striking aspect of Schultz' findings are the many underutilized instruments available to the German government for the promotion of core labor rights. For example, German companies have access to voluminous export financing facilities and investment guarantees. While this government support is conditional on the adherence to core labor rights, the review processes for environmental and social impacts ignore these rights. Other examples include the state-owned companies in the portfolio of the Ministry of Finance. While some of them, e.g. Deutsche Telekom, have been accused of violating labor rights at their subsidiaries abroad, the ministry denies responsibility. Schultz' examination of the CETA text comes to the conclusion that not only does the labor chapter in the trade agreement fall short on fulfilling the necessary criteria for effectively safeguarding the agreement itself, but also puts pressure on co-determination rights in the service sector where fundamental rights are already frequently violated.

The issue of labor chapters in trade agreements is the focus of *Madelaine Moore*'s contribution. Through assessing the existing studies on the impact of these chapters on labor rights conditions in supply chains, she concludes that there is little conclusive evidence of their effectiveness. Key to this is the lack of enforcement of the existing provisions in labor chapters. The enforcement of social chapters requires political will, attitudinal change and the presence of strong independent trade unions. Once there is the political will, then the design of the social clause can make a difference. As civil society and social partners play a crucial role in the functioning of labour provisions, they must be involved from the early stages. Moore argues that the agreements need to be coherent on numerous levels: concerning content (referring to the ILO core labor rights), the ministries involved in implementing the provisions of the chapter and the dispute settlement procedures. Furthermore, timeframes and outcomes need to be prescribed in the agreement in as clear and direct language as possible to avoid miscommunication or different interpretations. Consistency on these levels, Moore argues, is more important than sanctions.

The final chapter looks at the obligation for corporate due diligence arising for companies from intergovernmental human rights treaties. The UN Guiding

Principles on Business and Human Rights, which were endorsed by the Human Rights Council in 2011, introduced the concept of due diligence as part of corporate responsibility to respect human rights. *Christian Scheper* discusses the meaning and political significance of the concept, and assesses its effectiveness. He argues that the failure to specify the concrete obligations for companies and a lack of economic incentives for the comprehensive implementation of due diligence, renders this instruments rather ineffective. If it remains such a weak instrument, it might even increase transnational companies' political authority in the field of human rights interpretation instead of strengthening human rights along the supply chain. He also points out that a human rights policy that relies on corporate due diligence might become dependent on corporate forms of knowledge generation about labor rights conditions in transnational production networks. To become effective, Scheper argues, obligations have to be clearly specified and accompanied by clear sanctions if companies fail to meet them. In addition, transparency has to be guaranteed.

In sum, the volume shows that many instruments are available to governments but as long as the political will to make effective use of them is lacking, the enforcement of human rights along the supply chain remains unacceptably deficient. This in turn means that political pressure has to be built up to make it costly for political actors to ignore the plight of workers in labor-intensive segments of supply chains.

Literature

Greven, Thomas, 2012: Anforderungen an Legitimität und Effektivität von Sozialkapiteln in Handelsverträgen, in: Christoph Scherrer und Andreas Hänlein (Hrsg.), Sozialkapitel in Handelsabkommen. Begründungen und Vorschläge aus juristischer, ökonomischer und politologischer Sicht, Baden-Baden, Nomos, 83-102.

Khan, Mohd Raisul Islam and Christa Wichterich, 2015: Safety and labour conditions: the accord and the national tripartite plan of action for the garment industry of Bangladesh, Geneva: Global Labour University working paper No. 38.

2. Economic Arguments for International Workers' Rights

Christoph Scherrer

While international trade has resulted in great affluence for advanced capitalist countries, the ongoing liberalization of trade has not been accompanied by increases in prosperity everywhere. In many emerging market economies, working conditions, wages, and environmental standards have deteriorated, particularly in the plants producing for export. Every year, the International Trade Union Confederation (ITUC) documents widespread abuses of workers' rights.

According to the International Labor Organization (ILO), the following workers' rights are fundamental: freedom of association (Convention No. 87); the right to organize and bargain collectively (Convention No. 98); and prohibitions of forced labor (Convention Nos. 29 and 105), discrimination in employment (Convention Nos. 100 and 111), and child labor (Convention Nos. 138 and 182). The workers' rights covered by these core conventions are an inseparable part of human rights because they were adopted by consensus of ILO members, because they were ratified by most member countries, because they are covered by UN covenants and several human rights declarations, and because they have been reaffirmed again and again at international summits.

The problem with the ILO's conventions is not only that ratification is voluntary but that compliance is essentially also voluntary since the ILO has no enforcement mechanism to speak of. The court of public opinion is called upon through cautiously worded ILO reports on violations of individual countries.

The international labor movement has reacted to the ILO's ineffectiveness in dealing with labor rights abuses in the context of a rapidly globalizing economy by calling for a so-called social clause, i.e., a labor rights provision to be embodied in the World Trade Organization (WTO) and more recently in bilateral trade agreements. The Trans Pacific Partnership, initiated by the heads of the participating countries in October 2015, contains such a clause.

Predictably, employers' associations, many governments and the overwhelming majority of economists contend that trade agreements are not an appropriate means of enforcing minimum standards. However, critics do not stop at the question of how to enforce international social standards but also cast doubt on the usefulness of international standards in principle (e.g. Grossmann/Michaelis 2007). It is, therefore, necessary to examine whether international labor standards serve a useful economic purpose.

The question of whether international workers' rights are economically justified touches upon the fundamental economic understanding of the nature of the market as a social regulatory mechanism. In highly simplified terms, the various concepts of the market can be reduced to two paradigmatic approaches: the neo-classical and the neo-institutional »schools«.

From the neo-classical standpoint, welfare-increasing efficiency gains can be achieved in foreign trade only if unhindered trade permits product specialization on the basis of comparative cost advantages. Even in the case of infant industries, protection is considered to be a suboptimal policy. Any domestic distortions should be addressed by subsidies, rather than protection. The neo-institutional approach, by contrast, points to the destructive potential that market mechanisms can have in trade between nations because of the absence of a central regulatory authority at an international level. According to that view, foreign trade should, therefore, be flanked by domestic social legislation and regulated externally by multilateral agreements.

If criticism on purely ideological grounds is to be avoided, it is necessary to challenge these approaches on their own »home domain«. Therefore, I will show that, despite the prevalent opposing view among neo-classical economists, even neo-classical economics lends itself to theoretical justifications of international labor rights. Practitioners of institutional economics, of course, provide many reasons for taking the »high road« on labor rights. However, even an institutional viewpoint cannot rule out short-term costs for countries adhering to higher standards. In contrast to most economic treatises on international labor rights, I will argue that the question of competitiveness is not a North-South issue, but a South-South issue. Even small increases in costs due to higher standards will put the respective countries at a competitive advantage vis-à-vis their competitors at a similar level of industrial development. Therefore, developing countries are limited in their ability to raise labor standards on their own. This competitive situation, however, is the very reason why labor rights have to be negotiated internationally. Raising standards will have to be done in conjunction with other countries by multilateral agreement.

Neoclassical Defense of Workers' Rights

The criticism of social standards from a development perspective comes in two forms. The »hard« variant takes the position that industrial development requires a repressive employment regime. This has been promoted by Gary Fields but enjoys little support in the economic profession. The »soft« variant only demands that the employment regime contains no minimum standards that slow down development. It enjoys support among the majority of neoclassical economists.

The soft variant of the criticism takes issue with international standards mainly in the areas of pay, health, and safety at work (standards under consideration for some codes of conducts and social labeling programs), but also in the field of workers' rights. As a rule, it is argued that every officially imposed increase in production costs harms the prospects of sales in the world market, and hence the development prospects of the countries concerned. Every increase in labor costs supposedly jeopardizes the developing countries' main comparative advantage, namely abundant labor.

Core workers' rights can, however, also be justified within the neoclassical paradigm, mainly as responses to specific market failures. For example, freedom of association is a means to counterbalance the market power of employers. The bargaining power of an individual worker may be very limited faced with a powerful corporate employer or group of employers. The prohibition of forced labor and the exploitation of children belong to the core principles of the neoclassical market order: the market is defined as an exchange of goods among free persons. Furthermore, the adherence to these rights can enhance market efficiency. If discrimination is practiced, employment and earnings opportunities are allocated based on considerations not related to how well someone does a job. Anti-discrimination measures may facilitate the employment of individuals in jobs for which they are best suited. Collective bargaining institutions allow efficiency gains by encouraging workers to share their views with management about the running of the enterprise (Freeman/Medoff 1984).

Market failure is also to be found on the world market. Due to the leveling effect of competition, violations of core workers' rights in some countries can lead to their disrespect in one's own country (Leebron 1996: 54). In the extreme, a race to the bottom can ensue, pushing the standards of all trading partners to the lowest level. Most neoclassical economists reject the argument of a »race to the bottom« (e.g. Klevorick 1996). The term »destructive competition«, however, has been used within the neoclassical paradigm (Bator 1958; for a discussion within the debate on international labor standards, see Krueger 1996). If, for whatever reason, market exit is difficult, supply might stay the same or even expand despite lower prices. Destructive competition takes place in the labor market when workers offer their labor power at wages that do not cover their reproduction costs. An industrial worker, who cannot afford to send his children to vocational training programs, has not given his labor power according to his reproduction needs.

Rapid population growth contributes to a structural oversupply of labor power in the non-OECD world. Insufficient social standards are among the causes of population growth, especially the discrimination of women in education and in employment. Without welfare measures for old age, having a large number of children may remain attractive. Even without population growth labor power can be in oversupply. This is the case when industrial agriculture or world-class manufacturing meets subsistence or traditional industry. The displacement of the low-productivity subsistence agriculture or of inefficient industry (which had been protected by high transport costs or high tariffs) can release workers faster than the more productive market-oriented agriculture or modern manufacturing industry can absorb. This oversupply of labor power is exacerbated by impediments to market exit. The »doubly free« wage laborer usually lacks an alternative to wage labor. Once the subsistence economy has been left, return is almost impossible. For one, the subsistence agriculture will be pushed from the more fertile soil by the more productive industrial agriculture. The remaining pockets of subsistence agriculture will increasingly be less able to support its population and even less any returnees from urban areas. In addition, those who have left frequently find the hard work in traditional agriculture even less attractive than a life on the margins of big cities.

The lack of a social safety net as well as falling wages increase the need to expand the supply of labor power. Without corrective intervention, the impoverishment of large segments of workers can turn into a self-supporting downward spiral: an increase in labor supply forces real wages down, lower wages in turn increase the labor supply in the next round. In extreme cases, children are forced to work in order to secure the survival of the household. The more children are employed, the more adults are made redundant, which in turn forces them to send their daughters and sons to work. If the budget for education were to be cut because of a debt crisis, the number of children working would increase. This causal connection has been well documented, for example for Peru (Pollmann/Strack 2005: 26-27).

In order to restore an economic equilibrium according to market logic, some suppliers have to exit the market. Some neoclassical welfare theorists have rejected this solution even in the case of industrial plants. They argue that if the momentarily underutilized capacities would find demand at a later point in time, but if at that time it would be very costly to rebuild these capacities, then the regulation of competition is justified (Kahn 1971: 175). Market exit is not a viable solution for most wage earners for the above-mentioned reasons. Therefore, the regulation of competition is to be preferred, i.e. limitations on working time. In a historic perspective, this has been the answer to the oversupply of labor power during industrialization: the struggle for the eight-hour day, the prohibition of child labor, and (from today's viewpoint more problematic) the displacement of women from gainful employment. If such collective solutions are not available, the destructive competition can cross borders via trade (see below).

Neo-institutional Arguments: Workers' Rights for Sustainable Development

From an institutional perspective in economics, workers' rights contribute to long-term sustainable development. Both demand-side and supply-side arguments are put forward to demonstrate the stimulatory growth effects of workers' rights. From a demand-oriented perspective, highly unequal income distribution is regarded as an obstacle to sustainable development (Herr/Ruoff 2015). First, it is argued that such inequality impedes the emergence of a mass market in durable consumer goods, so that developing countries cannot emulate the »Fordist« growth model of the United States and Western Europe. Second, the concentration of national income in the hands of a few people produces an excessively high savings ratio, so that growth-stimulating investment is too low. It also increases the likelihood of capital flight (Boyce/Ndikumana 2002). Freedom of association and the right to collective bargaining are necessary preconditions for a more equal distribution of income (Gross et al. 2015).

The supply-side institutionalists cite two reasons why minimum social standards and resulting higher wages have a positive effect on a country's economic development prospects. First, higher wages promote the development of »human capital«, without which no economic development is possible. Wages close to or below the minimum subsistence level make it impossible for workers to invest in their own education, or that of their children, and are often insufficient to pay for necessary health care. Higher wages, on the other hand, would not only enable workers to maintain and enhance their qualifications but would also increase the incentive to attend school and adopt performance-oriented behavior (Sengenberger 2005). There is evidence that the early involvement of children in work can have serious consequences for their health and development (UNICEF 2009).

Second, they argue that social standards are necessary for making the transition from an extensive to an intensive use of labor. Under the prevailing system of sweatshops, employers have no particular interest in using labor intensively because workers are paid based on how many items are produced; hence, no fixed labor costs arise. Capital stock is usually small and consists of outdated machinery that cannot be used more efficiently. The resulting low labor productivity in turn precludes raising wages. In such a situation, minimum social standards could increase interest in measures to raise productivity by changing the structure of incentives for firms and workers. For firms, they would make the extensive use of labor less attractive; for workers, they would make it more rewarding to strive for the success of the firm. If, for instance, a strategy of »flexible specialization« is to succeed, certain preconditions must be met to ensure that workers can earn better wages, show themselves to be cooperative, and acquire professional qualifications. Social standards could help create those preconditions (Piore 1994). As the minimum wage in Puerto Rico increased, for example, turnover and absenteeism declined, job applicants were more thoroughly screened, and »managerial effort« improved (Robertson et al. 2009: 9-14).

Studies conducted by the ILO (2009), which look specifically at certain international labor standards, seem to be in line with the institutionalist argument. They show that compliance to labor standards positively contributes to a country's competitiveness and good economic performance. Other studies have argued in a similar direction (cf. Dehejia/Samy 2009). However, given the persistence of violations of core labor rights, the question remains whether violations are the result of competitive pressures. Unintentionally, the study co-authored by David Kucera raises some doubts about the validity of these studies. Kucera has won great merits for the operationalization of labor standards by developing a set of indicators for these standards (Kucera 2007). The study he conducted together with Ritasch Sarna shows, in line with the institutionalist argument, that weak labor rights do not correlate positively with strong export performance. However, the study identifies one exception: East Asia. The authors do not consider these countries to be representative: »[...] the East Asian experience is anomalous in the broader global context« (Kucera/Sarna 2004: 25). This move to fortify the general argument is not convincing. Global competitive pressure originates exactly from this region (Berik/van der Meulen 2010). A second look at the above mentioned studies reveals that they treat all countries the same in their regression analysis, and neither account for global market shares nor for changes in these shares.

Head-to-Head: South-South Competition

While almost all countries have ratified some ILO conventions, the new export nations in particular have been slow to ratify even core conventions. Some of the motives for not signing on to the ILO conventions are political in character. Dictatorships have good reasons to believe that trade unions might become places of government opposition (e.g. Solidarnosc in Poland). There are also economic reasons. While the »high road« promises long-term benefits, it may incur short-term costs. The amount of these costs, their impact on competitiveness, and their long-term rewards are difficult to appraise (Dehejia/Samy 2004). ILO studies conducted in India suggest that as a portion of the final price of carpets to the consumer, labor-cost savings realized through the employment of children are between 5 and 10 per cent for carpets (Anker et al. 1998).

However, the likelihood of higher wages does not automatically translate into higher production costs. According to the institutional argument mentioned above, the observance of labor rights will lead to greater efficiency, which compensates for higher wages. In the short-term, higher costs are nevertheless likely before the efficiency gains are realized. Given that most export goods from developing countries are sold to wholesalers or transnational corporations, which command a strong market position vis-à-vis the producers, even small differences in production costs can be expected to be decisive for market success.

The competition among the countries in the South has not received nearly as much attention as the North-South trading relationship. However, theoretical arguments as well as empirical evidence suggest that competition is fiercer along the South-South than the North-South axis (Ghose 2000). The greater the similarity between the competing regions with regard to factor endowment and market position, the more acute this danger (Mosley/Uno 2007). The extent of competition among Southern countries is influenced by the following factors: (a) simple production techniques which allow for easy market entrance, (b) fast growing labor forces because of a crisis in subsistence agriculture, (c) foreign indebtedness which forces countries to maximize export earnings, and (d) the ability of transnational corporations to switch supply sources and to relocate production facilities. The latter is more likely in labor intensive, low skill industries such as the toy or garment industries.

In a number of product lines, fierce competition has led to an environment conducive to violating core workers' rights. The search for cheap labor is well documented for the garment industry. Pressure originates from brand-name manufacturers as well as large retail chains (Anner/Hossain 2015). Because of fair trade campaigns, brand-name buyers are trying to enforce certain labor and environmental standards on their suppliers. However, they seem not to be willing to pay for the extra compliance costs of their suppliers (Zhang 2011).

Will the South Suffer Under Global Rules?

The objective of global rules for workers' rights is to take them out of the competition among producers. If efforts succeed to make these rules binding for every country, the competitive situation among countries will change. Individual countries will no longer fear that they will suffer competitive disadvantages by adherence to these rights. Instead, they will be able to assume that their labor competes under similar conditions.

The need for international agreements is demonstrated particularly well in the case of child labor. Some authors see only two alternatives for children in economic problem areas: work or starvation. Since exploitation is better than starvation, they opt against prohibiting child labor (Bhagwati 1994: 59). However, such harsh alternatives exist only under ceteris paribus conditions; that is, when the rules for competition have not changed. If child labor were to be prohibited in just one region in, say, carpet weaving, there is of course the risk that the carpet companies in that region will lose their market share. By contrast, if child labor were to be prohibited in all regions, then a loss in market share is not likely. Then family living wages could be paid to adults. Indian carpet makers would no longer be in competition with Pakistani carpet makers on labor costs but with industrial manufacturers of carpets. In this hypothetical case, the risk is whether the higher prices for carpets, which all carpet makers could charge, would lead to a diminishing overall demand for hand-made carpets. To answer this question, the substitution or demand elasticity has to be known. Experts are not of one mind concerning the degree of demand elasticity for products from the South.

Even if a »correct« value for the price elasticity of demand could be established, it would probably not reflect the reality of many exporters in the South. The elasticity of substitution and demand would vary considerably from product to product. Hand-made carpets, handcrafts, and tropical agricultural products can be substituted for products from the North only to a limited degree. Thus, demand for these goods is rather insensitive to changes in prices. The income elasticity of demand for these products will be quite high, since they do not belong to the group of staple goods. The demand for these goods will depend on the business cycle. Furthermore, their production costs are rather low relative to the final sales prices. This is also true for garments and footwear items. For some brand-name products, production costs are unrelated to sales prices. For cotton jeans made in Honduras and sold in the USA under a brand name, apparel assembly workers take home only 4 per cent of the sale price (Anner/Hossain 2015). Increases in production costs can be easily absorbed by distributors or retailers. Most child labor occurs in labor-intensive industries. It can, therefore, be safely assumed that the prohibition of child labor would not infringe upon the export opportunities of the South in the North.

Demand elasticity would be much more pronounced for complex industrial supplies from the South. These products are in direct competition with those from the North. Since they usually would not yet have reached the same quality levels, they would compete mostly on price. These kinds of products are produced in emerging economies, some of which violate core workers' rights. Nevertheless, it can be assumed that higher wages would not necessarily translate into higher prices. Compared with the hand-made products mentioned above, the higher degree of capital intensity keeps the share of wages to total production costs lower. In addition, the efficiency wage argument is applicable at this higher level of industrial development. Workers' qualifications and their motivation are important for mastering complex production processes. The general increase in wages can also be beneficial for the development of domestic demand, which in turn accelerates the move up along the industrial learning curve and helps realize economies of scale. Nevertheless, the more effective enforcement of workers' rights may carry with it adjustment costs in the short term.

Higher costs in the short term, however, are not likely to influence the long-term growth of developing countries. Growth prospects are more dependent on the education level of the workforce and on technology transfer than on the level of wage compensation. Even where minimum standards are maintained, wage costs are significantly lower than in the OECD countries. In addition, higher labor costs do not necessarily lead to higher prices for consumers in the OECD countries. They could be either neutralized by currency devaluation or absorbed by export price profit margins (Erickson/Mitchell 1998: 179).

In sum, the more an economy is capital, research, and service intensive, the less it will be affected by violations of core labor rights. Workers in Greece or Portugal will enjoy greater material benefits from the worldwide enforcement of core workers' rights than will workers in Germany or Japan. The main benefits would, therefore, accrue to the developing countries. Developing countries trying to respect these rights and improve working and living conditions are the most vulnerable to being undercut in world markets by countries seeking comparative advantage through the suppression of workers' rights. Often the victims are young and unorganized female workers in export processing zones that advertise the absence of trade union rights in order to attract investment. For these reasons, developing countries cannot raise their social standards in isolation but only in conjunction with other countries by multilateral agreement.

Conclusion

International core labor rights are human rights and as such to be respected. In addition, they can also be justified on economic grounds. In the academic debate, the arguments of advocates of internationally binding workers' rights are based on a neo-institutional view of the market mechanism, while those of their critics stem from a neo-classical approach. If criticism on purely ideological grounds is to be avoided, it is necessary to challenge these approaches on their own »home domain«. It can be demonstrated that, core workers' rights can also be justified within the neoclassical paradigm. They are constitutive for markets (since the market is defined as an exchange of goods among free persons) and address market failures such as power imbalances or barriers to market exit. They are an important precondition for the development of »human capital« and therefore contribute to economic efficiency.

If standards are as beneficial as some claim, why are they not voluntarily adopted? Some of the motives for not signing on to the ILO conventions are political. There are also economic reasons. Although the »high road« promises long-term benefits, it may incur short-term costs. While attempts to assess the cost impact of adherence to ILO conventions have not delivered reliable results thus far, even small differences in production costs can be expected to be decisive for market success. Most export goods from developing countries are sold to wholesalers or transnational corporations, which command a strong market position vis-à-vis the producers. This competitive situation, however, is the very reason why social standards have to be negotiated internationally. As long as it is possible for an economic region to gain competitive advantage by undercutting the social standards in other regions, these other regions are in danger of losing market share and hence employment opportunities. The greater the similarity between the competing regions with regard to factor endowment and market position, the more acute is this danger. It will be particularly high if market success depends on a single factor, namely low-skilled labor. In such a case, the danger from lower standards cannot be offset by other factors. This situation is particularly true of developing countries, which face the constant risk that new regions with an even larger reservoir of cheap labor will break into the world market. For these reasons, developing countries cannot raise their social standards in isolation but only in conjunction with other countries by multilateral agreement.

There is no need to fear a decline in the overall demand for goods from the developing countries, as their long-term growth depends primarily on the training level of their workers and on transfers of technology. International standards can, therefore, plausibly be justified in terms of development theory.

References

Anner, Mark/Hossain, Jakir (2016): Multinational Corporations and Economic Inequality in the Global South: Causes, Consequences and Countermeasures in the Bangladeshi and Honduran Apparel Sector, in: Alexander Gallas/Hansjörg Herr/Frank Hoffer/Christoph Scherrer (eds.): *Combating Inequality: The Global North and South*, London/New York: Routledge, 95-110.

Anker, R./Barge, S./Rajagopal, S./Joseph, M. P. (1998): *Economics of Child Labor in Hazardous Industries of India*. New Delhi: Hindustan Publishing Corporation.

Bator, Francis M. (1958): The Anatomy of Market Failure, in: *Quarterly Journal of Economics,* 72(3): 351-379.

Berik, Günseli/van der Meulen, Yana (2010): Options for Enforcing Labor Standards: Lessons from Bangladesh and Cambodia, in: *Journal of International Development* 22(1): 56-85.

Bhagwati, Jagdish (1994): A View from Academia, U.S. Department of Labor, Bureau of International Labor Affairs, in: *International Labor Standards and Global Economic Integration: Proceedings of a Symposium,* Washington DC: GPO: 57-62.

Boyce, J. K./Ndikumana, L. (2002): Africa's Debt: Who Owes Whom? Political Economy Research Institute, University of Massachusetts, Amherst, Working Paper 48.

Dehejia, V./Samy, Y. (2009): Trade and Labor Standards: New Empirical Evidence, in Ravi Kanbur/ Jan Svejnar (Eds.): *Labor Markets and Economic Development*. Abingdon, Oxon, UK: Routledge.

Dehejia, V./Samy, Y. (2004): Trade and Labor Standards: Theory and New Empirical Evidence, in: *Journal of International Trade and Economic Development*, 13(2): 179 – 198.

Erickson, Christopher L./Mitchell, Daniel J.B. (1998): Labor Standards and Trade Agreements: U.S. Experience, in: *Comparative Labor Law and Policy Journal*, 19(2):145-183.

Freeman, Richard B./Medoff, James (1984): *What Do Unions Do?* New York: Basic Books.

Ghose, Ajit K. (2000): Trade Liberalization, Employment and Global Inequality, in: *International Labor Review*, 139(3): 281-305.

Gross, Tandiwe/Hoffer, Frank/Laliberté, Pierre (2016): The Rise of Inequality Across the Globe: Drivers, Impacts and Policies for Change, in: Alexander Gallas/Hansjörg Herr/Frank Hoffer/Christoph Scherrer (eds.): *Combating Inequality: The Global North and South*, London/New York: Routledge, 15-30.

Grossmann, Harald/Michaelis, Jochen (2007): Trade Sanctions and the Incidence of Child Labor, in: *Review of Development Economics*, 11(1): 49-62.

Herr, Hansjörg/Ruoff, Bea Maria (2016): Labor and Financial Markets as Drivers of Inequality, in: Alexander Gallas/Hansjörg Herr/Frank Hoffer/Christoph Scherrer (eds.): *Combating Inequality: The Global North and South*, London/New York: Routledge, 61-79.

Kahn, Alfred E. (1970/1971): *The Economics of Regulation: Principles and Institutions*, Vol. 2. New York: John Wiley.

Klevorick, Alvin K. (1996): Reflections on the Race to the Bottom, in Jagdish Bhagwati/Robert E. Hudec (eds.): *Fair Trade and Harmonization. Prerequisites for Free Trade? Vol. 1: Economic Analysis*. Cambridge, MA: MIT Press.

Krueger, Alan B. (1996): *Observations on International Labor Standards and Trade*. Cambridge MA: NBER – NBER Working Paper Series, Nr. 5632.

Kucera, David (Ed.) (2007): *Qualitative Indicators of Labor Standards: Comparative Methods and Applications*. Dordrecht: Springer.

Kucera, David/Sarna, Ritash (2004): How Do Trade Union Rights Affect Trade Competitiveness? Working Paper No. 39 Policy Integration Department, Statistical Development and Analysis Group. International Labor Office, Geneva.

Leebron, David W. (1996): Lying Down with Procrustes: An Analysis of Harmonization Claims, in Jagdish Bhagwati/Robert E. Hudec (eds.): *Fair Trade and Harmonization. Prerequisites for Free Trade? Vol. 1: Economic Analysis*. Cambridge, MA: MIT Press.

Mosley, Layna/Uno, Saika (2007): Racing to the Bottom or Climbing to the Top? Economic Globalization and Collective Labor Rights, in: *Comparative Political Studies*, 40(8): 923-948.

Piore, Michael J. (1994): International Labor Standards and Business Strategies, U.S. Department of Labor, Bureau of International Labor Affairs: *International Labor Standards and Global Economic Integration: Proceedings of a Symposium*, Washington, DC: GPO: 21-25.

Pollmann, Uwe/Strack, Peter (1995): Zwischen Überlebensnotwendigkeit und Ausbeutung, in: Hans-Martin Große-Oetringhaus/Peter Strack (eds.): *Verkaufte Kindheit. Kinderarbeit für den Weltmarkt*. Münster: Westfälisches Dampfboot – terre des hommes book.

Robertson, Raymond/Brown, Drusilla/Pierre, Gaelle/Sanchez-Puerta, Maria Laura (Eds.) (2009): Globalization, Wages, and the Quality of Jobs. Five Country Studies. Washington, DC: World Bank.

Sengenberger, Werner (2005): Globalization and Social Progress: The Role and Impact of International Labor Standards. A Report Prepared for the Friedrich-Ebert-Stiftung, second revised and extended revision, Bonn.

UNICEF (2009): Progress for Children – A Report Card on Child Protection, Number 8, September.

Zhang, Hao (2011): Hegemonic Authoritarianism: The Textile and Garment Industry, in Christoph Scherrer (Ed.): China's Labor Question. Mering: Rainer Hampp Verlag.

3. Overview of Enforcement Instruments for Workers' Rights along Supply Chains

Stefan Beck and Christoph Scherrer

While international trade has resulted in great affluence in some advanced capitalist countries, the ongoing liberalization of trade has not been accompanied by increases in prosperity everywhere. In many emerging market economies, working conditions, wages, and environmental standards have even deteriorated, including the plants producing for export (Marx et al. 2015). Every year, the International Trade Union Confederation (ITUC) documents widespread abuses of workers' rights.

The debate about international trade and labor rights at least goes back to the beginning of the last century and led to the establishment of the *International Labour Organization* (ILO) in 1919. As of 2015, the ILO has 186 member states and has adopted 189 conventions, including 8 fundamental conventions, which are part of the *Declaration on Fundamental Principles and Rights at Work* adopted in 1998, at the 86th International Labour Conference. The fundamental conventions are: freedom of association (Convention No. 87); the right to organize and bargain collectively (Convention No. 98); and prohibitions of forced labor (Convention Nos. 29 and 105), discrimination in employment (Convention Nos. 100 and 111), and child labor (Convention Nos. 138 and 182). The workers' rights covered by these core conventions are an inseparable part of human rights because they were adopted by consensus of ILO members, because they were ratified by most member countries, because they are covered by UN covenants and several human rights declarations, and because they have been reaffirmed again and again at international summits (Salem/Rozental 2012).

While the ILO conventions have not prevented the erosion of workers' rights in many countries, it is most likely that without them the erosion would have been much more pronounced. In countries that have ratified conventions, they have become national law and are therefore in principle enforceable through the national legal systems. Furthermore, they have been frequently invoked in defense of workers' rights. The court of public opinion should not be underestimated ("boomerang"). Nevertheless, given the manifold violations of workers' rights, there is an urgent need to develop mechanisms that effectively protect labor rights throughout the world. One way would be to strengthen the enforcement mechanisms of the ILO (e.g. Hepple 2006). Another way is to look for instruments beyond the ILO. The international labor movement and labor friendly NGOs have reacted to the ILO's limited effectiveness in dealing with labor rights abuses in the context of a rapidly globalizing economy by pursuing many different strategies.

In this chapter we want to provide an overview of some of these initiatives and assess on the basis of secondary sources their contribution to improving working conditions throughout global production networks. We start out with the long-standing demand for a so-called social clause, i.e., a labor rights provision to be embodied in the World Trade Organization (WTO) and more recently in bilateral trade agreements. The Trans Pacific Partnership, initialed by the heads of the participating countries in October 2015, contains such a clause. We move on to assess the following instruments for the improvement of working conditions: public procurement policies, Global Framework Agreements between global union federations and transnational corporations, codes of conduct of corporations, and civil society initiatives such as social labels. We also look at the recently pronounced United Nations Guiding Principles on Business and Human Rights which call on companies to adopt human rights due diligence processes. Finally we take a brief look at the very recent G7-supported German initiatives for "responsible supply chains" including a 'Vision Zero Fund' for occupational safety. Both, the UN Guiding Principles and the German initiatives, are treated in more detail in this volume, see Scheper and Schultz respectively.

Labor Chapters in Trade Agreements

Multilateral Agreements

There have been several initiatives to bring labor standards into the World Trade Organization (WTO). At the 1996 Singapore Ministerial Conference the United States and some other developed countries advocated a "Social Clause", but after heated debates and the resistance of mostly developing countries, which saw it as protectionist measure, it was defeated. In the Ministerial Declaration the member states agreed that core labor standards are recognized, but should not be brought into the WTO. The assignment of the WTO would be the regulation of trade, whereas the ILO would be the appropriate body to address labor issues. Another attempt followed at the Seattle Ministerial Meeting in 1999, but the Meeting ended before any agreement was reached (Turnell 2001; Brown 2000). Until today the WTO itself does not deal with labor issues; it only cooperates with the ILO in a non-binding way.

The legal WTO framework contains no explicit references to labor standards, except GATT Article XX(e) which allows countries to deviate from GATT obligations in respect of products made by prison labor. An implicit link is GATT Article XX(d) that allows "measures necessary to secure compliance with laws or regulations not inconsistent with the GATT". However, its application to labor standards was rejected during the negotiations of the Havana Charter (Anuradha/Dutta 2012). There are a few other GATT articles that possibly could be used to link labor standards to several trade disciplines (Brown 2000), but these links have not been invoked so far:

- *Anti-Dumping (GATT Article VI):*"Exports maybe subject to an anti-dumping duty if a product is exported at a price below its normal value and the sale of the product can be shown to be causing or threatening to cause material injury to domestic producers." This requires proof of either price discrimination or pricing below production cost. *Social dumping* as a consequence of lower labor standards and, therefore, lower production cost is not covered by this Article (Brown 2000: 105; cf. also Turnell 2001).

- *Countervailing Duties (GATT Article XVI)*: Government-enforced low wages and labor standards depressing the cost of production could be considered as an export subsidy subject to countervailing duties. But again, lower labor standards do not meet the criteria of a subsidy according Article XVI, because there is no income transfer from a public authority to the company (Brown 2000: 106).

- *Nullification and Impairment Provisions (GATT Article XXII)*: If by any measure a member impairs or nullifies the benefits that would otherwise be forthcoming under GATT rules, another member may submit the case for dispute resolution. But even if poor labor standards would fall under this Article, it does not provide for any remedy (ibid.).

In other words, to establish a link between labor standards and trade that could be used to act against low labor standards the GATT would have to be changed – against the prevailing will of the majority of WTO member states.

As argued above, the strict separation of international trade and labor standards leads in some instances to a lowering of labor standards. Liberalizing trade (GATT), services (GATS), and public procurement (GPA), without leverage to ensure labor rights, creates incentives to use labor standards and institutional deregulation as a means to gain a competitive advantage (cf. Turnell 2001).

Bilateral Trade Agreements: Justification for Labor Clauses

In contrast to the WTO treaties, many recently concluded bilateral trade and investment agreements include labor provisions. In particular, since the adoption of the North American Free Trade Agreement (NAFTA) and the attached North American Agreement on Labor Cooperation (NAALC) the number of trade agreements including labor provisions increased significantly. In June 2013, 58 of 248 trade agreements in force and notified to the WTO contained labor provisions (IILS 2015: 20).

Figure 3.1: ILO member countries with trade agreements including labor provisions by region, 2013

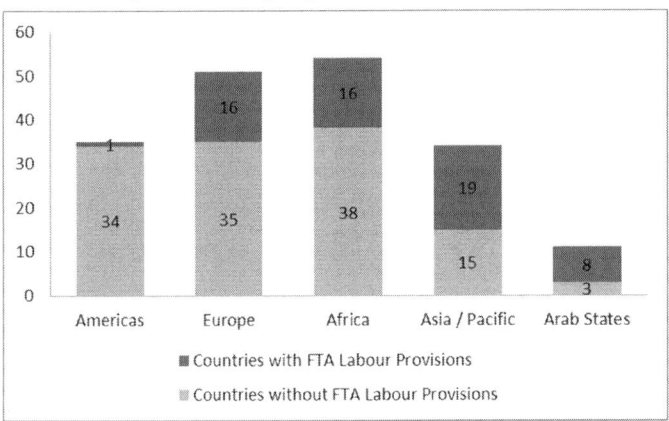

Source: IILS 2015: 20

In particular, in the Americas, in Europe, and in Africa the majority of ILO member countries is party to at least one free trade agreement that contains labor provisions. Overall, about 60 percent of all ILO member countries with trade agreements notified to the WTO are party to at least one agreement containing labor provisions (IILS 2015: 21).

While the GATT compatibility of these labor provisions has not been tested in a dispute settlement procedure, a legal assessment by Claudia Hofman and Andreas Hänlein (2012) came to the conclusion that even within the GATT rules there is room for a labor rights clause in bi- or plurilateral Free Trade Agreements. However, as they point out, the avoidance of a violation of GATT principles depends on the concrete design of the particular labor rights clause. "Weak" social clauses, which lack binding quality and enforcement mechanisms, are less likely to collide with GATT principles. Depending again on the wording and content, labor rights clauses with stronger enforcement mechanisms could potentially violate the principle of most favored nation treatment (Art. I:1 GATT) or the prohibition of quantitative restriction (Art. XI:1 GATT). Hofman and Hänlein argue that as Core Labor Rights are part of a common international consensus of values, Article XX (a) GATT (measures necessary to protect public morals) can be invoked for sanctions in response to violations of these rights. Article XX (b) GATT (measures to protect human life or health) covers measures with regard to the prohibition of child or forced labor. Its coverage of collective bargaining or non-discrimination aspects may be disputed. The opening clause of article XX GATT (the so-called "chapeau") allows for the pursuit of legitimate national aims under certain conditions: The particular measure must not result in an unjustifiable or arbitrary discrimination and the measure must not lead to a disguised restriction of international trade (Hofman / Hänlein 2012: 132).

Bilateral Trade Agreements: Promotional or Conditional Labor Clauses

The current labor provisions in bilateral trade agreements vary widely in scope and content. The most basic difference is whether they are only promotional or also conditional (Anuradha / Dutta 2012: 32):

- *Promotional elements*: These focus mainly on supervision and/or capacity building provisions in relation to labor.
- *Conditional elements*: These are linked to economic consequences, in the form of legally enforceable provisions accompanied by incentives, sanction mechanisms as well as dialogue and monitoring.

Figure 3.2: Increase in number of labor provisions in bilateral and regional trade agreements, 1990 - 2013

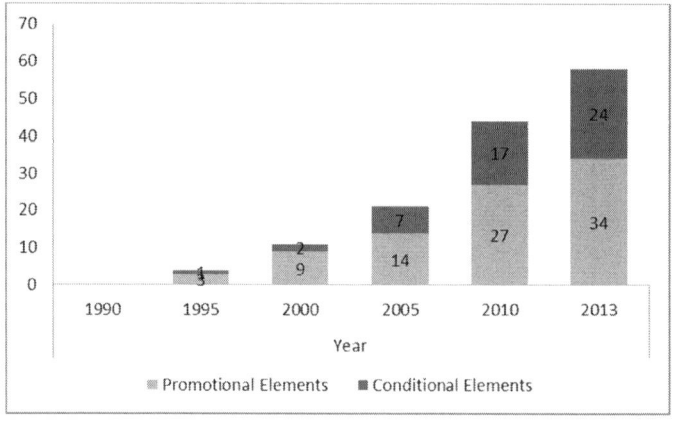

Source: IILS 2015: 19

Figure 3.2 shows that the majority of free trade agreements including labor provisions still rely on promotional elements. In the last decade, however, the number of agreements that also include conditional elements increased progressively.

Table 3.1 below shows that, interestingly, despite labor provisions having been integrated for the first time in NAFTA already in 1993, even concluded later, 13 out of the selected 26 trade agreements do not have any labor provisions et all. And second, also after NAFTA already comprised conditional elements, i.e.

enforcement procedures like a dispute settlement, with one exception (Canada – Chile), only the US-Agreements encompassed those elements regularly. Table 3.1 provides taxonomy of the different types of labor provisions:

Table 3.1: Labor Provisions in US Preferential Trade Agreements

Name and date of entry into force of the trade agreements	Reference to ILO instruments	Scope and content of labor provisions	Enforcement mechanisms
NAFTA/NAALC (1994)	No	Strive for a high level of national labor laws in the area of CLS, as well as minimum working conditions and migrant rights Enforcement of labor laws in these areas	Fines up to US $20 million/0.07 of total trade volume (goods) (only in the case of non-application of national labor law in the field of child labor, occupational safety and health and minimum wage)
Trade Agreement with Jordan (2001)	ILO 1998 Declaration	"Strive to ensure" CLS (except non-discrimination and minimum working conditions) Enforcement of labor laws in these areas No encouragement of trade or foreign direct investment through weakening labor laws.	Regular trade sanctions under the regular dispute settlement mechanism of the agreement
Trade Agreements with Chile (2004), Singapore (2004), Australia (2005), Morocco (2006), Bahrain (2006), Central America-Dominican Republic (CAFTA-DR) (2006), Oman (2009)	ILO 1998 Declaration, Convention No. 182	"Strive to ensure" CLS (except non-discrimination) and minimum working conditions Enforcement of labor laws in these areas No encouragement of trade or investment through weakening of labor law in contravention of the labor principles contained in the agreement	Fines up to US $15 million in the case of non-application of national labor law in these areas (to be aid into a special labor rights fund)
Trade Agreements with Peru (2009), Panama, Colombia, and the Republic of Korea (not yet into force)	ILO 1998 Declaration, Convention No. 182	Ensure respect of CLS as contained in the ILO Declaration, and enforcement of related national laws No weakening of labor law in a manner affecting trade or investment if this contravenes CLS	Regular trade sanctions or monetary assessment under the regular dispute settlement mechanism of the agreement

Source: R.V. Anuradha/Singh Dutta, Nimisha 2012: 20

The NAFTA-NAALC agreement is by far the most extensively assessed agreement. While the NAALC is the most elaborate agreement, several studies rated it as ineffective (c.f. Bourgeois/Dawar/Evenett 2007: 45-51). In particular, the effects of NAALC decreased significantly after 2000. Not only had the number of cross-border cooperative activities decreased, but also the outcomes of submissions to the national administrative office (NAO) of the United States and Mexico. More and more cases have been declared inadmissible, withdrawn, or stalled in the review or consultations phase (IILS 2015: 47, 80). Furthermore, several studies assessing the impact of NAFTA on workers came to the conclusion that the US as well as Mexico registered job and wage losses and witnessed increased inequality after 1993 (cf. Weisbrot/Lefebvre/Sammut 2014; Raza et al. 2014).

In the pursuit of a labor rights clause in bilateral trade agreements, the United States suffers from a legitimacy deficit because it did not ratify most of the core conventions (Anuradha / Dutta 2012). But also the European Union does not display a coherent stance on labor rights (Velluti 2015). In addition, its current economic governance is in conflict with fundamental labor rights (Hendrickx / Pecinovsky 2015).

A study by R.V. Anuradha and Nimisha S. Dutta (2012) compares the trade agreements of the United States and the European Union. Both approaches differ in several ways. The US-Agreements contains stricter dispute settlement enforcement provisions, whereas the EU prefers consultations. Labor rights in U.S. agreements refer to ILO conventions only in the more recent agreements; most of them refer to rights mentioned in U.S. domestic labor law for the aforementioned reason of not having ratified a number of core ILO conventions (Anuradha / Dutta 2012; for a comparison of the various labor chapters, see also IILS 2015; Lukas/Steinkellner 2012; Zimmer 2012).

The U.S.-Cambodia Textile Agreement is frequently mentioned as a more effective instrument for the protection for workers. It came into force in 1999 after the GATT Multi Fibre Agreement expired and lasted until 2005. Its innovative features include "the alignment of government and business interests through the use of positive incentives: verified compliance with labor standards was rewarded with increased export quotas" (Anuradha / Dutta 2012). The ILO monitored compliance, the precondition for obtaining an export license. As a result labor conditions improved. Employment, wages and exports increased (Robertson, 2011; Wells 2006) and even after the global financial crisis compliance slipped only marginally (Brown et al. 2012).

Compared to the U.S. agreements, the EU labor chapters refer to ILO conventions, prefer consultation to enforcement and sanctions, and emphasize social development objectives such as gender equality and health within a cooperative framework (see table 3.2). A "soft" form of dispute settlement was the first time implemented in the EU Agreement with Caribbean countries (CARIFORUM), but "compensation or trade remedies [may not] be invoked against a Party's wishes." (Anuradha / Dutta 2012: 23). Consultations and Monitoring – eventually with participation of stakeholders and the ILO – still have priority. In the recent EU-Korea Agreement, again, there is no resort to dispute settlement; disputes shall be resolved by a Panel of Experts.

Table 3.2: Different types of labor provisions in EU trade agreements

Name and date of entry into force of the trade agreements	Reference to ILO instruments	Scope of provisions	Enforcement action
Trade Agreements with Palestinian Authority (1997), Morocco (2000), Israel (2000), Algeria (2005), Cameroon (2009)	No	Cooperation and/or dialogue on selected issues related to labor standards	
Trade Agreement with Chile (2003)	ILO Declaration on Fundamental Principles and Rights at Work, 1998	Commitment to give priority to the respect for basic social rights, including through the promotion of ILO. Fundamental Conventions and social dialogue cooperation on various labor and social issues	
Trade Agreements with South Africa (2000), ACP Countries (2003)*	ILO Declaration on Fundamental Principles and Rights at Work, 1998	Reaffirms the parties' commitment to the ILO CLS Cooperation on various labor and/or social issues	
Trade Agreement with the EU-CARIFORUM (2008)	ILO Declaration on Fundamental Principles and Rights at Work, 1998; ILO Core Labor Standards, internationally recognized labor standards	Commitment to (i) ensuring compliance with ILO CLS, (ii) not weakening or failing to apply national labor legislation to encourage trade or investment	Consultation and Monitoring framework with stakeholder participation, optional ILO consultation for amicable solution of differences. If dispute cannot be solved through consultation, appropriate measures other than trade sanctions may be considered.
EU-Korea (2011)	High levels of labor protection consistent with international standards Reference to ILO's Decent Work Standards.	Commitments to consult and cooperate on trade-related labor and employment issues of mutual interest.	Government to Government consultations; Reference to the Committee on Trade and Sustainable Development; Panel of Experts for making recommendations; No resort to dispute resolution provisions of the FTA.

Source: Anuradha / Dutta 2012: 24

The recently negotiated Comprehensive Economic and Trade Agreement (CETA) between the European Union and Canada also lacks an effective enforcement mechanism. In its labor chapter CETA refers to the fundamental conventions, the 1998 ILO Declaration on Fundamental Principles and Rights at Work, the 2008 ILO Declaration on Social Justice for a Fair Globalisation, and in addition (chapter on Sustainable Development) to the 2006 Ministerial declaration of the UN Economic and Social Council on Full Employment and Decent Work as well as the OECD Guidelines for Multilateral Enterprises. The parties of the Agreement "shall not fail to effectively enforce its labor law", and shall not lower "the levels of protection embodied in domestic labor law and standards", as an encouragement for trade or investment. Points of contact shall serve the exchange and provision of information, cooperative programs and be the recipients of submissions. Furthermore, domestic advisory groups, comprising representative civil society groups, shall be consulted or established, and for matters that have not been sufficiently addressed through government consultations a Panel of Experts may be convened to examine the matter, issue reports and make recommendations. In cases of non-conformity the parties shall identify appropriate measures, or decide upon a mutually satisfactory action plan. In case of disagreement a party may request further government consultations. Government consultations can include the expertise of the ILO or other experts or stakeholders. Effective enforcement mechanisms, however, are not available. Seen as a kind of template for the Transatlantic Trade and Investment Partnership (TTIP), the CETA labor provisions could already set standards for a large part of total world trade.

The differences between the EU and the US have also come to the fore in the most recently concluded trade agreements with Vietnam (August and October of 2015). While the labor chapter in the agreed upon text EU-Vietnam Trade Agreement emphasizes promotion of workers' rights, the binding side-letter to the Trans-Pacific Partnership Agreement is much more stringent. The U.S. won form the one-party state of Vietnam the assurance to ratify ILO conventions on freedom of association and the right to collective bargaining. Within seven years Vietnam has to create the legal framework for independent trade unions. If Vietnam's government does not comply with this obligation, the U.S. could suspend trade privileges (Schweisshelm 2015).

These new trade agreements revive the debate about the effectiveness sanctions versus cooperation: Are labor provisions with conditional elements and enforcement mechanisms more effective than provisions with promotional and cooperative elements? Empirical evidence suggests that both approaches can have some merits as well as shortcomings and their effectiveness is context dependent. There are two types of conditional labor provisions: a so-called "pre-ratification conditionality" and a so-called "post-ratification conditionality". *Pre-ratification conditionality* usually requires an improvement of labor law and standards prior to ratification, whereas post-ratification conditionality aims at the enforcement of existing law. In particular since 2006 pre-ratification conditionality became part of US trade agreements and contributed in several cases to labor law reforms. In response to concerns raised by members the United States Congress, Morocco, Bahrain and Oman reformed their labor laws ahead of concluding the trade agreements with the USA. The reforms concerned, e.g., the right to organize and to bargain collectively, anti-union discrimination, and child labor. In Peru, Panama and Columbia more specific reforms were undertaken in similar areas of domestic labor law. However, reform plans have not always been fully or sufficiently implemented. In some cases they were weakened by accompanying deregulations in other areas of labor law (IILS 2015: 29-42).

In spite of the higher number of trade agreements with post-ratification conditionality, not enough time has passed for a definite assessment of their impact. Most cases have been filed under the complaint mechanism of NAALC. Dominant issues of submissions against Mexico have been freedom of association, occupational health and safety, and minimum working conditions. Submissions against the United States particularly focused on the situation of migrant workers. While between 1994 and 1997 more than half of the cases reached the level of ministerial consultations, the corresponding share dwindled to less than one fifth after 2002 and more cases have been declared inadmissible. Until 2013 no case had reached stage 3, the creation of an evaluation committee of experts, not to mention stage 4, the appointment of an arbitral panel, and stage 5, the imposition of sanctions. In several cases the complaint mechanism was useful in addressing the problem. However, as mentioned above, a couple of studies rated NAALC as rather ineffective. The success of a complaint depends on several factors, like political attention, the monitoring by the NAO concerned, the presence of advocacy campaigns, supporting transnational organizations and coalitions, and the quality of the legal arguments put forward (IILS 2015: 43-57).

Complaints under trade agreements other than NAFTA most often deal with trade union rights. They were on the whole not successful. Improvements were more likely in the area of labor inspections. Sometimes domestic authorities became more aware of labor standards and more willing to engage with the ILO. Overall, the complaint mechanisms' effectiveness was rather limited so far. Pre-ratification conditionality (foremost concerning freedom of association) appears to trigger more fundamental changes, but also does not guarantee a sufficient implementation or compliance with labor law. Both approaches, pre- as well as post-ratification conditionality crucially depend on the political will of the country concerned and on accompanying advocacy coalitions (IILS 2015: 43-57).

Promotional provisions are more common than conditional provisions, in particular in North-South and in South-South trade agreements. Usually promotional conditions take the form of diverse cooperative activities like technical assistance, institutional capacity building, or forms of dialogue and policy development, sometimes including the involvement of social partners or the assistance of the ILO. Labor provisions, however, vary significantly across these agreements, ranging from simply reaffirming existing international obligations to substantial commitments on labor standards. Recent EU agreements, e.g. combine commitments to fundamental ILO conventions with an institutional framework encompassing cooperative activities, monitoring and dialogue mechanisms. Furthermore, some regional integration agreements like MERCOSUR involve tripartite elements to monitor and foster labor issues or carry out promotional activities. The Dominican Republic-Central America Free Trade Agreement (CAFTA-DR) agreement with the U.S. established an external verification body led by the ILO Sub-regional Office to monitor progress on labor standards. In the case of a dispute recent EU agreements provide State-to-State consultations or the option to submit the issue to an expert body, which issues findings and recommendations.

Cooperative activities include several projects, e.g. improving the capacities of labor ministries and labor judiciaries, campaigns against child labor, or centers providing legal assistance to workers. So far there is not enough research to provide reliable assessments concerning the efficiency of promotional labor provisions and several cooperative activities. Even in the case of CAFTA-DR Agreement, which contains rather extensive cooperative activities, studies conclude that "it appears that these activities have not substantially changed working conditions in the countries concerned" (IILS 2015: 81).

Bilateral Trade Agreements: Model Chapters

So far, experience indicates that there is no optimal design of labor provisions that fits all cases. Against this backdrop, Karin Lukas and Astrid Steinkellner drafted two sample texts for social standards of a sustainability chapter, one for bilateral free trade agreements with developing countries and one for such an agreement among industrialized countries (2010, 2012; a recent somewhat similar model for a Human Rights Clause was developed by Bartels 2015). In addition, they differentiate between minimum, average and maximum requirements (see table 3.3).

For a labor rights chapter Lukas and Steinkellner (2010: 9-12) list the following basic elements:

Normative framework: The social orientation should already be part of the preamble of a bilateral free trade agreement. This preamble should refer to more than the core ILO conventions. It should include references to the main international human rights documents.

"Non-lowering of standards" clause: In line with the ILO Declaration 2008 on Social Justice for Fair Globalization, the labor chapter should contain the obligation to maintain all existing labor and social legal standards comprehensively and under all circumstances.

Table 3.3: Comparison of Basic Elements for a Labor Chapter

		With developing country		Among industrialized countries
Standards	Minimum	Core Labor Standards		Core Labor Standards + Priority Conventions
	Average	Priority Conventions		Minimum wage, working hours, health & safety in the workplace, non- discrimination of migrants
	Maximum	Decent Work Agenda		Decent Work Agenda
Implementation Mechanisms	Minimum	Social standards part of dispute resolution		Social standards part of dispute resolution
	Average	Program for improving working conditions		

Source: Lukas / Steinkellner 2010: 13

Shield function: According to this human rights principle, universally accepted human rights should be given priority over commercial law obligations.

Sustainability impact assessment: The participants of the impact assessment should include employee and employer representatives as well as NGOs. Its recommendations should be made available prior to the start of the negotiations. Once the agreement is ratified, impact assessments should be carried out in regular intervals. In case of a severe negative impact, the agreements should be modified.

Monitoring: Independent committees of experts and consultative fora for the exchange of information between governments, social partners and other important stakeholders should monitor the effective implementation of the agreement and the compliance with the obligations following from it.

"Non-execution" clause: The same standard mechanisms should be used for resolving conflicts on labor and social matters as for all other chapters of the agreement.

Sanctions: Sanctions incentivize compliance with labor standards. The extent of the sanctions, however, should follow the principle of proportionality. They should not disadvantage employees who have already suffered from labor rights violations. Therefore, the primary form of sanctions should be payments in a fund for promoting standards and capacity building. Only in case the government refuses to make payments, trade benefits should be withdrawn (or in case of progress, trade benefits should be increased).

To this list of basic elements for a labor rights chapter one can add that in the case of developing countries pre-ratification conditionality and promotional provisions appear to be more effective than post-ratification conditionality.

Finally, trade unions, NGO's and other civil society actors should be involved in the negotiation process in a more formalized and institutionalized way. The same actors can also play an important role in cooperation activities and support the implementation and monitoring process of labor standards. In recent years, several civil society actors – e.g., human and labor rights organizations, technical inspection organizations, private initiatives – gathered experience in particular concerning monitoring, verification, and certification activities.

Based on the experiences of the Better Factories Cambodia program, Drusilla Brown and her co-authors would add to the above list subsidizing one-time investments to bring factories into compliance in order to overcome management's uncertainty about the benefits of better working conditions (Brown et al. 2012: 26).

Public Procurement

In recent years an old instrument for promoting good labor standards, public procurement, has been rediscovered (McCrudden 2007). Public authorities at all levels of the European Union spend about 1/5 of total EU Gross Domestic Product. This represents significant market power which can be strategically employed for social purposes. Already in 1949 the ILO adopted a specific convention on "Labor Clauses in Public Contracts" (Convention number 94). It stipulates that workers hired in contracting companies do not receive less favorable conditions than those laid down in appropriate collective agreements or other forms of pay regulation. However, only a limited number of countries have ratified this convention (in 2015: 63 countries, ILO Normlex).

The use of public procurement to pursue social aims is not limited by the disciplines of the World Trade Organization. While the GATS mandates negotiations on government procurement and services, these negotiations have not yet reached any results. Only countries that are party to the plurilateral Agreement on Government Procurement (GPA) may be subject to the disciplines of that agreement for those sectors they have listed in the annexes of their GPA. Public authorities in the European Union, however, are bound to the rules on competition. These rules as interpreted by the European Court of Justice limit public procurement conditionality on pay (Schulten 2012). Nevertheless, a whole range of other social conditions are permissible according to Article 26 of the EU Directive of 2004. In 2010, the European commission even published a long list of possible requirements for socially responsible public procurement. This list covers the ILO core conventions and some additional conventions and includes explicitly ethical trade issues in tender specifications (Schulten 2012: 6). In Germany, many Länder have adopted ecological and social criteria for their procurement policies. The pattern of adoption reveals the political contestations around social conditionality. Wherever the explicitly pro-business friendly party, the Free Democrats, was part of the ruling coalition requests for conditionality were rejected (Sack / Sarter 2015).

In the case of the procurement of goods, the social or ecological criteria in the tendering process have to be strictly product- and not supplier-related. It is not sufficient to show that the supplying company violates labor rights or standards. It has to be demonstrated that the offered product was produced under conditions that violated ecological or social criteria. Provider-related codes of conduct or certifications are not enough; the certifications have to be product-specific (cf. Beck 2013; CorA 2010).

These hurdles and the political contestations raise the question of how effective the social conditionality of public procurement has been so far. To our knowledge, little research has been done on the impact of such conditionality. A research team at the University of Lausanne has recently carried out a large scale study on the effects of the International Finance Corporation's Performance Standards which include workers' rights. Their findings show that the impact of these standards on the IFC inclined businesses behavior towards labor was "marginal at best" (Cradden et al. 2015: 2). The more striking finding was that almost all workers interviewed had been unaware of their employer's commitment to uphold the IFC performance standards (ibid.).

Global Framework Agreements between TNCs and GUFs

Given the obstacles for including effective social chapters in international trade agreements, the global union federations (GUFs) have pursued agreements with transnational corporations (TNCs), the so-called Global Framework Agreements (Müller et al. 2008). The rationale for these agreements is twofold: on the one hand the transnational corporations control much of world trade and occupy a powerful position within global production networks. Thus, they are a potentially powerful actor for enforcing labor rights throughout the production networks. On the other hand, who is best positioned to monitor a company's behavior and to the present the interests of those whose rights are violated but trade unions? These framework agreements usually include (a) mutual recognition of actors on both sides, (b) reference to all or to some of the ILO core conventions and some additional ILO conventions (i.e. working time), (c) processes of conflict resolution, and (d) specify the organizational domain to which they apply. In 2014, 103 global framework agreements were considered to be active (Fichter 2014).

A research team headed by Mike Fichter from the Free University of Berlin has conducted extensive case studies on the effectiveness of global framework agreements. They identified a number of cases in countries such as Brazil, India, Turkey and the USA where local trade unionists were able to make effective use of such a framework agreement to redress the violations of their rights (Fichter / Helfen 2011; Fichter et al. 2013). This involved agreements signed by global union federations such as BWI, IndustriALL, and UNI. However, in many cases local trade unions in dispute with local management were not aware of the existence of such agreements or were unable to link their strategies to the avenues made available by the agreements. On the basis of their findings, Fichter and Stevis recommend (a) to involve local actors from the initiation to the information implementation of the framework agreement, (b) to develop proactive approaches especially for countries not familiar with the European social dialogue, (c) to communicate and practice their framework agreements as a joint management and labor instrument accompanied by training practices for local management and workers representatives, and (d) to integrate the agreements' principles into the procedures of the contracting TNC (Fichter / Stevis 2013: 41-42).

Corporate and NGO Initiatives for Labor Standards

In the last decades, a variety of civil society initiatives concerning environmental or social standards emerged. Those initiatives are not necessarily linked to trade agreements and related enforcement mechanisms (if there are any), but rather try to monitor and improve standards along global value chains.

The most common approaches are the formulation of *codes of conduct* by individual companies or business associations, *corporate social responsibility* programs, the provision of *certificates* or *labels* by commercial or non-profit organizations, and *campaigns* organized by networks, organizations – including e.g. trade unions, research organizations, human rights organizations – or consumers.

Comparing the "business-driven" codes of conduct and certificates and the initiatives of NGOs or networks, it is not difficult to see, that the motives differ. Companies use those instruments to save or restore consumer confidence, i.e. their market share, whereas NGOs try to improve working conditions and development opportunities. Social labels and codes demand significantly higher standards but also limit the managerial power of control. They need therefore public attention and support to convince or pressure the management, and they have to pursue cooperative approaches (unions, workers, management, networks). As seen in some cases of the Clean Clothes Campaign, this can feed different interpretations, interests and reduce the efficacy of the initiative.

Business-driven Codes of Conduct

The development and formulation of codes of conduct can be seen as a reaction of companies to the discovery and publication of labor rights violations. The codes of conduct are supposed to signal that the company intends to adhere to certain environmental, social or human rights standards. In most cases subcontractors and suppliers are asked to adopt the code of conduct of the lead company. In some cases several companies of the same branch teamed up to develop a common code of conduct. One example is the *Electronic Industry Citizenship Coalition* (EICC), initiated in 2004 by eight companies. Today, the EICC comprises more than 100 electronics companies and in 2015 version 5.0 of its code of conduct went into effect (cf. www.eiccoalition.org). The EICC code of conduct refers to the UN Guiding Principles on Business and Human Rights, the UN Universal Declaration of Human Rights, the ILO Declaration on Fundamental Principles and Rights at Work, the ILO Guidelines on Safety and Health, the OECD Guidelines for Multinational Enterprises, ISO and SA standards. Implementation and Monitoring of the code shall be ensured by a management system, including self-assessments and the Validated Audit Process (VAP).

However, several incidents in the last few years, e.g. related to Apple and Foxconn (cf. China Labor Watch 2012, SOMO 2012, SACOM/MakeITfair 2012), both members of the EICC, have shown that codes of conduct like the EICC code cannot guarantee compliance with high labor standards. The standards of the EICC code of conduct itself as well as of the monitoring and auditing process are still not sufficient. The code only refers to the ILO Declaration on Fundamental Principles and Rights at Work and national law, but not to the ILO core conventions. Particularly, in countries with an insufficient or restrictive labor law and controlled or weak unions, Freedom of Association and Collective Bargaining are not sufficiently ensured (cf. SOMO 2012). The code also refers to local minimum wages but not to living wages. Furthermore, the code only mentions the next tier suppliers and does not cover the whole supply chain.

As investigations and interviews with workers have shown, in practice the monitoring and auditing processes often do not hold what they look like on paper. As a part of the management system, monitoring is largely based on self-evaluation and controlled by the company. In the past, the participation of suppliers in the monitoring process was rather low and controls took place randomly and were often superficial. Likewise, the review of audits revealed several shortcomings, in particular concerning freedom of association and collective bargaining. Companies often treated union rights as less important or they were neglected in the audit. In other cases different understandings and interpretations of standards, the issue at hand or of several indicators reduced the efficacy of the auditing process and the consequences in cases of non-compliance – if non-compliance is recognized at all. Audits are costly and often there is a time constraint. Not always the best qualified audit-teams are hired, only a few interviews are conducted, or the auditing focuses on less complicated issues. In particular, lacking knowledge about local conditions, insufficient participation of stakeholders or lacking independence of workers' organizations can be a cause for misinterpretations. Finally, sometimes companies know about an upcoming audit and can cover deficiencies (SOMO 2012; China Labour Watch 2012; Barrientos / Smith 2007).

The decree to which codes of conduct are implemented depends on local circumstances. Companies spent more efforts on implementation where it is comparatively easy, i.e., where a strong compliance culture, an educated workforce and few vulnerable groups of workers exist. In other words, countries with the highest decent work deficit receive the least attention from corporate standard setters (Klink 2015).

Some companies developed in addition to the EICC code of conduct a more far reaching program of *Corporate Social Responsibility* (CSR), including, e.g., the approval of the ILO core conventions, human rights instruments, or diverse certifications (Lukatsch 2010; Chahout 2011). Besides ISO-certifications, another one is the TCO certification by the Swedish non-profit-organization TCO Development. After ecological criteria, in 2009 social criteria also became part of the TCO certification. The requirements of the TCO certification require (cf. http://tcodevelopment.com):

- compliance with the eight ILO core conventions,
- compliance with Article 32 of the UN Convention on the Rights of the Child,
- compliance with national laws with regard to health and safety, labor law, minimum wages, and social security,
- the membership or a proof of compliance with the EICC code of conduct and SA 8000.

Compliance shall be verified by annual independent inspections and at least one annual and independent report about manufacturing facilities, where the certified products are produced. By its explicit reference to the ILO core conventions, more attention paid to union rights and eventually existing restrictions, and more explicit monitoring rules, the TCO certification can be seen as an improvement compared to the EICC code. But also the TCO certification has some shortcomings. For example, only the final production and the delivery of certified products are covered. The certification of specific products, however, makes the TCO certification interesting for public procurement relating to social criteria.

Overall, the governance gap left by governments and intergovernmental agencies has not been closed by private codes. The confusing amount of various standards "offers businesses the opportunity to choose the stringency level of standards and audits." (Pekdemir et al. 2015) As Richard Locke has persuasively argued, private codes of conduct, to be effective, need support from public authorities is crucial (2013).

Consumer-driven Codes of Conduct

Besides these rather "business-driven" codes of conduct and labelling programs, there are also "consumer-driven" codes of conduct and labelling programs provided by NGOs or civil society networks. The main goals of those initiatives are the promotion of "Fair Trade", worker's rights and to improve working and social conditions.

One of the best known initiatives, the *Clean Clothes Campaign* (CCC), is an alliance of European organisations, including NGOs and unions, cooperating with similar organisations and campaigns worldwide (http://www.cleanclothes.org). The campaign promotes labor standards based on the ILO conventions, the ILO Declaration of Fundamental Principles and Rights at Work, and on the Article 23 of the Universal Declaration on Human Rights. Furthermore it seeks to empower workers by taking seriously their right to be informed and eventually educated about their rights, and by their entitlement to organise themselves and being involved in cases of rights violations.

The brand name companies should adopt a code of conduct that follows the CCC model and should promote it throughout the production chain. Implementation and verification of the code of conduct should be done with the participation of multi-stakeholder initiatives. Companies should sign international framework agreements to facilitate the social dialogue with trade unions. Trade unions are especially important at the local level for these campaigns (Merk 2009: 608). Besides the implementation and verification activities, CCC launches public campaigns and appeals, which are documented in annual reports.

The Clean Clothes Campaign is an ambitious initiative with far reaching goals regarding the improvement of labor standards, the empowerment of workers, and the participation of civil society organisations or multi-stakeholder initiatives in the implementation and verification process. This decentralized and participative approach, however, has its own difficulties. The local projects are very heterogeneous. Working conditions, the readiness of companies to implement and to comply with the code of conduct, the composition and participation of multi-stakeholder initiatives and other actors, and the labor law can differ. As a consequence, implementation and verification processes, as well as the success also vary. CCC has therefore started to target also state actors (Kryst 2012).

Another known initiative is *Rugmark*, a label for carpets without child labor (http://www.goodweave.net). Rugmark gives licenses to carpet manufactures and exporters who stop employing children under 14 years old and pay the minimum wage to the adults who work for them. The carpet exporters receive a limited number of labels to tag the carpets, so every carpet can be identified and traced back even to the machine that was used. Rugmark inspectors check the factories regularly and unannounced. If producers were found to employ children and do not end this immediately, they will lose their license. Exporters pay 0.25% of their export revenues to finance the inspections, whereas the carpet importers pay 1% of the merchandise value to support the children who have lost their jobs.

Rugmark is a strongly specialized initiative with the sole goal to stop child (wage) labor in the production of carpets in India. This approach makes monitoring easier. The problem, however, is that it does not stop exporters from using child labor and unfair working conditions elsewhere and pursuing a strategy of price differentiation, i.e., higher prices for the morally conscious, upscale customer, and lower prices for carpets made by child labor for price-conscious customers independent of actual production costs.

A third approach is the use of Fair Trade labels to improve working and social conditions. Under the umbrella of *Fairtrade International* a couple of National Fairtrade Organisations merchandise the Fair Trade products and provide the seal in their countries. The basic principles and Fairtrade standards, however, are developed by Fairtrade International. Seen as an alternative to conventional trade, the concept of Fair Trade is designed to improve the terms of trade, address power imbalances, and offer better trading conditions to marginalized producers and workers. Fair trade is meant to provide minimum prices, decent wages, and a premium to use to improve social, economic and environmental conditions (http://www.fairtrade.net).

The basic wage labor standards are spelled out concretely in the current version of the *Fairtrade Standard for Hired Labour*. Based on the ILO Declaration on Fundamental Principles and Rights at Work and several ILO (including all core) conventions as reference for decent working conditions, the standards are:

- Freedom from Discrimination (ILO Conventions 97 and 143),
- Freedom of Labor (ILO Conventions 29 and 105),
- Child Labor and Child Protection (ILO Conventions 182 and 138),
- Freedom of Association and Collective Bargaining (ILO Conventions 87, 98, 135, 141 and Recommendation 143),
- Conditions of Employment (ILO Conventions 95, 100, 110, 102, 121, 130, 183 and Recommendation 115),
- Occupational Health and Safety (ILO Conventions 155, 184, 77, 78 and Recommendations 164, 102).

The several standards are specified by their respective intent and scope, the requirements to which companies have to adhere, guidance on how to interpret them, and the number of years the company has until it is audited against the requirement. Audits and certification will be conducted by the independent certifier FLOCERT. Before a product will be certified the producer must go through an initial on-site audit. After the certification the producer will be audited at least twice in a three-year certification cycle (http://www.fairtrade.net).

An overall assessment of the Fair Trade initiative on labor standards is still difficult, in particular since the recent revision of the Fairtrade Standards for Hired Labour. Fair Trade is overwhelmingly seen as an alternative trade and development initiative, its impact on labor standards is rather treated as secondary. However, there is no proof that the higher Fair Trade labor standards endanger the success of the initiative because of higher entry barriers, and second, there is no proof that the programs to empower workers are a threat to organized labor (cf. Davenport/Low 2012; Raynolds 2012). The initiative not only sets higher and more elaborated standards, but also provides detailed guidance how to apply and interpret them. And, in contrast to the Clean Clothes Campaign, the Fair Trade initiative also provides a coherent set of standards and application rules.

Finally, there are a couple of civil society organizations, networks, and research institutes, which can provide critical assessments, monitoring assistance, and help to develop or improve codes of conduct. Some examples are the Fair Labor Association (FLA), the non-government organization SACON in China, CEREAL in Mexico, the SOMO-Center for Research on Multinational Corporations, or the GoodElectronics network, which formulated common demands on the electronics sector. However, this heterogeneity complicates the development of coherent standards and guidelines (cf. Inkota-Netzwerk e.V. 2012; Ascoly/Oldenziel/Zeldenrust 2001).

Multi-stakeholder Initiatives: Bangladesh Accord

The combination of labor-driven (see section 5) and consumer-driven (see section 6.2) initiatives holds some promise for enforcing labor rights. The case in point is the Accord for Fire and Building Safety in Bangladesh (the Accord). This Accord was signed in the aftermath of the Rana Plaza disaster of 24th of April 2013 when a building complex for garment factories collapsed, leaving more than thousand workers dead and more than two thousand injured. Signatories to this Accord are over 180 retailers and brands from 20 countries from around the world and the Global Union Federations IndustriAll and UNI Global. It is a legally binding agreement which obliges the company to pay an annual fee of up to $500,000 per year for five years. The money is supposed to be spent on safety training, inspections and for structural repairs on buildings. The steering committee consists of representatives chosen by the trade unions and companies in equal representation plus a representative of the International Labor Organization as a neutral chair. Representatives of the government of Bangladesh and of labor-oriented NGOs are among the members of the advisory board (Accord 2013).

The Rana Plaza disaster demonstrated the ineffectiveness of social auditing programs. The Business Social Compliance Initiative had audited and certified some of the factories in the Rana Plaza complex. While the shock of the disaster certainly facilitated the signing of the Accord by the retailers and brand companies, the driving forces were the Global Union Federations and the protagonists of consumer-driven codes of conduct, i.e., the Clean Clothes Campaign and the Workers' Rights Consortium. The trade unions were able to make use of their previously established contacts to the giant brand companies through Global Framework Agreements and of their negotiating skills. The NGOs contributed their campaigning skills targeted at the reputation of the brand companies. As Reinecke and Donaghey have shown in their study, the synergies and complementarities between these actors brought about the Accord. Of course, the co-operation was not always without tension: "At ... times, aggressive campaigning against the brands with whom unions were in negotiations was perceived as hindering the dialogue." (Reinecke / Donaghey 2015).

It is a bit too early to make the final judgment upon the impact of the Accord. An in depth evaluation of the impact of the Accord in the first half of 2015 comes to mix conclusions. Working conditions in the second-tier factories, the factories that supply to the signatory companies of the Accord, have somewhat improved, especially in the area of occupational safety and health. However, despite a clear commitment in the Accord, the signatory companies did not offer funds to these second-tier suppliers to implement expensive measures to make the buildings and workplaces safer. In addition, the focus on health and safety left others aspects of the labor conditions untouched such as low pay, long working hours and especially issues of workers' collective action, i.e., freedom of association and collective bargaining (Khan / Wichterich 2015).

The UN Guiding Principles on Business and Human Rights

In 2011 that United Nations Human Rights Council adopted unanimously The Guiding Principles on Business and Human Rights which have been prepared under the leadership of John Ruggie as the special representative of the UN Secretary-General on Business and Human Rights. The Guiding Principles consist of three pillars. The first one highlights the prime responsibility of states to protect human rights. The second pillar covers the corporate responsibility to respect human rights (with an explicit reference to ILO core labor rights) and the third pillar calls for access to remedies if governments do not observe their duty to protect human rights. These Guiding Principles are international soft law and, therefore, lack sanctioning power. However, given the broad consensus behind them, they provide legitimacy to more comprehensive action by governments and businesses in the protection of human rights. The United Nations member states have committed themselves to develop so-called National Action Plans for the implementation of the guidelines (see Scheper in this volume). The Leaders' Declaration of the G7 summit held in Germany in 2015 highlighted the support of G7 nations for the UN Guiding Principles and welcomed the efforts to set up substantive National Action Plans (G7 declaration 2015).

The specific novelty of the guidelines pertains to extending the responsibility to respect human rights to corporations. Companies are asked to practice due diligence in handling human rights risks in their own responsibility, going beyond the respect of national laws. The companies are called upon to take proactive steps to clarify and understand how their activities may impact the human rights of stakeholders. Thereby, the Guiding Principles break new legal and political ground. It is therefore not surprising that many issues are yet to be clarified: the distinction between duty and responsibility, the instruments available for the integration of human rights into business procedures, and the degree of involvement of people affected by corporate activities. Companies are prepared to take responsibility but try to avoid any duties for the protection of human rights throughout their production networks. Many companies consider it impossible to monitor their subcontractors' subcontractors.

A number of software solutions are available for businesses to integrate human rights issues in their decision-making processes. However, as Brigitte Hamm and Christian Scheper point out, standardized procedures for human rights impact assessments focus too much on compliance with statutory standards (such as minimum wage laws which in some countries might be below the poverty line), neglect possibilities for social upgrading, and avoid engagement with those whose human rights might be violated. Hamm and Scheper, therefore, recommend that companies invite civil society actors in devising context specific, stakeholder inclusive human rights impact assessments (Hamm / Scheper 2012).

In a recent policy paper, Robert Grabosch and Christian Scheper (2015), argue that governments can in many ways support corporations to effectively respect human rights throughout their production systems. Their list of government action includes:

Policy statement: the government's policy statement on how to implement the Guiding Principles can on the one hand signal the business sector that the respect for human rights is important and on the other hand can give the business sector orientation of what is actually expected from it in terms of human rights due diligence.

Risk and impact assessments: the government can invite stakeholders to formulate guidelines for risk and impact assessments differentiated for human rights issues, business sectors, and company size.

Grievance mechanisms: a government should provide for the victims of human rights violations accessible mechanisms for redress. The National Contact Points for the OECD guidelines have proven to be insufficient. They are in need of reform.

Training: a government could provide help desks for business consultations on human rights issues and offer training sessions especially for SME.

Networks: a government can initiate or support networks for the stakeholders of global production systems. These networks can exchange information and foster solidarity across borders.

Support for any international treaty on the human rights obligations of businesses: a government can also go beyond the Guiding Principles by supporting the efforts of the UN Human Rights Council to develop a binding international agreement for business enterprises.

Public procurement: the 2014 EU guidelines for public procurement allow for sustainability criteria. Therefore, human rights issues should become part of the set of criteria for public procurement.

Export promotion: government support for exporters in the form of loans or investment guarantees should be made conditional on human rights due diligence processes.

Development cooperation: the expertise of actors in development cooperation can be employed for improving human rights impact assessments and for the support of business enterprises engaged in development cooperation. That support should be conditioned on the enterprises' commitment to human rights.

The list should be expanded to include a most vital element of improving working conditions: Government support for the right of workers to organize and to bargain collectively. A group of legal experts has studied the feasibility of making corporations responsible for the adherence to human rights in their supply chains by German law. Their study includes the draft for such a law (Klinger et al. 2016).

Even more desirable than individual national initiatives would be the development of an international legal framework on the basis of the Guiding Principles for combating workers' rights violations (for such a proposal, see Lukas 2012).

German Government Initiative for Sustainability in Global Supply Chains

In the wake of the collapse of the Rana Plaza building in Bangladesh, the German Minister for Economic Cooperation and the Minister of Labor and Social Affairs put forward an agenda for joint action by representatives from governments, businesses, social partners, international organisations and civil society along global supply chains (BMZ 2015). To ensure compliance with internationally agreed and binding labor, social and environmental standards in supply chains, the agenda includes the following measures:

• "Establishing a 'Vision Zero Fund' for global prevention, with the aim of reducing the number of people who are harmed by accidents at work as far as possible worldwide (e.g. by investing in fire safety measures, requisite training and accident insurance schemes);

• Promoting stakeholder alliances involving the private sector, civil society and trade unions for the implementation of agreed labor, social and environmental standards in all G7 countries;

• Giving small and medium-sized enterprises (SMEs) in G7 countries better support so that they can take on social responsibilities along global supply chains;

• Improving complaints mechanisms and arbitration processes to help workers in production countries in situations where standards are not upheld; and

• More transparency for consumers in order to foster sustainable consumption." (BMAS / BMZ 2015)

This agenda was intended for the G7 summit held in Germany in June of 2015. It was picked up by the leaders declaration at the G7 summit under the heading "responsible supply chains" (G7 Declaration 2015). The German government has started to implement some items of this agenda. It has set up an Internet platform where consumers can obtain information about the content of the various labels (www.siegelklarheit.de/). It has also initiated a stakeholder forum for the textile and garment industry, the so-called alliance for sustainable textiles (Bündnis für Nachhaltige Textilien). It aims at a common definition of environmental, labor and health standards as well as continuous implementation goals for reaching the standards. It will also work out policy recommendations for favorable conditions to pursue sustainability strategies in the countries of production as well as for German and European policymakers (Bündnis für Nachhaltige Textilien 2015).

After the government had committed itself to support only voluntary measures, thus ruling out legal obligations, about half of the companies engaged in production and distribution of textiles and garments in Germany joined this alliance together with NGOs and trade unions by October 2015. While the alliance cannot decide on any measures against the will of its business members (principle of unanimity), the progress made by business members will be regularly reviewed by a third party and, in case of noncompliance, can lead even to the expulsion from the alliance (Dohmen 2015).

Perhaps the most interesting part of this agenda is the "Vision Zero Fund". It will be established in cooperation with the International Labor Organization and will support its efforts in preventing and reducing workplace related death and serious injuries. Recipients will have to commit themselves to prevention measures. The sums so far pledged are, however, paltry: €7 million, of which €3 million come from the German government.[1]

The German-initiated G7 agenda remains at a voluntary level. As shown above, the 'business-driven' codes of conduct and Corporate Social Responsibility programs are rather weak (concerning labor standards) and remain management-controlled. Asymmetric power and wage relations, different labor and ecological standards have been drivers for vertical disintegration and the creation of global value chains – they are an integral part of today's business models. Multi-stakeholder initiatives were invented by unions, human rights organisations, other NGOs, but not by transnational corporations.

Summary

The chapter provided an overview of some, not all initiatives to improve working conditions throughout global production networks. Here they are summed up.

The World Trade Organization (WTO) has refused to lend its dispute settlement process to the enforcement of international labor rights. However, *labor chapters in bilateral trade agreements* are compatible with WTO rules under certain circumstances. In recent years, many of those agreements feature such a

---

[1] https://www.g7germany.de/Content/EN/Artikel/2015/10_en/2015-10-13-g7-arbeitsminister_en.html

chapter. Some chapters are promotional, some even conditional. The effectiveness of the conditional labor chapters are somewhat higher but far from perfect because the process leading up to sanctions is highly political. Among the conditional labor chapters the ones with "pre-ratification conditionality" are somewhat more effective than those with "post-ratification conditionality". Some scholars have drafted context specific model labor chapters which, if implemented, promise better results. Most effective are subsidies for one-time investments to bring factories into compliance in order to overcome management's uncertainty about the benefits of better working conditions.

The use of *public procurement* to pursue social aims is permissible under certain conditions in Europe (and especially for those states not members of the Agreement on Government Procurement, GPA). However, there is little awareness of its potentials and even less among workers of such requirements for their employers supplying the public sector or publicly funded projects.

Global Framework Agreements between global union federations (GUFs) and transnational corporations (TNCs) were successfully used in some instances to redress violations of workers' rights at subsidiaries and first-tier suppliers. However, in many cases local trade unions in dispute with local management are not aware of the existence of such agreements or were unable to link their strategies to the avenues made available by the agreements. Therefore, local actors have to be involved from the start in the negotiation and implementation of the framework agreements.

In response to negative publicity, many private companies voluntarily adopted *codes of conduct*. Over time these codes have increasingly included references to ILO conventions and guidelines from other international organizations. In practice, however, most monitoring and auditing processes fall short of the codes' promises. The departments for corporate social responsibility are clearly subordinated to the purchasing departments. Without legal enforcement, the codes are at best reminders for good behavior, at worst they amount to whitewash.

In comparison to these *"business-driven"* codes, *"consumer-driven"* codes demand significantly higher standards and also limit managerial discretion. They need therefore public attention and support to pressure management. Maintaining this pressure is very challenging.

The combination of labor-driven and consumer-driven mechanisms for the protection of workers holds some promise for enforcing labor rights. The best example is the *Accord for Fire and Building Safety* in Bangladesh. Over 180 retailers and brands and Global Union Federations signed a legally binding agreement which obliges the company to pay an annual fee of up to $500,000 per year for five years for safety training, inspections and for structural repairs on buildings. Until mid-2015, the working conditions in the second-tier factories have improved in the area of occupational safety and health. However, funds were not provided for the more expensive measures of making the buildings safer. The situation concerning pay, overtime and collective bargaining did not improve.

The United Nations *Guiding Principles on Business and Human Rights* cover also the corporate responsibility to respect human rights. Companies are asked to practice due diligence in handling human rights risks in their own responsibility, going beyond the respect of national laws. Since the Guiding Principles break new legal ground, many issues are yet to be clarified. However, governments can translate these principles into national law and thereby provide clear guidance for corporations to effectively respect human rights throughout their production systems.

In preparation for the G7 summit in 2015, the German Government put forward an agenda for a *stakeholder action* by representatives from governments, businesses, social partners, international organisations and civil society along global supply chains. The G7 declaration referred to it, but the agenda remains at a voluntary level. Asymmetric power and wage relations, different labor and ecological standards have been drivers for vertical disintegration and the creation of global value chains – they are an integral part of today's business models. Multi-stakeholder initiatives were invented by trade unions and human rights organisations, but not by transnational corporations. Therefore, such a G7 initiative may only serve to provide legitimacy to the struggle for better working conditions but does not contribute to it in practical terms. The miniscule funding provided for the 'Vision Zero Fund' to prevent work-related accidents reflects the limited political will to confront the business community with stricter rules for its conduct.

In sum, so far none of the many initiatives seem to be particularly effective. Global Framework Agreements seem to be quite effective as long as local actors are involved right from the start. The United Nations Guiding Principles hold some promise, if governments are willing to support and pressure companies to implement them. The same holds true for the social conditionality of public procurement. Most promising remains trade conditionality. However, if only a rather weak social chapter in a trade agreement is politically achievable, it risks justifying trade liberalization measures and the strengthening of investors' rights which will undercut the bargaining strength of labor. It is therefore not sufficient to discuss specific instruments for the promotion of labor rights along value chains; one also needs to address the general governance of international trade and investments.

References

Accord (2013): 'Accord on Fire and Building Safety in Bangladesh', Retrieved from http://bangladeshaccord.org/wp-content/uploads/2013/10/the_accord.pdf

Anuradha, R.V./Singh Dutta, Nimisha (2012): Trade and Labour under the WTO and FTAs, Centre for WTO Studies.

Ascoly, Nina/Oldenziel, Joris/Zeldenrust, Ineke (2001): Overview of Recent Developments on Monitoring and Verification in the Garment and Sportswear Industry in Europe, SOMO Centre for Research on Multinational Corporations, http://www.somo.nl/publications-en/Publication_3073/at_download/fullfile.

Barrientos, Stefanie / Smith, Sally (2007). Do workers benefit from ethical trade? Assessing codes of labour practice in global production systems. Third World Quarterly 28, 713–729.

Bartels, Lorand (2015): A Model Human Rights Clause for the EU's International Trade Agreements, Berlin, German Institute for Human Rights.

Beck, Stefan (2013): Sozial verantwortliche Beschaffung von Informationstechnik – Socially Resposible Public Procurement of Information Technology, ICDD Working Papers, No.6.

BMAS/BMZ (2015): Good work worldwide, Vision paper by Federal Minister Dr Gerd Müller and Federal Minister Andrea Nahles, http://www.bmz.de/en/publications/type_of_publication/information_flyer/information_brochures/Materialie241_lieferketten.pdf.

BMZ (2015): "Promoting decent work worldwide through sustainable supply chains" – Andrea Nahles and Gerd Müller open international G7 stakeholder conference, http://www.bmz.de/g7/en/aktuelles/150310_PM_Lieferkettenkonferenz/index.html.

Bourgeois, Jacques/Dawar, Kamala/Evenett, Simon J. (2007): A Comparative Analysis of selected Provisions in Free Trade Agreements, Brussels, European Commission.

Brown, Drusilla K. (2000): International Labor Standards in the World Trade Organization and the International Labor Organization, Federal Reserve Bank of St. Louis, pp. 105-112.

Brown, Drusilla K. / Dehejia, Rajeev / Robertson, Raymond (2012): Retrogression in Working Conditions: Evidence from Better Factories Cambodia. Better Work Discussion Paper No. 6.Geneva, International Labour Office.

Bündnis für nachhaltige Textilien (2015): Aktionsplan. http://www.bmz.de/de/zentrales_downloadarchiv/Presse/Textilbuendnis/Aktionsplan_Buendnis_fuer_nachhaltige_Textilien.pdf

China Labor Watch (2012): Tragedies of Globalization: The Truth Behind Electronics Sweatshops; http://chinalaborwatch.org/pdf/20110712.pdf.

CorA (2010): Bietererklärungen als Instrument zur Einbeziehung von Arbeits- und Sozialstandards in der öffentlichen Beschaffung; Berlin, www.cora-netz.de/wp-content/uploads/gutachten-webversion.pdf.

Cradden, Conor/Graz, Jean-Christophe/Pamingle, Lucien (2015): Governance by Contract? The impact of the International Finance Corporation's Social Conditionality on Worker

Organization and Social Dialogue, Working Paper, Université de Lausanne, Institut d'études politiques, historiques et internationales.

Davenport, Eileen/Low, Will (2012): The labour behind the (Fair Trade) label, in: *Critical perspectives on international business*, 8(4): 329-348.

Dohmen, Caspar (2015): Textilbündnis "Feigenblattprojekt", in Süddetusche Zeitung, 15. Oktober 2015. http://www.sueddeutsche.de/wirtschaft/textilbuendnis-feigenblattprojekt-1.2693534.

Fichter, Mike (2014): Global Framework Agreements: A New Strategy for Trade Unions? paper delivered at Conference Financialization and Labor, February 27 – 28, 2014, Wissenschaftszentrum Berlin. https://www.wzb.eu/sites/default/files/u7/08_fichter_international_framework_agreements.pdf

Fichter, Michael / Stevis, Dimitris (2013): Global Framework Agreements in a Union-Hostile Environment: The Case of the USA, Berlin, Friedrich Ebert Stiftung.

Fichter, Michael/Helfen, Markus (2011): Going local with global policies: Implementing international framework agreements in Brazil and the United States, in: K. Papadakis (ed.): *Shaping Global Industrial Relations. The Impact of International Framework Agreements*, Houndsmills: Palgrave Macmillan, 73–97.

Fichter, Michael/Kadire Zeynep Sayim/Özge Berber Agtas (2013): Organization and Regulation of Empoyment Relations in Transnational Production and Supply Networks. Ensuring Core Labor Standards through International Framework Agreements? Ankara: Friedrich-Ebert-Foundation.

Grabosch, Robert/Scheper, Christian (2015): Die menschenrechtliche Sorgfaltspflicht von Unternehmen, Berlin, Friedrich Ebert Stiftung.

Hamm, Brigitte/Scheper, Christian (2012): Human Rights Impact Assessments for Implementing Corporate Responsibility. Conceptual Challenges and Practical Approaches. INEF Research Paper Series on Human Rights, Corporate Responsibility and Sustainable Development 10/2012. Duisburg: Institute for Development and Peace, University of Duisburg-Essen.

Hendrickx, Frank / Pecinovsky, Pieter (2015): EU economic governance and labor rights: diversity and coherence in the EU, the Council of Europe and ILO instruments, in: Marx, Axel/Wouters, Jan/Rayp, Glenn / Beke, Laura (eds.) Global Governance of Labor Rights. Assessing the effectiveness of transnational public and private policy initiatives, Cheltenham, UK, Edward Elgar, 118-149.

Hepple, Bob (2006): 'Does Law Matter? The Future of Binding Norms' in: Politakis, G (ed.), Protecting Labour Rights as Human Rights: Present and Future of International Supervision Geneva, ILO, 229–30.

Hofman, Claudia/Hänlein, Andreas (2012): Verankerung von Sozialstandards in internationalen Handelsabkommen aus rechtswissenschaftlicher Perspektive, in: Scherrer, Christoph/Hänlein, Andreas (eds.): Sozialkapitel in Handelsabkommen, Baden-Baden, Nomos, 103-140.

IILS (2015): Social Dimensions of Free Trade Agreements, Geneva, International Institute for Labour Studies, International Labour Organization, Revised Edition.

Inkota-Netzwerk e.V. (2012): Outdoor Companies Profiles 2012, http://www.inkota.de/ fileadmin/user_upload/Themen_Kampagnen/Soziale_Verpflichtung_fuer_Unternehmen /Outdoor/Firmenprofile/CCC_Companies_Profiles-Outdoor_2012.pdf.

Klinger, Remo/Krajewski, Markus/Krebs, David/Hartmann, Constantin (2016): Verankerung menschenrechtlicher Sorgfaltspflichten von Unternehmen im deutschen Recht, Gutachten im Auftrag von Amnesty / Brot für die Welt / Germanwatch / Oxfam.

Klink, Dennis (2015): Compliance opportunities and the effectiveness of private voluntary standard-setting -lessons from the global banana industry, in: Marx Marx, Axel/Wouters, Jan/Rayp, Glenn / Beke, Laura (eds.) global governance of labor rights. Assessing the effectiveness of transnational public and private policy initiatives, Cheltenham, UK, Edward Elgar, 230-256.

Kryst, Melanie (2012): Coalitions of labor unions and NGOs: The room for maneuver of the German Clean Clothes Campaign, in: Interface: a journal for and about social movements Article, 4(2): 101 – 129.

Locke, Richard (2013): The promise and limits of private power: promoting labor standards in the global economy, Cambridge, Cambridge University Press.

Lukas, Karin (2012): Human rights in the supply chain: influence and accountability, in: Radu Mares (ed.) The UN guiding principles on business and human rights, Leiden, the Netherlands, Brill Nijhoff.

Lukas, Karin/Steinkellner, Astrid (2012): Sozialnormen in Nachhaltigkeitskapiteln bilateraler Freihandelsabkommen, in: C. Scherrer and A. Hänlein (eds.): Sozialkapitel in Handelsabkommen, Baden-Baden, Nomos, 157-179.

Lukas, Karin/Steinkellner, Astrid (2010): Social Standards in Sustainability Chapters of Bilateral Free Trade Agreements, Ludwig Boltzmann Institute of Human Rights and Chamber of Labour Vienna.

Lukatsch, Ilona Delamere S. (2010): Corporate Social Responsibility in der Supply Chain in China; Diplomica Verlag.

Marx, Axel/Soares, Jadir/Van Acker, Wouter (2015): The protection of international labor rights: a longitudinal analysis of the protection of the rights of freedom of association and collective bargaining over 30 years in 73 countries, in: Marx, Axel/Wouters, Jan/Rayp, Glenn / Beke, Laura (eds.) global governance of labor rights. Assessing the effectiveness of transnational public and private policy initiatives, Cheltenham, UK, Edward Elgar, 13-41.

McCrudden, Christopher (2007): Buying Social Justice, Oxford: Oxford University Press.

Merk, Jeroen (2009): Jumping Scale and Bridging Space in the Era of Corporate Social Responsibility: cross-border labour struggles in the global garment industry, in: Third World Quarterly, 30(3), 599–615.

Müller, Torsten/Platzer, Hans-Wolfgang/Rüb, Stefan (2008): Internationale Rahmenvereinbarung - Chancen und Grenzen eines neuen Instruments globaler Gewerkschaftspolitik. Friedrich-Ebert-Stiftung.

Pekdemir, Ceren, Pieter Glasbergen and Ron Cörvers (2015): On the transformative capacity of private fair labor arrangements, in: Marx, Axel/Wouters, Jan/Rayp, Glenn / Beke, Laura (eds.) Global Governance of Labor Rights. Assessing the effectiveness of transnational public and private policy initiatives, Cheltenham, UK, Edward Elgar, 209-229.

Raynolds, Laura T. (2012): Fair Trade Flowers: Global Certification, Environmental Sustainability, and Labor Standards, in: *Rural Sociology*, 77(4): 493-519.

Raza, Werner/Grumiller, Jan/Taylor, Lance/Tröster, Bernhard/von Arnim/ Rudi (2014): An Economic Assessment of the Claimed Benefits of the Transatlantic Trade and Investment Partnership (TTIP) in: Scherrer, Christoph (ed.), The Transatlantic Trade and Investment Partnership: Implications for Labor, Rainer Hampp Verlag, Mering, 41-99.

Reinecke, Juliana / Donaghey, Jimmy (2015): The 'Accord for Fire and Building Safety in Bangladesh' in response to the Rana Plaza disaster, 257-277.

Robertson, Raymond (2011): Apparel wages before and after Better Factories Cambodia, Better Work Discussion Paper No. 3, International Labour Office, Geneva.

SACOM/MakeITfair (2012): Sweatshops are good for Apple and Foxconn, but not for workers; 31.05.2015. http://makeitfair.org/en/the-facts/news/sweatshops-are-good-for-apple-and-foxconn-but-not-for-workers.

Sack, Detlef/Sarter, Eva Katharina (2015): Der Europäische Gerichtshof und die deutschen Bundesländer – Sozialpolitisierung und Rechtsunsicherheit im europäisierten Föderalismus, Universität Bielefeld, Manuskript.

Salem, Samira/Rozental, Faina (2012): Labor Standards and Trade: A Review of Recent Empirical Evidence, in: *Journal of International Commerce and Economics*, United States International Trade Commission, 1-36.

Schulten, Thorsten (2012): Pay and other social clauses in public procurement – a European overview, in: T. Schulten, K. Alsos, P. Burgess, K. Pedersen (eds.): Pay and Other Social Clauses in European Public Procurement, Düsseldorf, Hans-Böckler-Stiftung, 5-23.

Schweisshelm, Erwin (2015): Trade Union Pluralism through Free Trade? Vietnam's Trade Agreements with the EU and the US, Friedrich Ebert Stiftung, Perspective.

SOMO (2012): Freedom of association in the electronics industry; SOMO Paper, May 2012; SOMO - Centre for Research on Multinational Corporations; http://somo.nl/publications-en/Publication_3804.

Turnell, Sean (2001): Core Labour Standards and the WTO, https://www.mq.edu.au/__data/assets/.../Number203202001.PDF

Velluti, Samantha (2015): The EU's social dimension and its external trade relations, in: Marx, Axel/Wouters, Jan/Rayp, Glenn / Beke, Laura (eds.) Global Governance of Labor Rights. Assessing the effectiveness of transnational public and private policy initiatives, Cheltenham, UK, Edward Elgar, 42-62

Weisbrot, Mark/Lefebvre, Stephan/Sammut, Joseph (2014): Did NAFTA Help Mexico? An Assessment after 20 Years, Washington, Center for Economic and Policy Research.

Wells, Don (2006): "Best Practice" in the Regulation of International Labour Standards: Lessons of the U.S-Cambodia Textile Agreement, in: Comparative Labor Law & Policy Journal, 27: 357-376.

Zimmer, Reingard (2012): Sozialklauseln im Nachhaltigkeitskapitel des Freihandelsabkommens der Europäischen Union mit Kolumbien und Peru, in: Scherrer, Christoph/ Hänlein, Andreas (eds.): 2012: Sozialkapitel in Handelsabkommen, Baden-Baden, Nomos.141-156.

4. Instruments of German Foreign Economic Policy for Promoting Co-Determination along Supply Chains

Alison Schultz

The merits of the German co-determination system are widely acknowledged by the scientific, political and business communities in Germany (Biedenkopf, Streeck, and Wissmann 2006; Greifenstein and Kissler 2010). The extensive involvement of employees at both the plant and board level is not only a democratic requirement, but also leads to numerous economic benefits. Co-determination promotes a cooperative corporate culture, a stable workforce and offers companies great potential for innovation thanks to the high level of knowledge exchange (Biedenkopf, Streeck, and Wissmann 2006, 67–70; Greifenstein and Kissler 2010, 15; Streeck et al. 1998, 8). The German co-determination system has proved to be beneficial in adapting to new circumstances and mitigating economic uncertainty, particularly during structural change and global crises (Biedenkopf, Streeck, and Wissmann 2006, 67–70; Greifenstein and Kissler 2010, 15; Kraft and Stank 2004). In times of global capital mobility, the involvement of employees in company decisions helps to pursue long-term growth and employment interests rather than short-term yield-oriented incentives, thus providing a sustainable alternative to the shareholder model (Greifenstein and Kissler 2010, 141). This applies both to traditional sectors and particularly to modern, knowledge-based production, which benefits from a greater exchange of know-how, the involvement of highly qualified employees and their commitment to the company (Biedenkopf, Streeck, and Wissmann 2006, 50; Dilger 1999; Streeck et al. 1998, 8).

Despite its high reputation, the preservation of the German co-determination model is increasingly uncertain. In the wake of difficult global economic conditions, a declining relevance of the industrial sector (for which the co-determination legislation was originally implemented) and the shrinking of trade unions, new political and legal frameworks have emerged (Fichter 2005, 94; Greifenstein and Kissler 2010, 101–2; Streeck et al. 1998, 10). Through European regulations and the opening up of the market to foreign business forms, co-determination rights can be circumvented in the current system. (Biedenkopf, Streeck, and Wissmann 2006, 28–29; Keller and Werner 2007; Seyboth and Thannisch 2008; Sick 2015a; 2015b; Sick and Pütz 2011). This could be exacerbated by the current foreign trade policy, in particular by the (planned or already signed) new investment and trade agreements. So far little is known on the potential effects of these agreements on co-determination.

Broadening the view and considering the economic activity of German companies outside of Germany, an even more worrying image emerges. Companies that actively abide co-determination in Germany, often stand out for massive suppression of fundamental rights of co-determination, i.e. freedom of association, freedom of assembly and free bargaining, in other parts of the world. Such cases range from subsidiaries of German companies (e.g. T-Mobile in the USA or Volkswagen in Nigeria), to suppliers of German customers (e.g. kik suppliers in Bangladesh) and projects financed by German financial institutions (e.g. projects financed by the KfW bank; Handelsblatt 2016; International Trade Union Confederation 2016f).

The special design of the German co-determination system has historically grown within the German institutional architecture. The German model is even referred to as "the German special path" by some of its detractors (Biedenkopf, Streeck, and Wissmann 2006, 58). However, as part of the core labor standards of the International Labor Organization (ILO), the fundamental rights of co-determination are acknowledged by almost all countries and therefore must be guaranteed worldwide. This applies in particular to the right of association, the right to trade union freedom and collective bargaining (ILO Convention 87 and 98). Since the signing of the UN Guiding Principles on Business and Human Rights in 2011, German companies are obliged to respect these rights also in their business activities in other countries (United Nations Human Rights - Office of the High Commissioner 2011).

Co-determination occupies a special place among the rights of wage-earning employees. In addition to being workers' rights in themselves, co-determination rights as "enabling rights" put workers in the position to improve their own situation. Therefore, the guarantee of co-determination rights is a prerequisite for the establishment of further rights (Barrientos, Gereffi, and Rossi 2010, 7). In order to promote global labor rights, co-determination is hence of fundamental importance and should be at the center of efforts to improve the conditions of workers all over the world.

The current federal government has set itself the goal of "Good Work Worldwide" (BMZ 2015). Against the background of the success of the extensive co-determination rights in Germany, the concern for the preservation of this model and the risk of non-compliance with co-determination rights of German companies abroad, three considerations arise for the government:

Firstly, the German co-determination model could be of interest to other nations participating in the world market. Nevertheless, a defensive position prevails on the political side. While the concern for the preservation of co-determination has been discussed (Biedenkopf, Streeck, and Wissmann 2006; Sick 2015a) at the same time, the idea to expand a system that has demonstrated its positive effects or to promote it as a Best-Practice example, is surprisingly little present in the political debate. The federal government should pursue a more active approach here.

Secondly, it should be the goal of the Federal Government to maintain a successful system within Germany. Against the background of the conclusion of new mega-regional trade agreements with far-reaching consequences for labor legislation, more clarity should be given regarding the implications that upcoming trade agreements could have on co-determination, in order to make arrangements which do not jeopardize existing co-determination rights.

Thirdly, it is necessary to ensure that German companies abroad respect fundamental labor rights. A first and important step in this direction is the guarantee of basic co-determination rights, also in other countries.

The German government, through shaping different policy areas, can influence all three aspects, either negatively or positively. A particularly important area is foreign economic policy. Therefore, this study examines the extent to which co-determination rights can be protected and promoted through foreign trade policy. Current policies will be compared to the existing potential and concrete proposals will be presented on how the German co-determination system can be made known abroad and how co-determination can be guaranteed in German companies operating across the German borders. In addition, potential effects of the planned trade agreements TTIP and CETA on co-determination will be examined and suggestions will be introduced on how these trade agreements could promote co-determination instead of endangering it.

This chapter will proceed as follows: First, an overview of the German co-determination system and the current state of research on co-determination in Germany is presented. This is followed by an analysis of different policies of the Federal Government, which are relevant to foreign economic policy, for their potential to promote co-determination. Instruments of the Ministry of Economics and Energy (BMWi), the Federal Ministry of Finance (BMF), the Federal Ministry for Economic Cooperation and Development (BMZ), the Federal Foreign Office (AA) and the Reconstruction Credit Institute (KfW-Bank) are analyzed. Finally, the two forthcoming trade agreements, the Comprehensive Economic and Trade Agreement (CETA), which has already been signed by the European Union (EU) and Canada but is pending ratification by EU Member State Parliaments, and the Transatlantic Trade and Investment Partnership (TTIP) which is planned between the EU and the USA, will be investigated on their influence on co-determination rights. The focus is put on CETA, as the final text of the TTIP is currently in the negotiation phase.

The German Co-determination System

The following chapter presents the historical context and the essential features of German co-determination. It continues with a brief overview of the research on the impact of co-determination practices on democratic and economic factors and concludes with an outlook on the new challenges for employee participation and their possible reorientation in a Europeanized and globalized economy.

Historical Background and Legal Framework

Co-determination requirements and approaches in Germany can look back on a long tradition. Beginning with the futile proposals in the Frankfurt National Constitution (Frankfurter Nationalverfassung) on their introduction into the Weimar Constitution, co-determination together with the tariff autonomy, became the centerpiece of the German system of industrial relations after the Second World War (Verfassung des deutsche Reiches 1919, art. 159 and 165; Andersen 2013, 459–63; Streeck et al. 1998, 7).

Against the background of the end of the Second World War, the economic recovery and a critical phase of the Cold War, co-determination was the central program of trade unions. The latter succeeded to force through not only operational co-determination but also the enforcement of a joint participation in the supervisory boards of the iron and steel works. This was transferred in a weaker form to the whole economy in the 1970s despite the massive opposition of employers (Andersen 2013; Fichter 2005, 95–96; Greifenstein and Kissler 2010, 22).

Since then, employee co-determination in companies is regulated by law both at the plant and the board level; namely operational co-determination ("Betriebliche Mitbestimmung") and corporate co-determination ("Unternehmensmitbestimmung"). While the Works Constitution Act (Betriebsverfassungsgesetz) regulates the operational co-determination by a works council, corporate co-determination in companies with a workforce of over 2000 is provided in the Co-determination Act (Mitbestimmungsgesetz), for companies with 500 to 2000 employees in the One-Third Employee Participation Act (Drittelbeteiligungsgesetz[1]) and for companies in the coal and steel industry with over 1000 employees in the Coal, Iron and Steel Co-determination Act (Montanmitbestimmungsgesetz). According to this, companies with more than 2,000 employees are subject to equal representation of employees in the supervisory board. This parity is however weakened by the double vote of the board's chairman appointed by the employers and the binding participation of a senior executive on behalf of the employees. Employees fill one third of the supervisory board, in companies with 500 to 2000 employees. For large companies in the mining and steel sector, equal participation is required, which is provided by an independently elected member for stalemate situations as well as the appointment of a Labor Director in the company's board (Deutscher Bundestag 2013b; 2013b; 2015a; 2015a; 2015b; 2015c; 2015c).

---

[1] Until its adoption in 2004 the content of the One-Third Employee Participation Act was part of the Works Constitution Act (Betriebsverfassungsgesetz).

Research on German Co-determination
Since their introduction, both forms of co-determination have been of great interest for researchers. This is reflected both in theoretical papers, in particular research stemming from normative-democratic theories, as well as in empirical reviews with a wide range of questions (Greifenstein and Kissler 2010, 25). A third area of research is policy-related reports commissioned by the government.

Democracy and Co-determination

Co-determination is the main pillar of a democratic economic order. If democracy is the guiding principle of a society, the economy should not be organized in an anti-democratic manner. Therefore, dependent employees, as citizens, should not be regarded as "supplicants of a company" (Biedenkopf, Streeck, and Wissmann 2006, translation: KK; Biedenkopf, Streeck, and Wissmann 2006, 67–70).

In situations where individual enterprises decide significantly on the subsistence and life of their employees, the claim of wage-dependent employees on participation, coordination and cooperation should be granted based on democratic principles and the moral goal of humanization of the working world (Andersen 2013, 460; Demirovic 2008, 391). Co-determination is thus a realization of democracy as opposed to the authoritarian rule of capital's representatives. It thus puts under control the power of large companies and ideally creates an equitable relationship between capital and labor (Andersen 2013, 460). At the same time, it also serves as a means of further democratization (Vilmar 1973, 103).

In this context, co-determination ensures social peace and fulfills an integration function (Greifenstein and Kissler 2010, 12–16). This has already been confirmed in the early years of empirical co-determination research for corporate decision-making. Constructive cooperation in the supervisory board, transforms the latter in a conflict-free place for institutional integration of the workers who assume contributing tasks of supervision and advise the board in the early decision-making process. The influence of employee participation in corporate policy is reflected in a stronger emphasis on social aspects (Biedenkopf et al. 1970). However, as a problem concerning democratic claims, there is often a lack of possibilities to influence and a high level of informality, which limits both the controllability of boards and transparency efforts from external, regional and civil society forces (Greifenstein and Kissler 2010, 79).

The peacekeeping and integrative effects are also reflected in the operational co-determination. As stated in the report of the Co-Determination Commission (Mitbestimmungskommission) of 1998, operational co-determination is extensively used to implement tariff-contractual rules in a "situation-specific manner" (Streeck et al. 1998, 15, translation: KK). As a result, the works councils manage to enforce the interests of the workforce to varying degrees. An important success factor here is the participation of the represented (Greifenstein and Kissler 2010, 77–81). The low coverage of works councils, especially in small and medium-sized enterprises, is viewed as problematic. According to the Co-Determination Committee of 1998, it questioned the "functioning of the dual system of industrial relations as a whole" (Streeck et al. 1998, 15, translation: KK).

Despite its justification through democratic, societal and moral principles, the success of the German co-determination system is increasingly being measured by its economic success or failure, particularly because of attacks by the representatives of the Shareholder Value approach (Greifenstein and Kissler 2010, 25; Kocka 2006). A characteristic of the empirical research on the topic is that the interests of its initiators profoundly guide it. Greifenstein und Kissler, in their comprehensive overview of empirical research on co-determination, describe the debate between workers and employers about the economic implications of co-determination as "an interest-based mock fight" (Greifenstein and Kissler 2010, 77–81, translation: KK).

Co-determination - A Competitive Disadvantage?

The opponents of co-determination usually refer to price-theoretical arguments and emphasize the costs of participation, especially of board level representation. In this regard, a commission set up by the Federation of German Industries (BDI) and the German Confederation of German Employers' Associations (BDA) in 2004 criticized the specific design of German co-determination as too expensive. Following their report, both the committee work and the higher wages and social benefits associated with a strong workers' representation resulted in high costs. Coupled with the inefficiency of larger supervisory boards, co-determination was thus hindering economic growth and acting as a locational disadvantage in the international capital market (Greifenstein and Kissler 2010, 96–100; Stettes 2007). Some researchers consider the power of trade unions within supervisory boards as an impediment to employment; while others fear that the management has an incentive to behave opportunistically against employees rather than keeping an eye on the economic position of the company (Stettes 2007, 17).

Most empirical studies cannot confirm these economic disadvantages resulting from co-determination (Greifenstein and Kissler 2010, 99–100). Werner and Zimmermann (2005) do find a negative effect of corporate co-determination on employment. However, in contrast, Renaud (2008) finds a positive connection between corporate co-determination, profits and productivity. Vitols (2015) estimates its impact on productivity and competitiveness as generally neutral and finds neither grounds against equal representation nor evidence of a negative influence of trade union representatives on supervisory boards.

According to various further analyses, the German system is not in conflict with a capital market orientation (Höpner 2003; Zugehör 2003). German supervisory boards are no less competent than their counterparts in countries without co-determination, and the representation of employees on the supervisory board does not hinder their ability to function or to control. Nor does the larger number of supervisory board members constitute a clear competitive disadvantage. According to a study by Bermig and Frick (2011), a larger supervisory board has a negative impact on the return on equities but is associated with a higher market-to-book-ratio, whereas the impact on return on equity and interest rates remains insignificant. Based on the frequently occurring phenomenon that a supervisory board has more members than required by law, the authors conclude that the size of the supervisory board is hardly perceived as a competitive disadvantage. Moreover, there is no empirical evidence of opportunism within the management (Biedenkopf, Streeck, and Wissmann 2006, 17–18; 2006, 17).

A comprehensive analysis of various econometric studies by Jirhahn (2011) shows that overall, both operational and corporate co-determination tend to strengthen economic performance and productivity. After reviewing numerous empirical studies, Greifenstein and Kissler (2010, 141) conclude that rather than a locational disadvantage, co-determination could be seen as the "German response to globalization" (ibid., 141, translation: KK).. This assessment is supported by a survey among supervisory board members, business people and board of directors members in 2004, which does not show any fundamental rejection of employee participation and certainly no intention to abolish it (Biedenkopf, Streeck, and Wissmann 2006, 67–70).

Co-determination - A Competitive Advantage?

Advocates of the efficiency of employee participation argue based on a participation theory rather than on a price theory. They emphasize the advantages of a stable workforce and a socially integrated company organization (ibid., 67–70). Following their argument, a relaxed relationship between employees and management, accompanied by fewer strikes, leads to a productive and cooperative corporate culture that brings economic benefits. A further benefit mentioned is the greater understanding of the workforce of entrepreneurial needs (Streeck et al. 1998, 8). Co-determination is also expected to boost the innovative capacity of a company by exploiting internal resources and competencies of employees (Greifenstein and Kissler 2010, 15; Sperling and Wolf 2010; Ziegler and Gerlach 2010). This is empirically reflected in a better effect on modern forms of work, reorganization and further training measures, and in more filed patents (Hübler 2003; Kraft and Stank 2004;

Kriegesmann, Kley, and Kublik 2010; Zwick 2003). An important contribution to the innovation process is demonstrated in particular by works councils that consistently attempt to push through the interests of the employees despite oppositions from the management (Seibold et al. 2010). The possibility of activating, channeling and using a company's specific knowledge by means of their participation is currently fully exploited by a few companies (Kirner, Weißfloch, and Jäger 2010).

Therefore, the works council is credited as an "indispensable actor of strategic company management" and as a "co-manager of a modern corporate culture" (Greifenstein and Kissler 2010, 141; Kriegesmann, Kley, and Kublik 2010). Both institutions of co-determination have proved to act as an early warning system and valve in crises. They look for ways out in a non-bureaucratic, pragmatic and effective manner, thus supporting the company economically and in particular in the preservation of jobs (Bierbaum and Houben 2005; Greifenstein and Kissler 2010, 141). Although there is no empirical evidence for a general effect of co-determination on employment growth of companies (Koller, Schnabel, and Wagner 2008), works councils established during economic crises have a positive influence on employment and make company closures less likely (Jirjahn 2011).

Co-determination also has a sustainable element: the control of management in supervisory boards helps, especially in times of global capital mobility, to pursue long-term growth and employment interests rather than short-term profit-oriented incentives. Moreover, it assists in identifying implementation problems in the decision-making process at an early stage (Greifenstein and Kissler 2010, 141). Furthermore, the forced exchange between representatives of different parties within the company and in the supervisory board, contributes to a sustainable corporate culture since collective actors acquire knowledge that they would otherwise would not share and thus acquire higher competence (ibid., 12–16).

A business model with employer participation is based on long-term company affiliation (Dilger 1999), which makes human capital investment profitable (Streeck et al. 1998, 8). In the context of the increasingly knowledge-based production and the associated growing importance of individual performers for the company's success, co-determination plays an important role in binding competent individuals to the company (Biedenkopf, Streeck, and Wissmann 2006, 50)..

In summary, it can be stated that there are only few demonstrable effects of co-determination on economic factors. However, existing research tends to suggest a positive effect, whereas no negative effect is apparent (Greifenstein and Kissler 2010, 96–98). Anecdotal evidence, e.g. stemming from the German car industry, also suggests that companies that are particularly affected by employee participation are highly competitive and have adapted themselves successfully to new conditions during structural change (Streeck et al. 1998, 11) However, the results of empirical studies on co-determination should not be generalized. Few assertions can be made about the tertiary sector, which, despite its great importance for business and employment, is often still excluded from co-determination and underrepresented in research. The public sector, which is subject to a special regulation of employee participation, is also hardly a subject of current research (Greifenstein and Kissler 2010, 41–42).

New Challenges in the Globalized World Economy

The German co-determination system faces various challenges. The most important ones are, first, its exposure to the modern globalized world economy and, second, the expansion of the legal bases of German companies, in particular through European integration.

Challenges in a Globalized World Economy

The increased mobility of capital and labor, coupled with globalization, and the associated competitive constraints, outsourcing and job losses, are putting massive pressure on the co-determination system. The representation of the heterogeneous workforce in an international wage competition is becoming increasingly difficult and has been made even more difficult by declining union membership (Fichter 2005, 94; Greifenstein and Kissler 2010, 101–2). The co-determination system, as an institution created for the industrial sector, also suffered a loss of meaning in the structural change due to the increasing importance of the tertiary sector. This is also reflected in the distribution of employee participation. For example, the proportion of workers employed in the private sector who are neither represented on the operational nor on the corporate level has grown from about 50 percent in the middle of the 1980s to more than 60 percent in the mid-1990s (Streeck et al. 1998, 10). In 2015 only 42 per cent of the employees in West Germany and 33 per cent of the employees in East Germany were represented by a works council (Ellguth and Kohaut 2016).

On the grounds that the "German special path" was not up to the new challenges, critics welcomed the decline in employee participation and demanded a restriction of the rights to co-determination (Biedenkopf, Streeck, and Wissmann 2006, 56–60). On the other hand, supporters argued that "cooperative modernization" had proved to be a successful strategy of collaborative structural adjustment. The maintenance and further expansion of co-determination was therefore desirable and realistic (Streeck et al. 1998, 13). By means of employee participation, companies had succeeded in avoiding destructive measures, such as an overly strong orientation towards volatile financial markets. Instead, necessary restructuring was actively pursued and effectively shaped (Biedenkopf, Streeck, and Wissmann 2006, 54; Streeck et al. 1998, 13).

In order to cope successfully with new tasks arising from globalization and flexibilization, co-determination changed its functions: It shifted its focus away from protecting workers within a distributive struggle towards the goal of framing the conditions of the individual corporation or factory (Greifenstein and Kissler 2010, 105; Kleinschmidt et al. 1997).

In particular, operational co-determination has increasingly become co-management within the process of moving from standardized forms of work to project- and customer-oriented approaches (Streeck et al. 1998, 10). It is partly supplemented or replaced by various management-induced direct forms of participation (Andersen 2013, 463; Greifenstein and Kissler 2010, 113–15). Professionalized works councils gained importance in regards to corporate co-determination, especially in their role as an instance of controlled flexibility in consideration of employee interests (Ellguth and Ahlers 2003; Greifenstein and Kissler 2010, 106).

The stronger focus on representation on the plant level was considered in 2001 with a reform of the Works Constitution Act (*Betriebsverfassungsgesetz*), which takes account of the new tasks and framework conditions of operational co-determination (Rudolph and Wassermann 2001). Due to the successful prevention of plant closures by the strategic action of the works council (Detje et al. 2008), some in the scientific community see the opportunity to establish operational co-determination as a counterpart to shareholder capitalism (Martens and Dechmann 2010). However, it is also pointed out that the reductions in pay and restrictions imposed under pressure from job losses could undermine the peacekeeping and integrating functions of co-determination (Greifenstein and Kissler 2010, 17).

Challenges of a New Political and Legal Framework

In addition to the changed global economic conditions, the existing system has been called into question by new political and legal developments. This was mainly a result of deeper European integration. The future of German co-determination in the context of freedom of establishment in a European system of different co-determination regimes was regulated by various European legislation on corporate governance and decisions of the European Court of Justice (Biedenkopf, Streeck, and Wissmann 2006, 28–29).

Since 2004 and 2006 companies and co-operatives can be registered on a European level in accordance with EU Corporate Law as *European companies* (*Societas Europaea*; SE) and as *European co-operative society* (*Societas cooperativa Europaea;* SCE). Both corporate forms grant some co-determination rights on the operational and the corporate level.

These are less extensive than the German regulations (ibid., 30). However, the directive on European companies stipulates that when an SE is established by a change of the corporate form of a company the highest level of co-determination of the companies involved (Greifenstein and Kissler 2010, 22) applies. These relatively strict regulations are weakened by the fact that co-determination for European companies and cooperatives is regulated first and foremost by negotiation between representatives of the workforce and the management, and only in the case of non-agreement does a statutory fallback regulation take effect. The same applies to the cross-border merging of corporations (Biedenkopf, Streeck, and Wissmann 2006, 2006).

In the case of SEs and SCEs, there is a risk of circumventing corporate co-determination, in particular, when a German company changes its legal form before it exceeds a limit relevant to the German regulation. Co-determination at the corporate level is then "frozen" at the existing level, even if the threshold of 500 or 2000 employees is exceeded (Sick 2015a). It is estimated that in 2016 some 50 companies are avoiding equal co-determination using this strategy (Hans-Böckler-Stiftung 2016).

Another possibility to undermine the rules on corporate co-determination is the use of companies of foreign legal form. In 2004, the European Court of Justice (ECJ), in a ruling in reference to the right of freedom of establishment, allowed the free settlement of foreign companies in Germany. Governing law is that of the country of origin.

Hence, both German limited partnerships, which use a foreign general partner (such as Ltd & Co KG), as well as foreign corporations settling in Germany, remain unaffected by German co-determination legislation. Moreover, companies do not have to comply with co-determination rights even if they operate predominantly or even exclusively in Germany. This also applies to companies from Switzerland and since the signature of an agreement between Germany and the USA in 1954, to US corporations (Sick 2015b, 3).

In 2014, there were 94 companies in Germany, which circumvented corporate co-determination through foreign legal forms. These were more than four times as many as before 2000, when 20 companies used this evasive maneuver (ibid., 3).

The European regulations, together with the existing gaps in the co-determination legislation, can lead to the heterogenization of employee participation, the creation of company-specific industrial relations and a restriction of co-determination rights (Greifenstein and Kissler 2010, 93). At the same time, however, there is also the possibility that employees from other European countries with weak national regulations could fall under the protective framework of employee participation (ibid., 93).

This could be further promoted through the institution of the European Works Council (EWC), already established in the 1990s. This institution enables the European workforce of a transnational company to organize itself across national boundaries. In its implementation, there are still reports of numerous problems such as: power asymmetries between actors and the difficulty of working together against the backdrop of different historic trade union patterns of action (ibid., 93–94). Nevertheless, the EWC is increasingly establishing a sustainable policy of representation of interests and is respected by employees and the management likewise (Biedenkopf, Streeck, and Wissmann 2006, 95; Streeck et al. 1998, 18; 1998). Moreover, the EWC makes the co-determination by employees of different nationalities within a company at the plant level possible. On the board level, however, there has not been any regulation for German companies, which would have solved the problem of the sole representation of the German share of an international workforce (Biedenkopf, Streeck, and Wissmann 2006, 33–34).

There is also the legal possibility of setting up a 'Global Works Council', in which the various representations of employees in different countries coordinate and inform each other. It is not yet clear whether this institution will develop into a relevant movement (Rüb 2000).

The discussion of the new challenges for the German co-determination system shows that a national consideration of the system is no longer sufficient against the background of global economic interdependencies and the legal integration of Germany into European structures. Thus it is necessary to look at the challenges arising from the integration of Germany into the global economy. This will be done later in this work by examining the effects of the CETA and TTIP trade agreements on co-determination rights in Germany.

Furthermore, the impact of German economic activity on co-determination rights in other countries must be examined. It is particularly interesting to what extent Germany's foreign trade policy can contribute to the promotion of Germany's co-determination rights rather than suppressing them. For this purpose, the opportunities of German foreign economic policy to engage itself for the right to co-determination worldwide are scrutinized below. Following a general classification of these possibilities, selected instruments of this policy field are examined in more detail.

Ways the Federal Government Could Promote Global Co-determination Rights

German companies operating within national borders are legally obliged to respect extensive co-determination rights. The management of many German transnationally active corporations stands out as exemplary in the cooperation with employees. However, the management of subsidiaries of these corporations, such as the *Deutsche Telekom* subsidiary *T-Mobile US* in the southern states of the USA, is often less radiant (Handelsblatt 2016; Mey 2015; We Expect Better 2016). An even more severe suppression of co-determination rights is encountered in the suppliers of German corporations, such as the *KiK* supplying companies in Bangladesh (Ganguly 2015). Evidence for the suppression of co-determination rights in subsidiary companies or across the supply chain has been sufficiently documented (BMWi 2007; 2014a; 2014c; 2014d; 2014e; 2015; Ganguly 2015).

In order to avoid such cases and to contribute to the promotion of co-determination rights, the German Federal Government should, firstly, step up the efforts to convince German companies to respect co-determination rights throughout the entire supply chain. Secondly, in order to prevent the infringement of rights by companies in countries that do not politically protect the co-determination rights of their citizens, the German government should intensify the exchange with the respective governments.

A study published on behalf of the World Bank identifies four tasks to be undertaken by governments in order to effectively force companies to respect rights along their supply chain. The duties of the state are: to mandate effective standards (mandating), to assist companies in their implementation and facilitate the latter as much as possible (facilitating), to participate in the establishment of standards (partnering) and to honor good practices (endorsing) (Fox, Ward, and Howard 2002, 3–6).

For foreign economic policy this implies that foreign trade and investment promotion must be designed in such a way that it effectively obligates or incentivizes a company to comply with co-determination rights (mandating). At the same time, corporations are supposed to receive as much support and assistance as possible in order to meet this task (facilitating). Therefore, these two aspects will be taken into account in the chapter on foreign trade and investment promotion, which deals with export financing aids, export credit, investment and untied loan guarantees, chambers of commerce abroad and *Germany Trade and Invest*. The two aspects are also considered in the investigation of *develoPPP.de*, a project sponsored by the BMZ for private development cooperation.

In order to set a good example, the state should introduce Best Practice behavior in its own companies and in public procurement (partnering). This is dealt with in more detail in the chapters on public procurements and state-owned companies. Several platforms, such as the *UN Principles for Responsible Investment* or the *Partnership for Sustainable Textiles*, already provide support for exemplary behavior (endorsing). Both the approaches are therefore also examined in this study. In order to keep an eye on the dialogue with other countries, embassies are considered as the starting point. The *National Action Plan for Business and Human Rights* (*Nationaler Aktionsplan für Wirtschaft und*

Menschenrechte), which was concluded by the end of 2016, could have provided a useful platform for a meaningful coordination and coherent application of the numerous instruments. It will therefore be treated as the first instrument for the purpose of this study.

For each instrument, a connection to co-determination is established and possible channels for its promotion are presented in detail. The framework conditions under which these channels can be effective will be pointed out. The considerations are compared with current policy. Consequently, concrete proposals for action are deduced. In order to point out clear responsibilities, the various instruments are grouped under the competent Ministry. If a number of competencies are involved, the choice falls on the Ministry that is most responsible for the task of promoting co-determination. Despite the fact that the German Foreign Ministry has been the prime mover of the instrument discussed in the next chapter, the *National Action Plan for Business and Human Rights*, the decision on the final plan depended on the various ministries involved since it provides a framework for the work of all ministries. Therefore, the instrument will not be categorized under a specific ministry.

The National Action Plan for Business and Human Rights: A Coherent Framework for Government Policies?

The German *National Action Plan for Business and Human Rights* was concluded in December 2016 by the German Federal Government within the framework of the *UN Guiding Principles on Business and Human Rights*. The plan was developed under the leadership of the Federal Ministry of Foreign Affairs (AA). Involved in the process were also the Federal Ministry for Economic Affairs and Energy (BMWi), the Federal Ministry of Labor and Social Affairs (BMAS), the Federal Ministry for Economic Cooperation and Development (BMZ), the Federal Ministry of Justice and Consumer Protection (BMJV) and the Federal Ministry of Finance (BMF).

UN Guiding Principles on Business and Human Rights

The UN Human Rights Council adopted the *UN Guiding Principles on Business and Human Rights* unanimously in June 2011. The 31 principles developed by John Ruggie under the three pillars Protect (the state duty to protect human rights), Respect (the corporate responsibility to respect human rights) and Remedy (access to remedy for victims of human rights violations), oblige the signatory states to prevent human rights violations by corporate misconduct and to ensure the detection and punishment of violations and the compensation of their victims. Through National Action Plans (NAPs), the guiding principles are to be implemented by the signatory states into concrete policies (United Nations Human Rights - Office of the High Commissioner 2011).

As criticized by the German Trade Union Confederation (DGB) in its statement on the guiding principles, the framework does not explicitly point to the instrumental role of statutory co-determination in the protection of human rights (Deutscher Gewerkschaftsbund 2009, 4).

However, co-determination is important for the content of the guiding principles and their implementation in two major ways. Firstly, the rights to freedom of association, freedom of trade unions and freedom to set rates are the basis of co-determination. As *ILO core labor standards* they are guaranteed in the principles as central working rights to be respected by companies ('Respect'; United Nations Human Rights - Office of the High Commissioner 2011). Secondly, the guiding principles emphasize the importance of the involvement of the relevant stakeholders at several points in their *operational principles* (which articulate the provisions of implementation for states and corporates).

For instance, companies should involve "relevant stakeholders" when drafting a human rights commitment (Guiding Principle 16), as well as when tracking the effectiveness of improvement proposals (Guiding Principle 20) and when communicating externally how they address their human rights impact (Guiding Principle 21). Concerning "Remedy", non-State based grievance mechanisms (Guiding Principles 28 and 29) are referred to as mechanisms developed with stakeholders and managed by multi-stakeholder groups. One of the effectiveness criteria for non-judicial grievance mechanisms (Guiding Principle 31) is that they build on exchange and dialogue with stakeholder groups (ibid.). In the corporate context, employees and their interest groups are among the most important stakeholders. The involvement of the latter is therefore at the core of the UN Guiding Principles (Hadwinger et al. 2016, 181).

For example, the involvement of co-determination bodies in accordance with the above principles, can be implemented by providing works councils with guidance and information on risk analysis and impact assessment, or by developing, improving and managing grievance mechanisms in partnership with the company (ibid., 181–87).

Possibilities for the Promotion of Co-determination through the National Action Plan

The *smart mix* of different measures – national or international and mandatory or voluntary, as suggested by the guidelines, can be interpreted very differently by governments in terms of liability and entitlement (Grabosch and Scheper 2015, 10). Like many others, the German Federal Government has adopted a National Action Plan (NAP), which should implement the guiding principles through different concrete practices.

If designed appropriately, the NAP could have promoted co-determination through two channels. Firstly, it had the potential to oblige or incentivize German companies to enforce operational co-determination in subsidiaries and suppliers. Secondly, the design of the German NAP is of great interest to governments that are in the early stages of the same process since provisions for employee participation could serve as a model for other action plans and thus it could stimulate discussions outside Germany to establish co-determination. The following section explains the potential of the first channel. It then examines the extent to which the adopted NAP uses this potential.

In order to make the enforcement of operational co-determination in subsidiaries and suppliers outside Germany more effective, a framework that makes the introduction of co-determination attractive for German companies should have been created. Despite the expected positive long-term effects of co-determination, the introduction and, in particular, the safeguarding of rights across the entire supply chain will lead to short-term and company-specific costs. A purely voluntary provision could create competitive disadvantages for companies that are concerned with the effective implementation of labor rights (ibid., 43). Empirical studies of voluntary commitments are not very optimistic about their effectiveness (e.g. Anner 2012; Banerjee 2014; Vogel 2005, 164).

If, therefore, the Federal Government was willing to commit itself to the enforcement of the guiding principles, and thus of human rights in business, as stipulated in the coalition agreement (CDU Deutschland and CSU-Landesleitung 2013, 125), the respective regulation should either contain binding obligations with effective sanctions for non-compliance or positive incentives for compliance. Practical proposals existed for both practices prior to the adoption of the German NAP.

Binding Regulation and Sanctions: Enforceable Human Rights Due Diligence

The UN Guiding Principles in themselves are non-enforceable. Only with the appropriate political support of national governments can they be instrumental in filling the existing regulatory gaps in the area of the global protection of wage-earners' rights and thus for co-determination. A central instrument in this direction is the introduction of 'Human Rights Due Diligence' as stipulated in the *UN Guiding Principles*, provided that these are incorporated into national law.

Extensive proposals for their political and legal design have been laid down by Grabosch and Scheper (2015). Due diligence determines the requirements that members of a professional group must fulfill in a situation, in order to counteract infringements of the rights of third parties (ibid., 26). In the event of damage, i.e. in case of infringement of rights due to negligent due diligence, responsible companies can be brought before a court of law.

Due diligence is already legally anchored in a wide range of economic sectors. The innovation in the context of the *Guiding Principles* is represented by the relation to human rights and their global application. Human rights due diligence could for instance force parent companies to create framework conditions under which suppression of co-determination rights in supplier companies is prevented.

There are already numerous 'soft laws' with recommendations to companies in this area. Their complexity and the lack of clarity of the current legal situation, however, place big challenges on companies that want to implement measures to prevent human rights violations in subsidiaries or suppliers outside Germany. Against this background, many companies under competitive pressure avoid the often costly changes and ultimately prefer to accept the violation of human rights and the minimal risk of legal disputes (ibid., 27).

Therefore, in order to establish legal certainty, it is necessary to make clear that companies must also exercise human rights due diligence in businesses abroad and in accordance to international law. For instance, a violation of *ILO core labor standards* should clearly be interpreted as a lack of due diligence. In addition, minimum requirements for human rights due diligence should be regulated and different measures should be conceded to companies of different backgrounds (ibid., 6).

Specifically, the legislator could indicate substantive themes and leave the further design to multi-stakeholder initiatives. Existing institutions such as *Human Rights Impact Assessments* could be used to facilitate the implementation. The extent to which a German company is obliged to comply to human rights due diligence could be made dependent on the industry-specific risk of rights violation, the durability of business relations, and the level of influence the company has on the conditions of production (ibid., 63).

Moreover, a system of 'safe harbors' and 'sure shipwrecks' could be introduced to restrict legal grey zones in complex situations. 'Safe Harbors' are rules that allow the compliant party under obligation to escape sanctions (e.g. when a company has adhered to 'best practice' proposals). 'Sure shipwrecks', on the other hand, are clear transgressions, which unless the company can prove in a concrete case that the damage would have occurred anyway, would lead regularly to sanctions (e.g. the non-existence of a due diligence concept) (ibid., 63).

The judicial sanctioning of extraterritorial legal infringements is officially possible in Germany since 2009 and the Rome II Regulation at the latest. According to the current legal situation, judgments are usually pronounced according to the law of the country in which the damage occurred. In this case, if designed as described above, human rights due diligence would have to be taken into account to some extent. Alternatively, in the case of a design of due diligence as overriding mandatory provisions, foreign law would be replaced by human rights due diligence clauses (ibid., 63).

A binding regulation should be complemented by a supporting institutional framework, which would assist companies, in particular through information, to assess the risk of their supply chain and to apply their due diligence. Such an institutional framework can be supported, for example, by the German embassies and chambers of commerce abroad as outlined in later chapters (ibid., 64).

An argument which is often put forward suggests that parent companies could not be held responsible for human rights violations or the restriction of co-determination rights in subsidiary and supplier companies, since supervision in global supply chains was impossible per se or only achievable through a disproportionate effort. In practice, this is however not confirmed. Examples of similar regulations (such as the regulation on conflict minerals in the US *Dodd-Frank Act*) suggest that such a law can be effective without overburdening parent companies. Regarding the *Dodd-Frank Act*, on the contrary, a systematic development of risk knowledge in the affected companies can be observed (ibid., 44–46).

Employee co-determination could, in turn, take a crucial position in a system of corporate due diligence. Co-determination within plants over the supply chain appears to be an effective means to prevent human rights risks of all kinds in subsidiaries and suppliers.

Voluntary Regulations Linked to Positive Incentives

Instead of sanctions, positive incentives could also be used for the enforcement of co-determination rights and other labor rights across the supply chain. One possibility for this is certifications, with which companies pledge good behavior for a positive image among consumers. It is important to note that these certifications are effective only in industries that are directly in contact with the end consumer. An instrument in this direction is the *Partnership for Sustainable Textiles*, which will be covered later in this study.

Alternatively, by setting out conditions for state subsidies, export or investment guarantees, a binding commitment for co-determination rights can be enforced for the companies wishing to obtain such support. Possibilities for how the German Federal Government can use such instruments are discussed in the sections on the Federal Ministry of Economics and Energy (BMWi).

A general proposition applying to both mandatory and voluntary measures was summarized by the head of the Economic and Human Rights Working Group at the Federal Foreign Office in a conference as follows: "Compliant behavior must be cheaper than non-compliant behavior for a company" (Bundesministerium für wirtschaftliche Zusammenarbeit und Entwicklung and Auswärtiges Amt 2015, 5–6, translation: KK). To this end, the Federal Government must clearly communicate its requirements for human rights due diligence, as well as actively support companies in dealing with human rights risks (ibid., 5–6).

The wise integration of existing structures and institutions, such as the *OECD Guidelines* or the *Global Compact*, is crucial for effective and realistic regulations for the enforcement of corporate co-determination in subsidiaries and subcontractors. The *OECD Guidelines* will be discussed below.

The German National Action Plan

The development phase of the German NAP was praised as exemplary by many sides. A comprehensive consultation process took place before the plan was drafted. The current situation regarding the guiding principles was presented in a detailed *National Baseline Assessment*, which also addresses the need for change and possible concrete starting points (Bundesministerium für wirtschaftliche Zusammenarbeit und Entwicklung and Auswärtiges Amt 2015, 2; Deutsches Institut für Menschenrechte 2015).

However, the adoption of the plan in December 2016 by the Federal Government did not keep its promise for the extensive involvement of civil society. Trade unions and NGOs expressed criticism regarding the fact that civil society and business representatives were abruptly relegated to an observer role after the consultation phase (Deutscher Gewerkschaftsbund 2016b, 1). Contrary to previous commitments, they were not included in the drafting of the plan and were no longer consulted before its adoption (CoRA-Netzwerk für Unternehmensverantwortung et al. 2016, 4). The lack of a serious involvement of important stakeholders is also reflected in the content of the NAP.

The action plan is divided into five chapters. These describe the process of its formulation, the expectations of the Federal Government to companies, important areas of action as well as plans for policy coherence and monitoring of the targets set. The most important "expectation" the Federal Government expresses to German companies is the compliance with human rights due diligence.

Human Rights Due Diligence in the NAP

The human rights due diligence of companies within the NAP, along with the *UN Guiding Principles*, foresees several steps. It requires the preparation of a statement of principle, the identification of potential negative impacts of a company on human rights and measures to prevent them, a reporting process and the establishment of a grievance mechanism.

These different elements of due diligence are partly based on the participation of employees. For example, it is stated in the NAP that the different perspectives of employees as well as trade unions should be included in the design and implementation of human rights due diligence (Deutsche Bundesregierung 2016,

8). The examination of negative impacts is to take place in on-site dialogue with (potential) stakeholders (ibid., 8). These should also be involved in the design of the grievance procedure (ibid., 11). However, beyond that, co-determination rights and mechanisms to secure them are not mentioned in the 43-page document at all. Despite the reference to the *ILO core labor standards*, co-determination in the NAP does not play a role. Its essential function for the global enforcement of labor rights is therefore ignored. Important global measures of co-determination such as *Global Framework Agreements*[2] are also disregarded (Deutscher Gewerkschaftsbund 2016b, 7).

In contrast to the international consensus, the German government's definition of human rights due diligence is limited to preventive measures. Reparation measures and compensation for affected persons are not foreseen (CoRA-Netzwerk für Unternehmensverantwortung et al. 2016, 3; Deutsche Bundesregierung 2016, 9–13).

A well-designed NAP could have created a 'level playing field' through a smart mix of voluntary and binding measures, in which compliance with rights does not penalize a company in competition. This potential is compromised by the non-binding nature of the foreseen obligations. The human rights due diligence is not legally anchored and its non-observance is thus not sanctionable. By 2020, however, at least half of all companies with more than 500 employees should have integrated human rights due diligence into business processes. This objective is marked as achieved when a company either complies with obligations or explains why it was not possible to do so ('comply or explain'). If the specified number of companies is not reached, the Federal Government will "examine further extensive steps that could extend to legal measures" (Deutsche Bundesregierung 2016, 12, translation: KK).

Apart from the fact that the examination of binding obligations was already a task of the 2014-2016 NAP process, civil society actors are concerned that such a deadline will lead to idleness on the part of corporations. This risk is particularly present, since binding measures are not clearly announced in the submitted final draft (CoRA-Netzwerk für Unternehmensverantwortung et al. 2016, 4; Deutscher Gewerkschaftsbund 2016b, 2). Due to the non-binding character, firms still cannot rely on a legally certain definition of global human rights due diligence. Only this certainty would however effectively incentivize firms to strive for the compliance with co-determination rights to minimize financial risks associated with possible lawsuits. In addition to involving all companies (instead of only a few large ones), binding and enforceable human

---

[2] Global framework agreements are agreements negotiated between trade unions and a multinational group at a global level. They are intended to protect the interests of the entire workforce of a globally operating company.

rights due diligence would hence be a big step towards creating a 'level playing field' (Deutscher Gewerkschaftsbund 2016b, 2).

Furthermore, the requirements on companies are subject to the condition of not creating disproportionate bureaucratic burdens. This is considered by unions and NGOs as part of an interest-driven debate, which, on the pretext of reducing bureaucracy, dismisses political decisions and labor and human rights as nonsensical or unnecessary (CoRA-Netzwerk für Unternehmensverantwortung et al. 2016, 6; Deutscher Gewerkschaftsbund 2016b, 4).

Binding human rights due diligence is not required even from companies that are particularly close to the government. Thus, no binding regulation applies to companies owned by the Federal Government or the states (Länder), to companies that receive export funding or other forms of subsidy or that produce for the public sector. Instead, existing standards for companies benefitting from public support, should place a stronger focus on human rights (Deutsche Bundesregierung 2016). The decision to not even include human rights due diligence as a binding requirement for state-owned companies nor make state support dependent on due diligence contradicts previous drafts and deviates from NAPs of other countries such as Finland or Sweden.

Even if due diligence is not legally prescribed according to the NAP, companies are expected to report on the impact of their business activities on human rights. To create transparency according to a company's impact, corporations should fulfill their non-financial and diversity reporting obligations which have already been established in the Corporate Social Responsibility (CSR) Directive, introduced in 2016. In the interest of active co-determination, already in the debate about the CSR Directive, trade unions demanded to include works councils in the preparation of the non-financial information (Deutscher Gewerkschaftsbund 2016b, 8). Their involvement, however, similarly to the Directive, is not stipulated by the NAP (Deutsche Bundesregierung 2016).

Access to Justice for Damaged Parties

Even prior to the adoption of the NAP and, similarly now, in spite of the non-binding nature of its measures, it has been theoretically possible for damaged parties abroad to take legal action against German companies. However, according to the *German Institute for Human Rights* and various NGOs, victims of human rights violations by German companies outside Germany, have access to German courts only in very rare cases. In comparison to their European colleagues, German lawyers' engagement is below average in complex cross-border cases related to labor rights. Further, the lack of possibilities for class-action suits as well as the seldom provision of residence for lawsuits hinders judicial action from foreigners.

These problems, as well as numerous suggestions for improvements by NGOs and trade unions, in particular the demand for the possibility of class-actions suits, are not taken up by the NAP. Instead, attention is drawn to the existing possibility to file a suit and the preparation of a multilingual information brochure. This timid measure will not change the situation for those affected in the global South. The latter will continue to be unable to hold German companies responsible for legal infringements and thus also for the suppression of co-determination (CoRA-Netzwerk für Unternehmensverantwortung et al. 2016, 2–3; Deutsche Bundesregierung 2016; Deutscher Gewerkschaftsbund 2016b, 8; Deutsches Institut für Menschenrechte 2016, 9–10).

According to the German NAP, in addition to internal company mechanisms, the *National Contact Point* of the *OECD Guidelines* (which will be explored in more detail later in this study) should be reformed and revaluated as a major non-judicial grievance instrument. This solution is welcomed by civil society actors. However, against the background of the criticism on the *National Contact Point*, it remains to be seen to what extent it will be able to perform the function of a relevant non-judicial grievance mechanism. Even after the reform planned in the NAP, the post of the *National Contact Point* will not be independent due to its incorporation into the BMWi. Coupled with the absence of stakeholder participation, this raises doubts as to whether it will be able to fulfill the effectiveness criteria that the *UN guiding principles* target to non-judicial grievance mechanisms (CoRA-Netzwerk für Unternehmensverantwortung et al. 2016, 2-3; 14; Deutsche Bundesregierung 2016).

Monitoring the NAP

Effective monitoring of the entire NAP is essential, in particular due to the numerous orders involved to further assess certain issues or measures. The Federal Government intends to set up an inter-ministerial committee, which reviews the planned measures. The monitoring process is to be attended by the NAP steering committee, which includes representatives from businesses, civil society and trade unions. The steering committee will be integrated into the existing *National CSR Forum*. Civil society and trade unions demand a new mandate, a new governance structure and clear decision-making processes for this body. In addition, it should ensure equal representation of the business community, trade unions and NGOs, as well as a permanent exchange with the inter-ministerial committee (CoRA-Netzwerk für Unternehmensverantwortung et al. 2016, 16).

The relatively extensive monitoring is, however, subject to the availability of funding. NGOs also criticize the fact that no independent and recognized institution, such as the *German Institute for Human Rights*, has been involved in the monitoring process. Moreover, the review of the implementation should extend beyond self-disclosed company reports. A justification of why certain points are not fulfilled ('comply or explain') should not be recognized as complying with human rights due diligence (CoRA-Netzwerk für Unternehmensverantwortung et al. 2016; Deutsche Bundesregierung 2016).

A number of assistance possibilities and voluntary initiatives are planned to help companies that are concerned about compliance with human rights due diligence. Different bodies will offer information and training programs to respect human rights across the supply chain and to expand the existing range of options. The German representations abroad, the German Chambers of Commerce Abroad and the portal Germany Trade and Invest will also provide support. This will be discussed in more detail in later chapters of this study. The NAP does not plan one central independent, generally accessible, counseling center with sufficient personnel, which was requested by NGOs as a contact point for companies with questions on human rights due diligence (CoRA-Netzwerk für Unternehmensverantwortung et al. 2016, 13).

In addition to consulting, the Federal Government intends to reward and make public best practice approaches by awarding a CSR prize. Furthermore, the introduction of a national guarantee mark, in addition to the European mark, is being considered. The CSR Prize could particularly support co-determination rights as selection criteria incorporate important elements of employee participation such as works councils and collective bargaining agreements (Deutscher Gewerkschaftsbund 2016b, 8). Nevertheless, it remains a selective measure (Deutsche Bundesregierung 2016).

Disappointing German NAP

Before its conclusion, at a conference on the German NAP in 2015, a member of the *UN Working Group on Business and Human Rights* stated that: "This is the NAP we are all looking for. It is expected to be a worldwide showcase" (Bundesministerium für wirtschaftliche Zusammenarbeit und Entwicklung and Auswärtiges Amt 2015). Looking at the adopted NAP, one year later, it can be argued that the plan remains far below expectations. Instead, it must be hoped that it will *not* serve as a model for other countries, since the federal government itself is failing to realize the promised "ambitious plan" (Bundesministerium für wirtschaftliche Zusammenarbeit und Entwicklung 2015, translation: KK). A comparison of European NAPs shows that the German plan falls behind the efforts made by many other countries (Germanwatch and Brot für die Welt 2016).

According to the *German Institute for Human Rights*, with a systematic refusal of binding requirements in favor of voluntary measures, the plan is "not as smart" as the *UN Guiding Principles* actually call for (Deutsches Institut für

Menschenrechte 2016, 5, translation: KK). While support for companies is guaranteed, binding requirements are just planned to be assessed (CoRA-Netzwerk für Unternehmensverantwortung et al. 2016, 3). Thus, no clear incentives were included for the observance of fundamental rights. On the contrary, compliance with co-determination rights across the supply chain can continue to appear as a competitive disadvantage for a company.

In the coming years, it remains to be seen whether the deficits of this plan can be offset by a committed implementation process by the Federal Government and other stakeholders (Deutsches Institut für Menschenrechte 2016, 12). If the NAP, as proposed by the DGB, is only a "first NAP" (Deutscher Gewerkschaftsbund 2016b, 1, translation: KK), followed by further plans with improved instruments, it could actually help to make co-determination across supply chains of German corporations a reality.

As indicated by different examples, the NAP links various measures from different areas and competencies. Many of these elements are revisited in the following chapters. An ambitious implementation of the plan would thus pave the way to making the German co-determination system known abroad. At the same time, it would offer a platform where different government initiatives with similar objectives could be coordinated. Moreover, it could lead towards a clear commitment to acknowledge human rights worldwide, also in the economic context. The next chapters explore the potential that each federal ministry offers in this direction.

Federal Ministry for Economic Affairs and Energy (BMWi) and KfW Group

The BMWi uses numerous instruments to promote foreign trade. Many of the funding possibilities anchored in the BMWi are offered in cooperation with the KfW-Bank (Reconstruction Loan Corporation). Before moving on to the analysis of individual instruments in the area of responsibility of the BMWi, the special role played by the state and thus the BMWi in the field of economic policy will briefly be discussed.

The Dual Role of the State As a Regulating Authority and Economic Actor

The government has a dual role within the economy. On the one hand, it regulates the behavior of market participants, for example through the legal anchoring of due diligence. At the same time, the state itself appears as a market participant in many occasions. In Germany, this happens in the roles of the *financial investor*, namely by financing exports and projects abroad, and its participation in companies as a shareholder, *the insurer*, namely by offering export and investment guarantees, and the *purchaser* of goods and services in public procurements.

The motivations for economic activity differ for the aforementioned functions. On the one hand, promotion of the economy and on the other, the acquisition of necessary goods and services. However, the different instruments are all impressive in size: The federally-owned KfW Bank is the largest state development bank in the world and the third largest bank in Germany (Deutscher Bundestag 2015d, 1). The Federal Government grants over 160 billion Euros for the insurance of exports ('state as insurer'; Euler Hermes Aktiengesellschaft 2015, 2) and the public sector spends annually over 350 billion euros ('state as purchaser'; Umweltbundesamt 2016).

In its role as a market participant the state simultaneously also sets rules. It decides how a business partner is selected, what requirements are being placed on him and how contracts are formulated. The combination of the two roles of the state, where for example, purchasing a service is at the same time regulated by strategic purchasing in order to achieve other objectives such as good working conditions, is known as a 'linkage'. In more general terms, 'linkage' describes the connection of different political goals (McCrudden 2004, 257).

The Use of 'Linkage' to Promote Co-determination

The private sector has great interest in doing business with the state. Whether for state financing, insurance or purchasing, companies benefit from conditions that are not offered likewise in the private sector.

These areas are therefore particularly suitable for *linkage*. Barry and Reddy (2008) distinguish three forms of linkage in the context of employment rights. *Evaluation linkage* is the joint evaluation of different sub-objectives in order to evaluate whether a general societal objective is achieved. The level of importance of these different objectives, which are included in the evaluation, should then influence the institutional design of policy instruments.

Agency linkage means pursuing different objectives with an instrument or through an institution. Finally, a *rights linkage* represents a situation where the obtainment of special rights is made dependent on a certain behavior.

In the context of foreign trade promotion and public procurement, the promotion of labor and co-determination rights could firstly be introduced as an objective in addition to economic advantage (*evaluation linkage*). Secondly, the existing institutions would be tasked with effectively pursuing both objectives and should be designed accordingly (*agency linkage*). Thirdly, private economic actors who benefit from public funds should only be allowed to continue doing so if they also respect and promote co-determination rights (*rights linkage*).

Linkage is useful for the enforcement of rights in the area of responsibility of German actors abroad and particularly for the guarantee of basic rights in supply chains. It provides the opportunity to close the 'compliance gap', which has emerged since the 1990s due to the establishment of ever more far-reaching voluntary agreements on compliance with standards across the global supply chain on the one hand and a lack of binding verifications to enforce them on the other. In areas where a government considers traditional regulation options of 'command and control' as unacceptable, unenforceable or ineffective, alternative forms of regulation can be established through *linkage* (McCrudden 2007, 2).

The following section explores the different possibilities offered by *linkage*, which could be used by the German government in its role as investor in foreign trade when granting export financing, as an insurer in the guarantee of exports and investments abroad, and as a purchaser in public procurements.

International Export and Project Finance of the KfW Bank

The funds of the *KfW-IPEX Bank* and the KfW's fully owned subsidiary *Deutsche Investitions- und Entwicklungsgesellschaft m.b.H* (German Investment and Development Company; DEG) are available to German companies for the purpose of financing exports, investments and projects abroad (BMWi and Referat Öffentlichkeitsarbeit 2016c). While the *KfW-IPEX Bank* was created primarily for export and investment promotion, DEG aims to keep development targets in focus.

KfW-IPEX Bank

KfW-IPEX Bank operates worldwide project, foreign investment and export financing, including structured financing for major projects (ibid.). With a credit volume of EUR 69.4 billion, in 2015, the "most successful year of the company's history" (KfW IPEX-Bank 2015a, 5, translation: KK), it represented approximately 15 per cent of the KfW loans in its "export and project financing" segment and generated a surplus of EUR 628 million (ibid., 5).

The main task of the bank is financing in the interest of the German and European economies. Among other tasks, it also aims at securing raw materials for domestic production. At the same time, IPEX claims to be clearly committed to social responsibility, to promote environmental and climate protection and the development of an economic and social infrastructure worldwide (ibid., 3).

In this commitment to social responsibility should also belong the safeguarding of co-determination rights. In this regard, a simple rule for *rights linkage* could be the following: Only those companies who ensure co-determination rights in their entire area of responsibility, especially in the new projects and investments, can take advantage of the favorable conditions of export and project financing.

In response to massive criticism for financing socially and ecologically problematic projects (Hamm, Scheper, and Schölmerich 2011; Heydenreich 2014; urgewald 2015), the *KfW-IPEX Bank* is trying to secure social and ecological responsibility in financed projects through its own sustainability guidelines. As shown in Figure 4.1, depending on the credit form, the guidelines refer to the *Equator Principles* or the *Recommendation of the Council on Common Approaches for Officially Supported Export Credits and Environmental and Social Due Diligence* (Common Approaches) of the *Organization for Economic Co-operation and Development* (OECD).

Figure 4.1: Review Process of KfW Bank's Export Financing

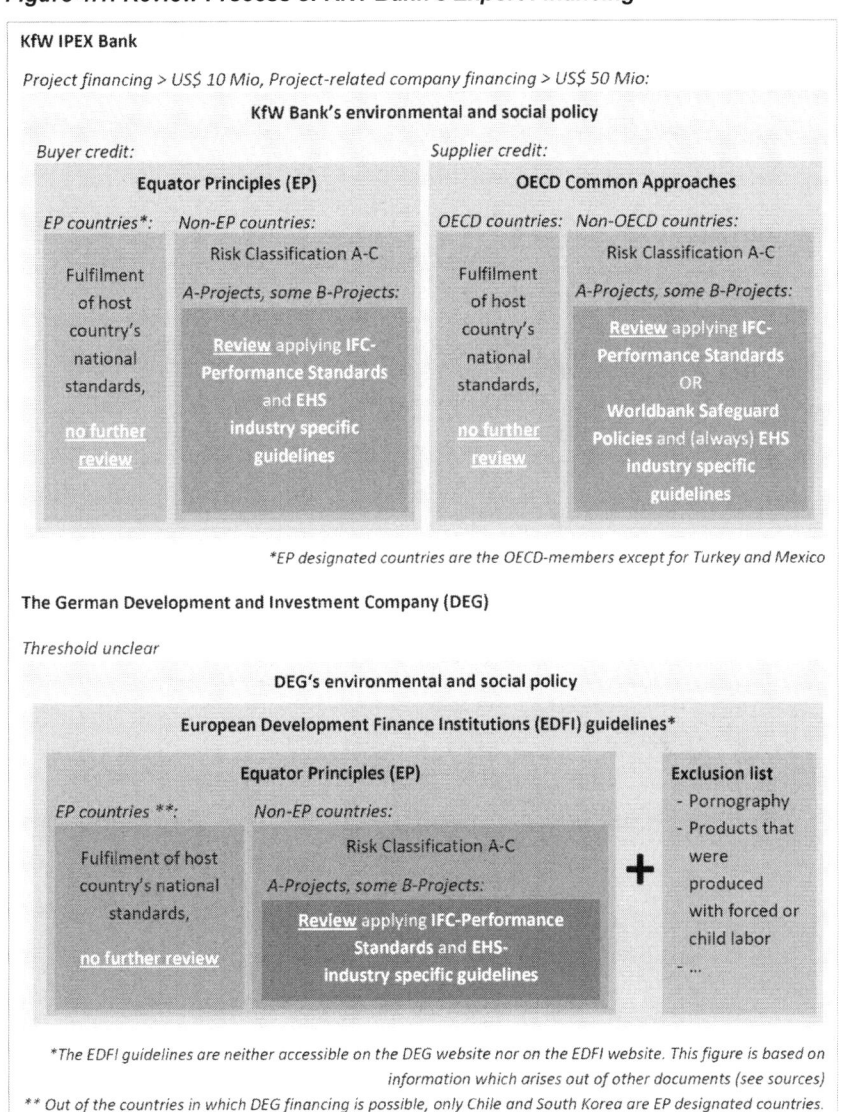

KfW IPEX Bank

Project financing > US$ 10 Mio, Project-related company financing > US$ 50 Mio:

KfW Bank's environmental and social policy

Buyer credit:		Supplier credit:	
Equator Principles (EP)		**OECD Common Approaches**	
EP countries*:	Non-EP countries:	OECD countries:	Non-OECD countries:
Fulfilment of host country's national standards, **no further review**	Risk Classification A-C A-Projects, some B-Projects: **Review** applying **IFC-Performance Standards** and **EHS industry specific guidelines**	Fulfilment of host country's national standards, **no further review**	Risk Classification A-C A-Projects, some B-Projects: **Review** applying **IFC-Performance Standards OR Worldbank Safeguard Policies** and (always) **EHS industry specific guidelines**

*EP designated countries are the OECD-members except for Turkey and Mexico

The German Development and Investment Company (DEG)

Threshold unclear

DEG's environmental and social policy

European Development Finance Institutions (EDFI) guidelines*

Equator Principles (EP)		**Exclusion list**
EP countries **:	Non-EP countries:	- Pornography
Fulfilment of host country's national standards, **no further review**	Risk Classification A-C A-Projects, some B-Projects: **Review** applying **IFC-Performance Standards** and **EHS- industry specific guidelines**	- Products that were produced with forced or child labor - ...

*The EDFI guidelines are neither accessible on the DEG website nor on the EDFI website. This figure is based on information which arises out of other documents (see sources)
** Out of the countries in which DEG financing is possible, only Chile and South Korea are EP designated countries.

Source: Own representation based on Deutsche Investitions- und Entwicklungsgesellschaft 2015; KfW IPEX-Bank 2015a; 2015b; OECD 2016; The Equator Principles Association 2011

Both frameworks initially foresee the categorization of a submitted project. If the project falls into a particularly risky category, in an environmental and social impact assessment, further information is collected, analyzed and assessed as to whether the project meets determined standards. For these standards, the equator principles refer to the *Performance Standards* of the *International Finance Corporation* (IFC). Depending on the project, the *Common Approaches* either refer to *IFC Performance Standards* or to the *Safeguard Policies* of the World Bank Group.

Although at first sight this method seems to be a comprehensive examination, a more detailed study of the impact on co-determination rights suggests otherwise. Firstly, the categorization of the projects from A ("high ecological or social risk") to C ("negligible risk") takes into account almost exclusively the external effects of a project. 'Category A projects', which are regarded as socially or ecologically problematic, are those which have particularly negative effects on the environment or the local population. Risks faced by employees involved in the project, such as a high risk of oppression of labor rights or an anti-union environment, are not taken into account.[3] In fact, projects with a considerable risk of the suppression of co-determination rights can completely circumvent the impact assessment, because only projects classified as A and a part of the projects classified as B are further investigated.

In addition, only projects which are located outside[4] the OECD are examined, since the IPEX assumes that OECD countries have "established authorization and monitoring practices in the environmental and social field, which are comparable to the strict German guidelines" (KfW IPEX-Bank 2015a, 46, translation: KK). This means that the risks of labor rights suppression in financed projects in countries such as Mexico or the USA, where trade unions are systematically repressed (International Trade Union Confederation 2016a, Lichtenstein 2013), are completely ignored.

---

[3] A list of exemplary category A projects also includes projects with "labor-intensive production processes". This could include projects where labor rights are particularly vulnerable. However, when looking at the classification in practice, it can be seen that projects classified as "A projects" are the ones considered to bear environmental and health risks, risk of population displacement and consequences for indigenous groups. This interpretation of the classification has been applied to export credit guarantees, for which a similar test procedure is foreseen. Unfortunately, the cases of IPEX financing that fall under the A category could not be analyzed because they are not available for the public

[4] As can be seen in Figure 4.1, only projects that are not located in OECD countries are reviewed for supplier credits. Buyer credits are checked for projects in countries that do not belong to the "Equator Principles Designated Countries" (EP countries). EP countries are all OECD countries except Turkey and Mexico.

Moreover, the entire Sustainability Guideline is valid only for project financing and advisory services with a value higher than USD 10 million. For project-related corporate financing even higher limit values apply (KfW IPEX-Bank 2015b, 3). As a consequence of these limitations, only 18 out of the 330 financing contracts[5] concluded in 2015 were examined (KfW IPEX-Bank 2015a, p. 47).

As mentioned above, the compliance of a project pending review with the standards applied is analyzed using an environmental and social impact assessment applying the *IFC's Performance Standards* or the *Safeguard Policies* of the World Bank Group, as well as the sector-specific *Environmental, Health and Safety (EHS) Guidelines* of the World Bank. As can be seen in Figure 4.2, the *IFC Performance Standards* point to the *ILO core labor standards* and thus also to employees' co-determination rights. The *Safeguard Policies* and the sector-specific *EHS Guidelines*, on the other hand, contain no provisions regarding the treatment of workers. In the case of projects using the *Safeguard Policies* instead of the *IFC Performance Standards*, further standards should be added according to the *OECD Common Approaches* (OECD 2016, 10).

Figure 4.2: The different evaluation standards

IFC Performance Standards (2012)	World Bank Safeguard Policies (2016)
1. Assessment and Management of Environmental and Social Risks and Impacts	1. Environmental Assessment
2. Labor and Working Conditions (Reference to ILO core labor standards including freedom of association, right to organize and collective bargaining)	2. Natural Habitats
	3. Forests
	4. Pest Management
	5. Physical Cultural Resources
3. Resource Efficiency and Pollution Prevention	6. Involuntary Resettlement
4. Community Health, Safety and Security	7. Indigenous Peoples
5. Land Acquisition and Involuntary Resettlement	8. Safety of Dams
6. Biodiversity Conservation and Sustainable Management of Living Natural Resources	9. International Waterways
	10. Disputed Areas
7. Indigenous Peoples	11. Use of Country Systems
8. Cultural Heritage	

World Bank Environmental, Health and Safety (EHS) Guidelines (2007) – Industry specific
1. Environmental
2. Occupational Health and Safety
3. Community Health and Safety
4. Construction and Decommissioning

Source: Own representation based on International Finance Corporation 2012; The World Bank Group 2007; 2016

---

[5] In the words used by the Sustainability Report of the KfW-IPEX, "72 percent" of projects classified as A or B outside the OECD were reviewed. As outside the OECD only 25 projects were classified as A or B, this amounts to 18 reviews KfW IPEX-Bank (2015a, 47–48).

Unfortunately, it is not possible to check how the review against the different standards is done in practice for the different projects. According to the *KfW Sustainability Guidelines,* companies must make their environmental and social impact assessment public (KfW IPEX-Bank 2015b, 7). However, the KfW IPEX-Bank does not disclose its financing, which precludes the identification of the companies and projects concerned.

Nevertheless, some conclusions can be drawn about the practical design of the environmental and social impact assessment. This can be done by considering the reviews of projects in the area of export credit guarantees (*Hermesdeckung*), which are based on very similar rules: Here, only one of the eight reports submitted for 2016 contains a statement on the rights of employees or their compliance in the planned projects. This single report, however, does not go beyond the recommendation that the "Human Resource Policy, Human Rights Policy, Code of Conduct, Workers Health and Safety Management Plan and Workers Grievance Mechanism" should be developed and enforced (Golder Associates Inc 2016, 63). In none of the reports, co-determination does appear in any form(Agaportal 2016a).

The already weak examination procedure is further weakened by the rules for accepting or rejecting the projects. The ministerial committee, under certain conditions, can still accept a project that does not meet the requirements.

Employees in financed projects should have the chance to complain if their co-determination rights are violated. The KfW Bank urges risky projects that have obtained funding to set up a grievance mechanism, maintain it and document the results (KfW IPEX Bank 2016, 46). However, due to the lack of transparency on project financing it cannot be established whether the concerned projects comply with this request. The published environmental and social impact assessments of export credit guarantee projects, which are based on the same rules, do not elaborate on such a mechanism (Agaportal 2016a).

In response to massive criticism, the KfW-IPEX Bank has set up an on-line mechanism where individuals, companies, organizations or other parties, which are negatively affected by a project financed by KfW IPEX-Bank, can file a complaint. However, it is questionable whether workers, whose rights of co-determination are restricted in a specific project, will address their complaints to the financing institution. Not only is the bank located in Germany, but its complaint procedure is not particularly well-known and is accessible only in German and English. The support of such complaints by NGOs or international trade unions would in turn require transparency on the subsidized projects, which is not given. The effectiveness of the established mechanism is therefore questionable.

To conclude: a closer look at the test practice raises doubts as to how serious is the KfW-IPEX Bank about its promise that "one of KfW-Bank's central objectives [...], is the environmentally and socially acceptable implementation of the projects it is financing" (KfW IPEX-Bank 2015a, 22, translation: KK). The same conclusion is drawn in a study conducted by the NGO urgewald in 2015, which examines various KfW-Bank projects and reveals massive human rights violations and environmental problems triggered by the funded projects (urgewald 2015). KfW IPEX Bank financed, among other things, the Brazilian mining company Vale, which was recognized as the most irresponsible company of 2011 for its human rights violations, inhuman working conditions and the exploitation of nature by the 'public eyes award' in 2012 (the public eyes awards 2016; urgewald 2015, 33). The urgewald study addressed problems, such as violent resettlement and displacement, environmental and climatic pollution as well as the destruction of livelihoods. These problems cannot be effectively prevented by the KfW-Bank's environmental and social impact assessment but are at least part of the review. This is not the case for the compliance with or the violation of co-determination rights.

The German Investment and Development Company (DEG)

DEG finances, promotes and advises companies that invest in countries of the global South. Its self-declared objective is to promote sustainable economic development through foreign direct investment in emerging and developing countries and to strengthen the financial sector of these countries (Deutsche Investitions- und Entwicklungsgesellschaft 2016b). At the same time, it acts as a promotional instrument for German foreign trade (BMWi and Referat Öffentlichkeitsarbeit 2016a).

Since its establishment, the Bank financed 719 projects in 79 countries, with a total sum of EUR 7.2 billion. In 2015, 115 German companies took advantage of DEG financing (Deutsche Investitions- und Entwicklungsgesellschaft 2015, 20–21). The Bank uses mainly its own funds, but can make use of a federal guarantee, which is very advantageous for the procurement of funds on the market. In 2015, it generated a surplus of 78 million euros after taxes.

In its annual report, DEG recognizes that investment in Southern countries offers considerable opportunities to improve environmental and social conditions on the ground but also involve risks. The assessment of environmental and social risks is therefore described as an "integral aspect of the overall risk assessment of DEG" (ibid., 17).

The assessment is in line with the common environmental and social principles of the *European Development Finance Institutions* (EDFI), a group of different European development finance organizations. Their standards developed in 2007 are similar to the IPEX procedure. They contain a categorization of the various projects, certain environmental and social due diligence requirements, as well as an exclusion list for non-fundable projects. For example, projects in the area of pornography or in areas that violate the prohibition of forced or child labor would not be funded. As shown in Figure 4.1, the standards applied by DEG refer to the performance standards of the IFC and the sector-specific *EHS Guidelines* of the World Bank (Ebert and Posthuma 2015, 7). Companies that want to obtain funding are contractually obliged to comply with the *IFC Performance Standards* and the *ILO core labor standards* contained therein, and thus also with the right to co-determination. In addition, DEG is a member of the *Extractive Industries Transparency Initiative*, which is committed to the transparency of money flows in the extraction of raw materials (Deutsche Investitions- und Entwicklungsgesellschaft 2016a).

It is unclear how exactly it is verified whether and how the obligations imposed on companies are respected. Since the common environmental and social principles are not published by the DEG or the EDFI, it is not comprehensible how the review will take place and which projects, for example, require an environmental and social impact assessment.

The annual report proudly mentions that all funds granted as of 2015 are published on the DEG website and contain company names, financing sum, risk category and justification (Deutsche Investitions- und Entwicklungsgesellschaft 2015, 11). This represents an improvement in transparency compared to KfW IPEX financing. It is questionable, however, why the social and environmental assessments of the projects are not published on the website as well, as is the case of export credit guarantees (Hermesdeckungen). This would be the only way to understand whether the required standards are actually met. If the assessments are as diligent as described in the DEG Annual Report, they must be available as DEG documents and could thus be made available to the public without further effort.

The uncertainty about the sustainability of the financed projects is further exacerbated when companies or infrastructure projects in other countries are financed through loans to financial intermediaries in other countries. In 2015, loans to the financial sector account for 39 percent of DEG financing.[6] The aim of the funding is to build sound local financial systems as the basis for investments.

If a financial intermediary acts as a mediator between the capital of DEG and the real economy in the country concerned, DEG cannot adequately control whether the funds are used in accordance with the company's own environmental and

---

[6] Not the entire sum of financings for the financial sector goes to financial intermediaries. Unfortunately, the financial sums granted to the financial sector are not further broken down in the annual reports.

social guidelines. KfW's sustainability guidelines stipulate that in the case of indirect financing, national laws should be adhered to and that environmental and social aspects should be "adequately respected". KfW's individual assessments are therefore no longer necessary. To guarantee this "adequate respect" the KfW actually checks only whether the financial intermediary has sufficient "organizational and personnel capacities" to conduct its own review of sensitive projects (urgewald 2015, 10).

The construction of a dam in Guatemala shows that the delegation of responsibility does not ensure the compliance with social and environmental criteria. After the DEG had not provided any funds due to the great social and environmental risks, the dam was later financed by an infrastructure fund in which DEG was directly involved (ibid., 10). In an investigation by the *Compliance Advisor Ombudsman* (CAO), the official complaints office for IFC projects, the involvement of financial intermediaries is generally regarded as extremely risky. As a result of the loss of control over financing, there is always the danger of contributing to ecologically and socially problematic projects (Office of the Compliance Advisor Ombudsman 2012)

Export and Investment Guarantee Scheme (Auslandsgeschäftsabsicherungen)

The German Federal Government offers state-run default coverage programs for foreign business transactions. This is particularly advantageous for transactions that lack access to insurance services in the private sector due to excessive uncertainty or long-term maturities. The coverage is granted as export credit guarantees (*Hermes-Deckungen*), investment guarantees (*Direktinvestition Ausland, DIA*) and united loan guarantees (*UFK-Garantien*). The auditing company *PricewaterhouseCoopers* (PwC) and the credit insurance company *Euler Hermes* have been mandated by the Federal Government as part of the consortium in charge of processing the three offers.

Export Credit Guarantees (Hermesdeckungen)

State export credit guarantees can be very helpful, if a company wants to "tap into" new "risky" markets, often to reach countries of the global South with its own products. Under the so-called Hermes cover, German exporters can obtain insurance for exports or maturities against economic and political risks in host countries not covered by private insurance as they are considered as "too risky" by the private sector.

The aim of the instrument is to ensure the competitiveness of the German export economy. In 2015, Germany assumed guarantee for contract values amounting to EUR 25.8 billion, the total authorization framework of credit guarantees amounted to EUR 160 billion. By way of comparison, this is more than half of the federal budget of the same year (Bundesministerium der Finanzen 2015a; Euler Hermes Aktiengesellschaft 2015, 2). The actual compensation paid in cases of insolvency of the customer for economic or political reasons totaled EUR 395 million. This sum was more than covered by the insurance fees and return flows, which generated an surplus of EUR 344 million for the federal budget (Euler Hermes Aktiengesellschaft 2015, 2).

The insurances apply only to transactions of German companies. Nevertheless, global labor rights can be influenced both in the production of the export goods and on the receiving hand. This is particularly true since 2015 when a change in the requirements for guarantees has allowed export products to contain more than 49 percent of foreign value-added. Consequently, export products rely on global supply chains. Moreover, many of the exports are destined for foreign large-scale projects, e.g. to establish large power plants. In these newly created projects labor rights might not be adhered to.

In order to prevent negative social and ecological effects of the project in the buyer country, Hermes guarantees require a social and ecological impact assessment. As it can be seen in Figure 4.3, the latter is based on the *Common Approaches* outlined above. Accordingly, an A-to-C categorization is provided, and is followed by an intensive examination of particularly risky projects based on the *IFC Performance Standards* or the *World Bank Safeguard Policies* as well as the sector-specific *EHS Guidelines*.

Figure 4.3: Due Diligence Procedure for Export Credit Guarantees, Investment Guarantees and Untied Loan Guarantees

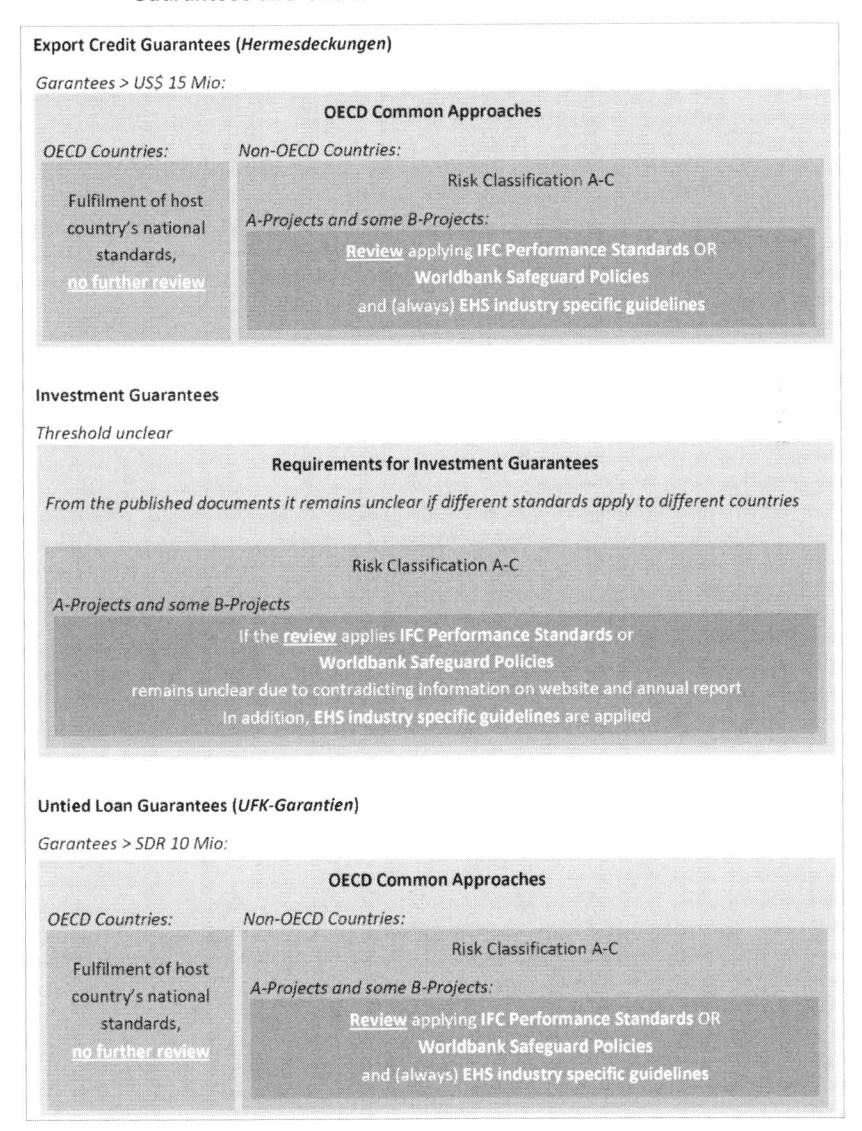

Export Credit Guarantees (*Hermesdeckungen*)

Garantees > US$ 15 Mio:

OECD Common Approaches	
OECD Countries:	*Non-OECD Countries:*
Fulfilment of host country's national standards, <u>no further review</u>	Risk Classification A-C *A-Projects and some B-Projects:* <u>Review</u> applying **IFC Performance Standards** OR **Worldbank Safeguard Policies** and (always) **EHS industry specific guidelines**

Investment Guarantees

Threshold unclear

Requirements for Investment Guarantees
From the published documents it remains unclear if different standards apply to different countries
Risk Classification A-C
A-Projects and some B-Projects
If the <u>review</u> applies **IFC Performance Standards** or **Worldbank Safeguard Policies** remains unclear due to contradicting information on website and annual report In addition, **EHS industry specific guidelines** are applied

Untied Loan Guarantees (*UFK-Garantien*)

Garantees > SDR 10 Mio:

OECD Common Approaches	
OECD Countries:	*Non-OECD Countries:*
Fulfilment of host country's national standards, <u>no further review</u>	Risk Classification A-C *A-Projects and some B-Projects:* <u>Review</u> applying **IFC Performance Standards** OR **Worldbank Safeguard Policies** and (always) **EHS industry specific guidelines**

Source: Own representation based on (Agaportal 2016a; 2016b; 2016c; BMWi, Euler Hermes, and PricewaterhouseCoopers 2016a; Euler Hermes Aktiengesellschaft 2013; 2015; OECD 2016; PricewaterhouseCoopers 2015)

If a project violates these principles, the inter-ministerial committee can still grant the export credit guarantee under certain conditions. The relevant Ministries, mandataries, experts from the business and banking industries and institutions that are important for the export industry compose this committee. The approval of a project is followed by a monitoring process only in the rare occasion of a particularly complex A category project (Euler Hermes Aktiengesellschaft 2013; OECD 2016).

The disclosure policy on Hermes guarantees proves that transparency on financed projects is possible. All projects with a cover volume of more than EUR 15 million are published on the website with the respective environmental and social impact assessments, which had to be carried out. Transparency on the environmental and social assessments of sensitive projects also leads to the above-mentioned disillusionment of these assessments. As of November 2016, of the 45 projects funded by more than EUR 15 million during the year, only eight had to prepare an environmental and social impact assessment, which was done by an external service provider. Their content was rather disillusioning. None of the projects, that received Hermes cover, were effectively assessed to determine whether co-determination rights were violated. The reports mention far too little regarding obligations to secure these rights, not to mention the verification of the obligations. Moreover, the assessment neglects completely all production steps preceding the export.

The right to co-determination is theoretically embedded in the ILO core labor standards contained in the IFC Performance Standards as a test standard for the provision of guarantees. Even if the World Bank Safeguard Guidelines are applied instead of the IFC Performance Standards, these are to be supplemented by further regulations such as the *ILO core labor standards*.

Nevertheless, none of the projects, that received Hermes cover, were effectively examined to establish whether co-determination rights could be endangered. Nor have any commitments been made in the reports, as to how these rights will be secured in future. All production steps preceding the export are also completely neglected in the assessment procedure. Although the BMWi states that the issues of environment and human rights in the area of credit export guarantees "are of great importance" (BMWi and Referat Öffentlichkeitsarbeit 2016a), little is done to use Hermes covers as an economic instrument to promote co-determination rights.

Investment Guarantees (Investitionsgarantien)

In order to secure the direct investment of German companies in countries of the global South against political risks, Germany offers investment guarantees. These act as insurance for an investment for fifteen years. The insurance covers risks such as system changes, discriminatory legal changes, state crises, turmoil, war or terror; in short: risks, which are normally not covered by private insurance companies. In 2015, insurance was granted to direct investments of EUR 2.6 billion, mainly in Russia, China, India, Colombia and Serbia. So far, fees and charges have covered compensation payments.

Direct investment in countries with low social and environmental standards always poses the risk of exploitation of the environment and the violation of labor rights. Apart from the minimum requirement for compliance with the national standards of the host country, projects with an extensive environmental or social impact are reviewed using the *IFC Performance Standards* and the sector-specific *EHS Guidelines* of the World Bank, similarly to the procedure of IPEX-Bank and Hermes covers. The only truly binding requirement is, however, compliance with the standards of the host country.

Decisions on the eligibility of the projects, which comply with national laws, but not with the *IFC Performance Standards* and the *EHS Guidelines*, are taken on a case-by-case basis. As with the Hermes covers, the final project approval is decided by an inter-ministerial committee with the participation of business experts.

Approved projects, which are environmentally and socially relevant must commit to the submission of an annual report on the investment situation, including environmental and social aspects. All applicants are also advised to comply with the *OECD Guidelines for Multinational Enterprises* and the *German Sustainability Code*; this is, however, not binding (BMWi and Referat Öffentlichkeitsarbeit 2016d).

Although applicants for investment guarantees have a much more direct influence on business practices abroad and similar impacts as Hermes covers, project-related data are not systematically published. This makes it difficult to understand whether the BMWi is able to counteract the violation of rights (Heydenreich 2014, 57).

Untied Loan Guarantees (UFK-Garantien)

Untied Loan Guarantees (*UFK Garantien*) aim at increasing the security of supply of German industry with raw materials (*Rohstoffvorhaben*) and the promotion of free market structures abroad (*Förderbankprojekte*). The guarantees are granted to banks in order to hedge an economic or political credit default risk of a raw material or banking business. The prerequisite for the approval of raw material projects is the conclusion of a long-term supply contract with a German purchaser. In practice, this means that a bank will be given a guarantee, if it finances a company that extracts raw materials for a German customer. Development bank projects are used to cover KfW loans to foreign development institutions, which transfer funds to small and medium-sized enterprises. For both types of projects, the guarantees are often awarded in conjunction with an IPEX or DEG financing (BMWi, Euler Hermes, and PricewaterhouseCoopers 2016b).

In 2015, only one of the proposed and approved UFK projects was ultimately realized due to falling raw material prices. A guarantee of over 96 million euros was granted. This is just two percent of the EUR 4.8 billion planned for UFK grants (Euler Hermes Aktiengesellschaft 2015, 79). The new export strategy pursued by the BMWi in 2016 therefore attempts to adapt the UFK guarantees to the needs of German business (BMWi 2016b, 3; 2016d; 2016e).

Both business units of the UFK guarantees are particularly sensitive to the compliance with co-determination and other labor rights. While it is very difficult to control the distribution of loans to foreign financial institutions as already explained, the violation of labor rights in the raw material sector is particularly frequent. The extraction of the raw materials listed as eligible for funding (including iron ore, copper, tantalum, gold, rare earth, natural gas and hard coal) is associated not only with major environmental problems, but also with massive violations of labor rights, especially trade union freedom. The International Trade Union Confederation (ITUC) reports of repeated, regular or systematic violations or the non-existence of fundamental rights of co-determination[7] in 13 of the 17 countries in which raw material projects have been financially guaranteed over the past few years[8] (Agaportal 2016c; International Trade Union Confederation 2016a). Reports from countries where employee participation is being suppressed show that this is often particularly serious in the mining sector. In most of the affected countries there are numerous reports of dismissed trade unionists and massive violence against trade unions (International Trade Union Confederation 2016e; 2016f; 2016i; 2016h; 2016b; 2016d; 2016c). For example, in 2015, the police fired at striking miners in an iron mine in Peru, killing one worker and injuring another 200 (International Trade Union Confederation 2016g). In South Africa, a mineworker of a platinum mine was killed by the police during a violent strike in February 2014 (International Trade Union Confederation 2016h).

---

[7] Namely, freedom of association, the right to strike and the right to collective bargaining.
[8] The *ITUC Global Rights Index* examines worldwide the guarantee of core labour standards. Civil rights, the right to collective bargaining, strike rights, freedom of association and procedural rights are given special consideration. The Index gives a rating of 1 (irregular violation of rights) to 5 (no guarantee of rights). The countries for which the UFK guarantees have been awarded in recent years are as follows: Iceland and Norway: 1 (irregular violation of rights); Canada, Macedonia, South Africa, Mozambique and Brazil: 2 (repeated violation of rights); Peru, Great Britain, Tanzania and Australia: 3 (regular violation of rights); Nigeria and the USA: 4 (systematic violation of rights); Turkey and Egypt: 5 (no guarantee of rights). No rating has been released for Mongolia and Guinea (International Trade Union Confederation 2016a).

It is therefore only logical for the Federal Government to state that, in addition to environmental and resource protection, health and safety issues should also be taken into account when awarding UFK guarantees (BMWi 2016c). Officially, the assessment of ecological and social effects is conducted based on the aforementioned *Common Approaches*, i.e. an A-to-C categorization with subsequent comparison of risky projects against the *IFC Performance Standards* and the *EHS Guidelines*.

However, on the website of the UFK guarantees it is only stated that an environmental study needs to be submitted upon application. It is unclear whether the actual environmental and social assessments contain labor rights and, in particular, co-determination rights, since the assessments of UFK guarantees are also not available to the public. Since the requirements are the same as those of the Hermes guarantees and, officially, only an environmental assessment is mentioned, it seems unlikely that labor rights would be part of the test. In unspecified cases, an environmental management plan with appropriate monitoring mechanisms must also be submitted and "appropriate social facilities and training facilities for the staff" must be introduced (ibid., translation: KK).

Whether the latter implies that UFK guarantees support an anti-union business practice as described above is unclear because of the lack of transparency. The cases are not systematically published; while the projects sporadically described in annual reports lack information on social and environmental impacts (Euler Hermes Aktiengesellschaft 2015; Heydenreich 2014, 57). The "Transparency Initiative" of the UFK Guarantees (Euler Hermes Aktiengesellschaft 2015, 82) initiated in 2015 consisted solely of the establishment of an internet presence with general information on guarantees and conditions of project awarding (ibid., 82). Under these circumstances it is very unlikely that co-determination rights are explicitly promoted through UFK guarantees.

New Export Strategy 2016

After an intensive dialogue with representatives of German industry, in 2016 the BMWi presented a new export strategy, which foresees an improvement of the various financing and hedging instruments. The aim of the strategy is to compete better with competitors on the global market, especially with China, and their comprehensive funding instruments. To this end, firstly, existing subsidies will be expanded. Secondly, OECD members will try to include non-members in the set of rules for export promotion initially created for the OECD. In order to make better use of the foreign trade promotion instruments, further guidance for companies will be given and a representative for a better coordination of the various instruments will be appointed in the BMWi. For strategically relevant projects, it will also be possible to actually circumvent the OECD regulations in order to compete with non-OECD countries on major projects. In doing so, the conditions of the competitor can be adopted (BMWi and Referat Öffentlichkeitsarbeit 2016e). This point raises doubts as to whether the ecological and social requirements laid down by the OECD will be completely ignored in favor of standards of competitors such as China. Environmental or social concerns are not addressed in the new strategy and have also been left out from the different workshops for the preparation of the strategy (BMWi 2016d, 3).

Conclusion: Underutilized Linkage

As discussed in the introduction of this chapter, foreign trade and investment promotion through export financing and foreign transaction insurance could contribute to the enforcement of co-determination rights in financed and insured projects. This can be achieved through various forms of linking human rights and instruments of external economic development (*linkage*). In the following section, a conclusion is drawn as to how far this has already been achieved in the promotion of investments abroad and where there is a need for action on the part of the government.

Evaluation Linkage

Based on the previous analysis it becomes clear that the promotion of co-determination is not an explicit objective of the funding instruments. Nevertheless, the goal of avoiding the suppression of co-determination rights is declared for all instruments. This objective is pursued while economic support is considered as a priority, thus relegating social and ecological concerns to a secondary goal. In this context, civil society has repeatedly stated that there is an inherent contradiction between the different objectives. For example, the objective of securing the supply of raw materials contradicts the promotion of an intact environment (urgewald 2015, p. 6). While this is a relevant argument in the field of ecology, this contradiction does not exist concerning co-determination rights. Quite on the contrary, the goal of supporting exports and foreign investment is very much compatible with the one of supporting labor rights. In sectors such as the extraction of raw materials, where co-determination rights are massively violated in many parts of the world, there is great potential for improving the situation, provided it is a clear policy objective. This clear objective should be anchored to both KfW's financing instruments and foreign transaction insurances, in order to reach an equal status to economic objectives.

Agency Linkage

The hierarchy of the different objectives in favor of economic advantages is reflected in the design of the foreign trade and investment promotion instruments. The various inter-ministerial committees, which have the final say on granting foreign trade and investment promotion (*Auslands-*

geschäftsabsicherung), are advised by representatives of the business sector. However, since the protection provided by the BMWi is supposed to only be granted if ecological and social concerns are not violated, civil society and in particular international trade union associations, should also be included.

In order to facilitate the safeguarding of co-determination rights in foreign companies, the companies mandated to manage the guarantee scheme, Euler Hermes and PWC, should be equipped not only with economic but also with human rights advisory competences. This way applicant companies can receive appropriate advice about the risks of violation of rights and their effective prevention (Grabosch and Scheper 2015, 23; Hamm, Scheper, and Schölmerich 2011, 4). The coordinating body introduced in the new export strategy and the mandated representative of the BMWi should not only advise on the use of the various instruments but also on the precautions to be taken to secure the rights of the employees on site.

Furthermore, as a supporting institution in foreign business transactions, the *German Mineral Resources Agency* (DERA) should also play a role in the prevention of labor injuries just as it does through the provision of economic advice on the extraction of raw materials. So far, its publications, which provide information on certain raw materials, do not even mention human rights aspects of mining and the associated risks (Deutsche Rohstoffagentur 2016).

In the context of forthcoming export promotion reforms, the BMWi should not only consult with economic experts and business communities as in 2016, but also involve civil society actors, in particular global trade union organizations and NGOs.

Rights Linkage

The existing requirements for the utilization of financing or guarantees already include a *rights linkage* approach. In fact, only those companies who comply with environmental and social regulations should take advantage of the instrument.

However, only in theory are these requirements applied to all projects. Very few projects, namely projects which are outside the OECD and which are subject to a high-risk classification, actually have to be assessed. Regarding co-determination rights, the non-assessment of projects within the OECD and projects of "low" risk classification are of particular concern here. In both cases, projects with a high risk of labor violations bypass the impact assessment. An additional problem is presented by the difficulty of assessing the wide range of standards and test mechanisms. The confusing diversity could be one reason why some standards remain unaffected in the environmental and social impact assessments, thus without being addressed by the relevant authorities (I.e. the BMWi, the KfW bank or the mandataries). The social test procedure could be majorly simplified by the clear requirement of a human rights due diligence over the whole supply chain for all financing and guarantees. The due diligence should place co-determination rights in the center and be legally enforceable before German courts. This would attract the attention of companies regarding the compliance with due diligence. Moreover, it would introduce a mechanism to demand fundamental rights and for complaints about violations without any additional bureaucracy. The planned measures of the *National Action Plan for Business and Human Rights* (NAP) discussed above are not sufficient. The plan foresees an intensification of the test procedures with regard to human rights issues. However, it does not contain a binding human rights due diligence for beneficiaries of the subsidy schemes.

Transparency regarding all financed and covered projects, including their social and environmental impact, would be fundamental to the functioning of such a regulation, but also in general for the improvement of the existing system. However, the NAP does not provide any useful approach in this direction.

If the current procedure is maintained, it is essential to monitor the agreed standards and the environmental and social management plans, which so far has taken place only in isolated cases.

The leverage effect of a *rights linkage* approach can only be effective, if projects that do not fulfill the requirements are consistently rejected. In this context, exemptions permitted by the inter-ministerial committees are obstructive. In view of the absence of enforceable due diligence, the grievance mechanism must be improved and made better known for all instruments. A new grievance mechanism foreseen in the NAP is the *National Contact Point*, which has been established in the context of the *OECD Guidelines for Multinational Enterprises* and which will be discussed in detail below. However, in order to fulfill this role meaningfully, the National Contact Point should be comprehensively reformed in a way that goes beyond the proposals of the NAP (Grabosch and Scheper 2015, 23). In addition, companies that do not participate in a mediation of the National Contact Point should be consistently excluded from funding. The NAP remains, however, vague on this matter.

With the appropriate application of all three forms of *linkage*, the various instruments of foreign trade and investment promotion could offer great potential for effectively incentivizing companies to bring their global business activities in line with co-determination rights.

Public Procurement

Each year, the Federal Government, states and the local authorities purchase goods and services worth over EUR 350 billion, i.e. 13% of the GDP (Kompetenzstelle für nachhaltige Beschaffung 2016). In the last few years, conditions of labor and environmental exploitation were repeatedly reported for goods produced for the public sector under (Heydenreich 2014, 59). For example, garment factories in Macedonia, which produce uniforms for the German Army, have been blamed for unpaid overtime and wages far below the subsistence level. None of the surveyed plants offered operational co-determination or trade union organization of any form to its employees (Erklärung von Bern, Südwind Institut, and Clean Clothes Campaign 2012). The massive economic incentive to win major government contracts makes public procurements a highly effective tool of *rights linkage* to prevent cases like the above and to promote compliance with co-determination right.

Public procurement is not a classical instrument of foreign trade policy. Socially responsible procurements however have been used for many years to improve national labor standards within a country. As early as the middle of the nineteenth century, the USA and France started using governmental purchases strategically, to pursue other objectives, such as the support of labor standards or the reduction of unemployment. The ILO Convention 94 from 1949, which has not been ratified by Germany, stipulates that public contracts should contain a clause to prevent social dumping. This would be achieved by prohibiting working conditions and wages in public contracts from being worse than the usual industry and regional standards (McCrudden 2004, 265).

Today, in the context of advancing privatization, socially responsible procurement is not only an instrument for improving but also maintaining existing standards within Germany. This practice could offset the dualization of the labor market pushed forward by privatization and the associated absence of trade union organization and co-determination in secondary labor markets (Emmenegger et al. 2012; Jaehrling 2015). According to studies, the strategy of socially responsible procurement is most effective when there are strong trade union structures and collective bargaining agreements in the country, which are however not implemented across the sectors. The main reason for the effectiveness of social procurement in the context of strong unionism is that the standards required in public contracts are often formulated with reference to the existing system, in particular to negotiated collective bargaining agreements. Furthermore, trade unions work towards a meaningful contract formulation and act as supervisory bodies in contracts already in place. These favorable conditions, strong trade union structure but no sector wide application of agreements, are given in Germany (Jaehrling 2015; Schulten et al. 2012).

Although public procurement, as already mentioned, is not a typical instrument of external economic policy, its practice has also an impact on global working conditions. The liberalization of public procurement markets achieved in Europe, which is being promoted through new free trade agreements around the globe, allows foreign companies to compete for German tenders. In addition, most German companies rely on a global supply chain. In either case, *linkages* can provide incentives for the enforcement of co-determination rights abroad.

The conditions for the award of public contracts must be set clearly in order to make *linkage* effective. They must secure existing co-determination rights in Germany and promote co-determination abroad at the same time. The practical design of social criteria and their verification must also be clarified. In addition, aid must be given in the implementation of socially responsible tendering (Deutsches Institut für Menschenrechte 2015, 23–24). The following section analyzes the extent to which this applies in Germany. Subsequently, possibilities are discussed, on how to make better use of the procurement, to secure and promote co-determination.

Socially Responsible Procurement in Germany

The German Federal Government through its procurement policy pursues three main objectives. Firstly, tax money that goes into public contracts should be spent as efficiently as possible. Secondly, the government seeks to create a competitive market, where no provider is arbitrarily preferred to another. Thirdly, this market has to be "embedded", in order to avoid neglecting social and environmental objectives, such as the compliance with co-determination rights.

From a legal point of view, these different objectives have different priorities. The procuring institution is obliged by national law to choose the most economical option, while by European non-discrimination rules it has to create a functioning competitive market. However, taking social or ecological aspects into account is not mandatory. This represents an improvement on the existing rules before 2014, under which, consideration of social and environmental aspects could lead to a lawsuit for the procuring authority for breaching the principle of non-discrimination.[9]

The federal procurement law, which has been in effect since April 2016, introduced two binding conditions for awarding public contracts: the compliance with the statutory minimum wage and with universally applicable collective agreements. The consideration of further social and ecological criteria is permitted in every phase of contract awarding, i.e. from the definition of the good or service to the determination of suitability and award criteria, and the specification of execution conditions (Portz 2016, 17). In its tendering procedure, a public contracting authority can demand compliance with *ILO core labor standards* throughout the entire supply chain. It can also express

---

[9] This was the case, for example, in the often cited "Rüffert" ruling in 2008. The condition of observance of wage contracts imposed by the Free State of Saxony on public procurement was considered as an infringement of the European Posting of Workers Directive and the freedom to provide services. (Jaehrling 2015, 151).

preference for a fair trade product, which is manufactured under consideration of the *ILO core labor standards*, even if the "fair" product is more expensive (BMWi and Referat Öffentlichkeitsarbeit 2016f, 4–5; Müller-Wrede 2015, 3).

Contractors that have violated environmental, social or labor regulations in the past, may also be totally excluded from the contract award procedure, if the contracting authority wants to (Haufe 2016). However, the award of the contract for the cheapest offer without examination of further criteria is still permitted. This is possible due to the non-binding character (*Kann-Bestimmung*) of the ecological and social criteria (Portz 2016).

The aforementioned federal rules are subject to EU Law, if contracts exceed a certain threshold value. Contrarily, when the value is lower than the threshold, additional state-specific regulations apply (BMWi and Referat Öffentlichkeitsarbeit 2015). With regard to the state level, compliance with collective agreements is also an obligatory criterion for awarding contracts in all federal states, except for Saxony and Bavaria. In addition, *ILO core labor standards* are mandatory in public contracts in nine states (Christliche Initiative Romero and Arbeitsgemeinschaft der Eine-Welt-Landesnetzwerke in Deutschland 2015, 11–12).

While compliance with the *ILO core labor standards* remains a target, it still begs the question as to how it can be verified within the tendering procedure. Evidence can be provided by submitting an independent certification, by becoming a member of a multi-stakeholder initiative, or by declarations of the companies themselves. The latter, however, do not permit effective control. Therefore, independent certifications or multi-stakeholder initiatives, which are designed to improve the working conditions along the supply chain in addition to compliance with the *ILO core labor standards*, seem preferable (Heydenreich 2014, 60). However, practical problems arise with these practices too. Certification is usually achieved through recognized quality labels such as the European Eco-label. In areas where there is no established certification procedure, proof of a "recognized quality label" is practically impossible. For instance, the Administrative Court of Baden-Württemberg declared the directives of a municipal cemetery statute to be unlawful because it had required from contracted companies the certificates Xertifix or Fairstone in order to comply with the *ILO core labor standards*. According to the court, these certificates did not contain any conclusive evidence for better practices (Portz 2016, 17).

A further practical problem arises in the control of the specifications. In fact, past experience with state tariffs and procurement laws shows that the majority of the contracting authorities has never, or rarely, checked whether the contractors have respected these.

It is within this context that the *Competence Center for Sustainable Procurement* was created in 2012. It supports procurement agencies at all levels, to apply criteria such as compliance with the *ILO core labor standards* in different stages of the award procedure and to effectively monitor them. The institution offers information online and via telephone, counseling, training and education on sustainable public procurement to contracting authorities at the federal, state and municipal level (Kompetenzstelle für nachhaltige Beschaffung 2016).

Making Socially Responsible Procurement Binding

The mandatory compliance with collective bargaining agreement introduced in the new General Local Authorities Code (*Vergabeordnung*) is to be welcomed. This can prevent social dumping in the award of public contracts and strengthen collective bargaining agreements. The award policy can thus support regulations in the field of industrial relations. At the same time, it must not constitute a substitute for generally binding rules. The circumvention of co-determination rights within Germany must be countered by active labor market policy and not just by social procurement alone.

Furthermore, the requirement of social criteria in the procurement procedure can no longer be classified as unlawful. This could have positive effects on working conditions outside Germany. However, the non-binding nature of the regulations raises doubts. As a result, socially responsible tendering takes place only when the agency decides actively to take the time and effort to consider social aspects and, if necessary, to change the procedure. It is incomprehensible that compliance with fundamental labor and human rights is made dependent on the decision of individual bureaucratic units. The binding inclusion of the *ILO core labor standards* across the whole supply chain should therefore be part of the procurement legislation.

Such a requirement is allowed within EU law (CoRA-Netzwerk für Unternehmensverantwortung 2015). Existing state-level regulations show that it is also possible in practice. Binding compliance with ecological criteria in procurement has already been demanded by the *Federal Environmental Agency* (Umweltbundesamt 2016).

Criteria should not be set based on the contractors' self-declarations. Certifications and multi-stakeholder initiatives are also of variable quality. For this reason, contracting authorities should be assisted in evaluating different labels and initiatives. The website of the *Competence Center for Sustainable Procurement* already contains information on existing labels. However, it is unclear and unsystematic. The integration of the website *Kompass Nachhaltigkeit* into the online presence of the Competence Center would be helpful. *Kompass Nachhaltigkeit* provides a comprehensive overview of different labels in all areas and provides information on how to evaluate these and which are compatible with the requirements of the different laws (Heydenreich 2014, 61; Kompass Nachhaltigkeit 2016). In the context of the unauthorized labels for gravestones, the *German Town and Municipality association* also proposes the creation of EU-wide and generally accepted quality labels for all relevant goods (Portz 2016, 17).

In addition to clear and ambitious criteria, effective and credible mechanisms need to be developed to review the criteria. To this end, the contracting authorities must regularly check company data. A successful example of such a review is the central control group set up by the State of Berlin (Heydenreich 2014, 61).

A contracting body can be quickly overburdened with the formulation of criteria, the evaluation of certificates or bidder declarations and the monitoring of the implementation. The *Competence Center* is therefore an important institution in order to support the establishment of a socially responsible procurement system, in particular for municipalities. The fulfillment of this task requires more personnel. In addition, the *Competence Center* should host a permanent exchange with experts from academia, development policy initiatives and environmental organizations. For this purpose, an advisory board could be established, as it has already been done in the state Bremen (ibid., 61–62).

Finally, it is unclear whether compliance with collective bargaining agreements and the possibility of incorporating social and ecological criteria in the award procedure are compatible with the CETA agreement. This question is addressed in the chapter on TTIP and CETA.

The potential of linking public procurement to social criteria should not be neglected. It is within the Federal Government's control to prevent the suppression of co-determination both at home and abroad. At the same time, the government would serve as an example of responsible purchasing for the private sector and consumers.

German Chambers of Commerce Abroad (Deutsche Auslandshandelskammern)

According to the *German Chambers of Commerce Abroad* they work "For the economy. Worldwide on site" (German Chambers of Commerce - Worldwide Network 2017). They " advise, support and represent German companies worldwide that wish to develop or expand their business activities abroad " (ibid.). They make use of numerous contacts and a good knowledge of the economic situation on-site to offer detailed information and concrete support for business activities in all important economies of the world.

Chambers of commerce abroad could act as ambassadors of co-determination, by informing newly established companies or companies already active in the host country about the risks of labor rights violations and their effective prevention. The chambers of the worldwide network could also select and accredit local certification bodies and auditors (Grabosch and Scheper 2015, 64). A similar service has already been established in the environmental field. Chambers of commerce advise on country-, sector- and company-specific issues of environmental protection and environmental law. Furthermore, they translate relevant legal texts, undertake environmental services such as performing registration and reporting procedures or the coordination and handle disposal and billing procedures.

Parallel to this, chambers of commerce could offer services to support the compliance with human rights and the introduction of co-determination rights in companies, subsidiary companies or supplier companies abroad. They could use their broad network of trade representatives, trade partners and manufacturers to expand their local databases with information on social aspects.

Since chambers of commerce are part of the economic development framework of the BMWi, their legal basis should be adapted in such a way to make them responsible for providing information on human rights (ibid., 64). The NAP provides that the *German Chambers of Commerce Abroad* will offer advice on human rights to a greater extent in the future (Deutsche Bundesregierung 2016, 34). It remains to be seen whether they will fulfill this task and whether co-determination rights will play a central role.

Germany Trade and Invest (GTAI)

The portal of the economic development agency *Germany Trade and Invest (GTAI)*, provides comprehensive background information and up-to-date reports for German companies selling their own products, purchasing intermediate products or investing abroad[10]. The information is organized under the following categories: economic climate, industries, business practices, law, customs and, depending on the country, procurement and development projects.

Labor rights risks that entrepreneurs face in a particular country when outsourcing production can be found in the existing portal only implicitly from a business perspective, focusing on increased labor costs associated with higher standards. For example, a report from April 2015 on Bangladesh, under the title "Rising Costs Reduces Competitiveness", states that larger production facilities are increasingly investing in working conditions. The latter coupled with the implementation of the minimum wage in 2013 according to the portal led to higher product prices, which in turn led many companies to change their production location (Germany Trade and Invest GmbH 2015). Another report from July 2016 welcomed the fact that, even though unemployment in Colombia

---

[10] The support of German companies that want to produce or export abroad is just one of the two main tasks of GTAI. The second task is to support foreign companies in their investments in Germany (Germany Trade and Invest GmbH 2016a)

was historically low, "employees for simple activities were numerous and cheap to hire" (Germany Trade and Invest GmbH 2016b, translation: KK).

Information on the risk of labor rights violations and indications for their avoidance could be included in the already existing structures with relatively little effort. The portal would only have to expand the previously purely economic reports, analyzes and recommendations also to social aspects. The NAP mentions that GTAI should also be responsible for human rights reporting and consulting (Deutsche Bundesregierung 2016, 34).

In addition to the numerous approaches that are provided in policy areas created for other objectives, to support co-determination rights, the German government can make use of instruments that have explicitly been created to improve working conditions. Two of these instruments, the *National Contact Point for the OECD Guidelines* in the BMWi and KfW's German network on *UN Principles for Responsible Investment* will be explored below.

Strengthening the National Contact Point for the OECD Guidelines

The *National Contact Point* for the *OECD Guidelines* is a body that the BMWi can use to promote co-determination. It is responsible for promoting the *OECD Guidelines for Multinational Enterprises* and for receiving complaints against violations of the Guidelines.

The *OECD Guidelines for Multinational Enterprises* are one of the most comprehensive instruments implemented for enforcing global environmental, labor and social standards. They refer to international agreements such as the *Universal Declaration of Human Rights* and *ILO core labor standards*, and provide recommendations in ten chapters for responsible corporate action in various areas, including human rights and employment policies. They are valid for the 34 OECD Member States and twelve other signatories.

Since the entry into force of the guidelines in 1976, they have been revised several times. In particular, in 2011, these revisions picked up long-term demands from trade unions and NGOs. The guidelines now include a human rights due diligence over the entire supply chain, as well as a human rights chapter, addressing issues of fair remuneration in transnational corporations.

The Guidelines are a voluntary instrument. Therefore, adherence to the formulated recommendations is non-binding. However, the institutional and organizational implementation of the Guiding Principles is mandatory for member states. To this end, *National Contact Points* (NCPs) have been set up to raise awareness of the *OECD Guidelines*, to consider complaints in the event of violation of the guidelines, to examine complaints and, if necessary, to initiate a mediation procedure. All "interested parties" can submit complaints. Trade unions and NGOs are the most active in filing them. In case of complaints, the contact points have no executive competence and serve rather as a mediating authority of a procedure, the result of which is not binding (Hadwinger et al. 2016, 32–33).

In contrast to the *UN guiding principles*, (operational) co-determination is explicitly mentioned in the *OECD Guidelines*. Within the framework, workers are entitled to establish trade unions and representative bodies of their choice and to be represented in collective bargaining. A multinational company should conduct constructive negotiations with these workers organizations either individually or through employers' associations in order to meet the targets set for the conditions of employment. In addition, the company should give workers' representatives the support they need to promote the conclusion of more effective collective bargaining agreements. Moreover, it should provide the employee representatives with the necessary information for a constructive negotiation of the terms of employment. Representatives must be informed about changes in business activity, such as closures or relocations, and must be included in the decisions that lead to them. Other matters of common interest are also to be discussed with employee representatives (Organisation for Economic Co-operation and Development 2011, chapter 5).

National Contact Points Track Record

Germany's *National Contact Point* (NCP) is located in the BMWi. However, decisions are taken in coordination with seven other ministries belonging to an inter-ministerial council (BMWi and Öffentlichkeitsarbeit 2015). The NCP could promote co-determination through its arbitration procedure for complaints. A successful settlement could lead the accused company to the implementation of more co-determination rights. The risk of a complaint could also have a deterrent effect on other companies, thus resulting in higher attention for co-determination rights in the future.

Since the establishment of the NCP in 2001, twenty-nine complaints have been filed (as of November 2016). Thirteen were extensively examined and sixteen were rejected because of lack of competence of the NCP or lack of evidence of a guideline violation. The accepted complaints had been filed by NGOs (5), trade union actors (5) or individuals (3). Six of the cases involved a direct or indirect violation of co-determination rights (BMWi 2016a).

A close look at the outcome of the mediation process shows a mixed picture for the six cases related to co-determination rights violations:

Three of the procedures led to a joint declaration by the complainants and the companies. In the case of one complaint regarding the violation of trade union rights in Indonesia by *Indocement*, a *HeidelbergCement* subsidiary, the resulting agreement consisted of two commitments. First, the withdrawal of formal warnings to trade unionists and second, a more or less firm commitment to respect their rights in the future (BMWi 2014c). In response to a complaint against *Bayer* about the replacement of a critical plant-level union to a pro-company alternative, the company paid compensation for lost trade union contributions. However, this was agreed on only under the condition that no further claims were made by the trade union side (BMWi 2007). Another complaint was filed by *UNI Global Union* and the *International Transport Workers' Federation* against *Deutsche Post-DHL* on account of the suppression of trade union rights in 13 countries. After the mediation procedure, *Deutsche Post- DHL* agreed to involve stakeholders and to carry out internal assessments of relations between employees and management, in individual cases. However, the NCP declared a large part of the allegations against the *Deutsche Post-DHL* as being without substance. Among other things, the suspension of a Colombian employee, who had posted information on labor rights on a bulletin board, was not considered a violation of the guidelines by the NCP. Moreover, the NCP did not acknowledge a violation in the dismissal of an employee who had urged superiors to talk about working conditions and neither in the dismissal of a worker who had shot videos of the bad working conditions. In these cases, the NCP argued that no violation could be present as a complaint had already been rejected by a local court or the local NCP (BMWi 2014b, 11).

Two more procedures ended without agreement: After the allegations of *IG-Metall* against *Hyundai* that it had hindered the works council, *Hyundai* decided to no longer participate in the mediation, so that the proceeding had to be terminated (BMWi 2015). In another complaint against *Adidas Salomon*, no agreement could be reached despite a constructive dialogue with the company (BMWi 2004).

The fact that the promotion of co-determination by voluntary negotiations would be quite possible is demonstrated by a sixth case, which was solved parallel to the NCP mediation procedure through direct contact between the two parties with the help of *UNI Global Union*. The conflict had occurred between the *Metro Habib Employee Union* and *Metro Cash and Carry*. The company was accused for not respecting employment contracts with regard to remuneration and working time arrangements, hygiene standards and safety regulations. Moreover, union members had been treated with hostility and threatened because of their union engagement. The negotiations resulted in a joint workshop on the management of all Pakistani *Metro* branches. The workshop dealt with the relations between employers and employees, social dialogue and intersecting relationships with employee representative. At the same time, the international umbrella organization *UNI Global Union* organized a meeting for local employee representatives with a focus on relationships with management. The workshops culminated in a joint dialogue, during which the management developed solutions to the problems at hand. This solution was carried out alongside the NCP procedure (BMWi 2014a).

Taken all cases together, the ones involving co-determination rights and the ones which do not, the overall impression of the German NCP is rather negative: Within a period of 15 years, only six complaints have led to any consequences that the NCP can take credit for. Considering all accepted cases, several weaknesses can be identified.

Firstly, cases, which have not already been settled by a national court or by another body, usually conclude with the company not found guilty on any account. The NCP often argues that German companies could not have assessed the situation on-site, or that their (unverified) requirements on suppliers were high enough. Another excuse given is that their commitment to other voluntary measures would already be exemplary. However, it is neglected that human rights due diligence of multinational companies would actually have to include additional expenditures for safety measures, the review of agreements with supplier firms or renouncing of measures with a negative impact on labor rights, such as extremely tight deadlines and cost pressure on suppliers. Even if mistakes by the companies are acknowledged, the consequences of the mediation are often not far-reaching and lead only to further voluntary obligations (BMWi and Öffentlichkeitsarbeit 2015; Hamm 2005; Heydenreich 2004).

The entire process of mediation is dominated by companies that can withhold important information or simply withdraw their cooperation as soon as they are dissatisfied with the process. Withdrawal from a procedure does not entail a large reputation risk because of the lack of public knowledge about the *OECD Guidelines* and the NCP. Reputation risk anyways exists only for companies in sectors that produce consumer goods or that depend directly on the end user.

In its present form, therefore, the grievance mechanism of the *OECD Guidelines* can specifically *not* fill the gap that has resulted from increasingly globally interweaved economic relations while maintaining national legal systems. Those victims of rights violations who are not heard through the official channels will most likely neither obtain compensation through the NCP process.

NGOs have further criticized the delay of cases and the lack of transparency in the existing procedure. The insufficient influence of civil society, in particular that of the global South, is also seen critically (Hamm 2005, 19–21). The criticisms are often linked to the fact that the NCP is affiliated to the BMWi and thus would inevitably focus on the interests of German companies rather than on the international rights owners. In addition, the outcome of the proceedings is dependent on the current government and on political dynamics (Hadwinger et al. 2016, 31–32).

With the 2011 revision of the Guidelines, the OECD sought to make the procedure more transparent. The integration of stakeholders in the process and access to the grievance procedure have been simplified (BMWi 2016d). The NCP is participating in a peer review process, which it has initiated itself in the context of the G7 process (Deutsches Institut für Menschenrechte 2015, 62).

Reforming the National Contact Points

The OECD Guidelines, in conjunction with the National Contact Points (NCPs), could provide a framework in which a multi-stakeholder dialogue can take place. However, in order to enable a dialogue to promote awareness of the employee's concerns in the company, further improvements are necessary.

First, an independent NCP with a quadri-partite organizational structure and decision-making power is required. Equal representation should be granted to the state, the private sector, trade unions and NGOs. In order to avoid individual and governmental bias from the proceeding, NGOs propose a binding code of practice which stipulates clear procedural rules and involves different groups (Hamm 2005, 23). A promising approach for a revaluation of the NCPs is provided in the NAP: The NCPs are to serve as a grievance instrument within the *Foreign Trade and Investment Promotion Scheme* in the future (Deutsche Bundesregierung 2016, 24). If this is to be done in the spirit of the *UN Guiding Principles,* a reform of the body as described above, which goes beyond the planned personnel increase and the creation of a separate organizational unit in the BMWi, is absolutely necessary.

The problem of a lack of effectiveness through voluntary action could be countered by linking the guiding principles to binding instruments. A *binding* compliance with the recommendations, or at least structured according to the comply-or-explain principle, could be considered a condition for foreign trade and investment promotion or export credit guarantees (Heydenreich 2004, 47).

In summary, the guiding principles are useful recommendations for companies. To encourage companies to adhere to these standards, however, external pressure and state control would be necessary (Hamm 2005). The OECD Guidelines lack both elements. Thus, as it is clear from the complaints filed at the NCP and the respective outcomes, the guidelines do not fill the legal gaps responsible for many of the sufferings of workers in the global market. They should therefore be used, in particular, as content documents in conjunction with more effective instruments.

German Network of the UN Principles for Responsible Investment

KfW Bank also has a number of initiatives aimed at preventing infringement of employment rights. One of these initiatives, the German network of *UN Principles for Responsible Investment*, will be examined below for its potential to promote co-determination.

The capital market orientation of globally operating corporations severely restricts their ability to seriously devote themselves to the interests of employees across the supply chain. For example, a company that has reduced profits to support labor rights expects losses in a volatile capital market, a risk that management usually tries to avoid.

In companies listed in stock exchange, this situation implies a dangerous division of responsibility. The management may have a personal interest in high social standards, but they cannot be enforced at the expense of shareholders. Investors, on the other hand, may neither be against human working conditions, but they are not in a position to decide on company policy. The shift of responsibility is even more present among institutional investors. A possible result is that, in a system in which actually all actors have the interest to promote social standards, no improvement takes place (Waring and Lewer 2004, 101–3).

Hence, in addition to management and consumers, private and institutional investors must be taken into account to secure co-determination rights globally. This is done by the *UN Principles* for *Responsible Investment* and its German network.

UN-Principles for Responsible Investment

The goal of the *UN Principles for Responsible Investment* (UN-PRI), adopted in 2006, is to develop principles for responsible securities management. This is to be done through the so-called ESG integration, i.e. the integration of *environmental*, *social* and *governance* criteria into the investment decision. Since its foundation, more than 1500 institutional investors have joined the initiative worldwide, including 60 from Germany (KfW Bank 2016b). In 2014, these investors managed 15 % of the globally invested capital (Aachener Stiftung Kathy Beys and Industrie und Handelskammer Nürnberg für Mittelfranken 2015).

By signing the six principles, members of the initiative voluntarily commit themselves to advocate sustainable investment in three different ways: Firstly, they integrate ESG topics into their own analyzes and investment decisions and produce the necessary information. Secondly, they seek to demand sustainable practices from listed companies. Thirdly, they cooperate with legislators to improve the regulatory framework for dealing with ESG issues. There are no minimum requirements or clear guidelines for all three commitments. The progress with the commitments, however, must be reported annually (Bundesministerium für Umwelt, Naturschutz und Reaktorsicherheit 2012, 25; United Nations Principles for Responsible Investment 2016).

A German PRI network was established in 2011 as an initiative of KfW-Bank. Its goal is to coordinate the co-operation of German signatories and to represent their interests in unison in the German market. The network is useful for contact management, but also provides a platform for the exchange of experiences, knowledge and strategies of various investment managers and asset managers (KfW Bank 2013).

Co-determination and PRI

Elements of employee participation are present in the PRI criteria for *social* and *good corporate governance*. For example, the category *social* entails several standards of decent work in the supply chain including freedom of association, employee relations and collective bargaining. Moreover, good corporate *governance* includes the rights of stakeholders and cooperation among them (KfW Bank 2016a; PRI Associations, UNEP Finance Initiative and UN Global Compact 2015, 4). However, how can responsible investment ultimately influence the reality of employees?

The literature on human resource management provides insights regarding this question: Referring to employee relations, Legge (2005) distinguishes between a 'hard' and a 'soft' approach to personnel management. The 'hard' approach pursues the goal of keeping labor costs as low as possible through efficiency and productivity, while the 'soft' attempts to grant employees development opportunities. This is intended to support a positive work ethos and bind employees to the company. Part of the second approach is the co-determination of wage-earning workers (Waring and Lewer 2004, 102). Particularly in listed companies, there is an increasing dominance of the 'hard' approach, which is (among other things) a result of tightening competitive pressure on the capital market (ibid., 100).

In this context, Waring and Lever identify three mechanisms how responsible investment can drive companies to respect the rights of their employees. Firstly, companies that apply 'hard', i.e. hostile personnel management should be excluded from the portfolio. The access to capital should therefore become more difficult, which serves as an incentive to improve the conditions. The increased demand for stock of responsible companies on the other hand should lead to a higher share price and be an incentive for other companies to position themselves responsibly. Secondly, the exclusion of a company from a responsible managed fund leads to a loss of reputation on the market and hints to problems with the management of the company. Listed companies worry about such signals and thus try to avoid them. Thirdly, particularly institutional investors such as the ones who are part of the PRI network, can benefit from co-determination rights regarding management strategies themselves. They can use their role as capital providers to submit resolutions in shareholder meetings and take part in decisions through their proxy votes. They could also run for board positions and therefore address aspects of employee participation.

A (not entirely selfless) survey of the sustainability rating agency *oecom* surveyed 199 companies from 30 countries and 34 sectors (oecom research 2013). The results show that sustainable investments motivate the majority of companies to become more involved in the environment and in the social sphere.

Promoting Co-determination through the German Network of the UN PRI

The mechanisms mentioned above for the promotion of co-determination rights through socially responsible investment can be effective only under three conditions. Firstly, sustainable investments must account for a large proportion of all investments. Secondly, they (and their screening processes) must be transparent and standardized, so that clear signals can be transmitted to the market. If companies remain unclear about what sustainable investors demand, they might ignore them. Similarly, a company cannot adapt to divergent criteria. Thirdly, the assessment schemes must be clearly committed to co-determination.

A positive example is set by the assessment criteria of the *Domini Social Equity Fund*. In this case, the factors of employee relations to be assessed by external auditors are *Strong union relations* ("the company has a history of notably strong union relations") and *Employee involvement* ("The company strongly encourages worker involvement and/or ownership through stock options available to a majority of its employees, gain sharing, stock ownership, sharing of financial information or participation in management decision making") (Waring and Lewer 2004, 104). The *Domini Social Equity Fund*, for instance, excluded Wal-Mart Stores Inc. from its portfolio for failing to fulfill these criteria (ibid., 99). An important aspect for international co-determination rights would be that these criteria relate to the entire supply chain.

Bearing in mind these three success factors– size, clarity, and centrality of participation rights – the Federal government should first of all seek to increase and therefore support responsible investment. This could be achieved, for example, through the obligation of private providers of government-subsidized pensions (*Riesterrente*) to join the PRI network. Secondly, the Federal Government should ensure the establishment of standardized screening mechanisms and set clear standards for them. For this purpose, a process for the development of a standardized screening process could be initiated within the German PRI network. A step in that direction was already made in 2014 by the guideline for consideration of ESG criteria (KfW Bank 2014). Thirdly, there is a risk that responsible investment will be abused for *greenwashing* and thus loses its potential. This is particularly dangerous because there are still no clear minimum standards for the members of the UN PRI. The government should advocate clear and ambitious standards, which explicitly include extensive co-determination rights.

Many investors rely on sustainability rates when picking which company to include in their portfolio. These ratings are, however, of very different quality. Sustainability rating agencies should therefore be bound by clear standards and supervised. In addition, there is the possibility to establish a state sustainability-rating agency in cooperation with European states. A state-funded agency would have several advantages. It could apply clear standards and standardized screening methods while maintaining its independence towards investors and from companies.

Federal Ministry of Finance (BMF): State-owned Companies

A large part of the state-owned enterprises is managed by the *Federal Ministry of Finance* (BMF). This chapter will deal with how these companies can be managed in such a way that the government does not participate in the violation of co-determination rights. As of the end of 2014, the Federal Government had stakes in 673 companies (Bundesministerium der Finanzen 2015b, 11). These include companies such as *Deutsche Bahn*, which are fully owned by the state, companies such as several airports in which the Federal Government has a share, and companies such as *Deutsche Post*, in which it holds shares indirectly via the KfW-Bank (ibid., 13).

The administration of federal participations falls within the competence of different ministries. With the exception of *Deutsche Bahn* (100% directly owned by the Federal Government), which is under the jurisdiction of the Ministry of Transport, all the following companies, which are active abroad, fall under the jurisdiction of the BMF: *Deutsche Post AG* (21% share via KfW), *Deutsche Telekom AG* (14.26% direct share and 17.44% indirect share via KfW), *Bundesdruckerei* (100% directly owned by the Federal Government) and *Commerzbank* (17.5% owned by the special funds of the *Finanzmarktstabilisierungsfonds*; FMS), *HypoRealEstate* (100% owned by the FMS)[11]. The majority of the rest of companies with federal participation are mainly or exclusively active within Germany (Bundesministerium der Finanzen 2015b; Heydenreich 2014, 50).

Co-determination in Federal Government-owned Companies

Accusations of violations of fundamental co-determination rights have been raised for several years against two of the six globally operating companies with federal shares.

As mentioned in the section on the NCP, a complaint was filed against *Deutsche Post-DHL* in 2012 for anti-union practices, which are in violation of the *OECD Guidelines*. The group was accused of violating the rights to establish and join trade unions, and of firing union members. In the cases of Deutsche Post-DHL

---

[11] Shares as of December 2014

in India, Colombia, Indonesia, Vietnam and Turkey, the accusation was accepted by the NCP. In Turkey, 37 employees were dismissed as a result of their trade union commitments. In a statement, *Deutsche Post-DHL* did not assume responsibility, but vowed to improve conditions. It promised to deal with the management of employee relationships in various countries and to improve them through measures such as a compliance program (BMWi 2016a).

However, an investigation from March 2016 shows that improvement has only partially been made, if at all. The study of the situation in DHL installations in Chile, Panama and Colombia, presented by the *International Transportation Workers' Union*, reports massive repression of trade union activity. Striking workers were shot, union activists were intimidated and subjected to hostile actions. Employees complained about illegal interceptions and bribery, which were used to force them into withdrawing from the union. According to employees, the mechanisms introduced by Deutsche Post-DHL for better communication did not bring any positive changes (Figueroa Clark 2016, 3). The image arises is that of a company that uses illegal methods to prevent the unionization of the workforce, and where trade unions are often portrayed as enemies (ibid., 27). Against this background, it is difficult to understand that in the reports published by the BMF on Federal Government share participation, there is no trace of the aforementioned issues. In fact, the government is obligated to report problems regarding the management of companies with state participation (Bundesministerium der Finanzen 2013; 2014; 2015b).

In response to a request by the Social Democratic Party (SPD) in 2013, the Federal Government at the time declared that there were no indications of violations of human and labor rights in companies with state participation (Deutscher Bundestag 2013a). At the time, however, not only the abovementioned *Deutsche Post* case was present. A complaint against *Deutsche Telekom's* largest subsidiary, *T-Mobile US*, had also been filed with the American NCP. The reason for the complaint was the restriction of the right to free and fair bargaining and the exploitation of weak labor laws in the USA by the *Telekom* group. In 2013, only 16 of the more than 38,000 employees of *T-Mobile US* were unionized. According to critics, this had occurred because of anti-union campaigns during working hours, explicit training of managers for the suppression of trade unions, increased control and dismissal of union members. The attempts of the American NCP to mediate were suspended due to the company's lack of co-operation (Heydenreich 2014, 50–52).

In spring 2015, a US court ruled that *T-Mobile US* had breached American law. A petition initiated by *ver.di*, which called on the Federal Government to ensure that the rights of employees in companies with federal participation are respected, was nevertheless ignored by the Petitions Committee. Since the formal quorum of signatures had not been reached within the specified time, a public hearing was rejected by the CDU. The (now governing) SPD supported this rejection on the basis of agreements in the coalition treaty. With the rejection of the petition, the Federal Government, which is the largest single shareholder of *Deutsche Telekom* with nearly 32 % of the shares, refused to exert any pressure even though *Telekom* obviously disrespected internationally recognized labor standards ratified by Germany (Mey 2015; We Expect Better 2016).

In the already cited reply to the SPD inquiry in 2013, the government at the time cited several reasons for its non-action. Apart from the denial of all allegations against the two companies, it explained that it couldn't influence the business practice in its role as shareholder. It continued by stating that the representatives of the government within the supervisory board of the company, just as any other shareholder, must mainly pursue the economic welfare of the company. According to the government at the time, however, "systematic violations of labor and human rights, which could have a negative impact on the company", should be reported (Deutscher Bundestag 2013a, 6, translation: KK). In other words, the infringement of fundamental rights is only to be opposed if the company itself suffers from it and if it is not a "sporadic" case. Referring to the *UN Guiding Principles*, the government argued that the recommendations for action on human rights due diligence are addressing only companies. States would therefore not be required to ensure their implementation (ibid., 3). As a consequence, "problems with the respect of human rights [did] not play a significant role in public shareholding management"(ibid., 5). The current Federal Government has not changed its stance, as it can be particularly observed in the rejection to discuss on the *ver.di* petition.

Legal Framework for the Administration of Companies with Federal Participation

The negligence of human rights due diligence appears to be contradictory. In fact, BMF's participation report clearly emphasizes that the Federal Government must pursue ethical values when managing its holdings (Bundesministerium der Finanzen 2015b, 17). The concrete foundations for this ethical-value orientation are rooted in the *Principles of Good Corporate Governance* published in 2009 and the *German Sustainability Code*.

However, it is exactly these *Principles of Good Corporate Governance* the government refers to in the aforementioned argument, that the state must prioritize the welfare of the company. Co-determination is mentioned in the principles, but only to the extent that it is required directly by German law (and therefore within Germany). In the *German Sustainability Code*, there is a link to securing co-determination rights in three areas (namely Criterion 9, which determines the identification of stakeholders, Criterion 14, which refers to labor rights, and Criterion 19, the observance of human rights over the supply chain). However, "compliance" with the Code is secured by 'comply or explain'. In case of non-compliance the company only needs to explain why implementation was not possible.

In order to ensure an ethical management of state-owned companies in line with the *UN Guiding Principles*, compulsory and far-reaching guidelines should be set. A possible way would be the obligation to enforce human rights due diligence over the supply chain. This would be particularly important for companies active in risk-prone human-rights-related areas, such as *Deutsche Telekom* with its mobile telephone production. In the case of financial institutions such as *Commerzbank* or *HypoRealEstate*, due diligence should also include conditionality for the provision of money and project financing (Heydenreich 2014, 53).

Furthermore, the Federal Government should contribute to the clarification and abolition of existing inconsistencies, taking seriously allegations against the NCP and petitions such as *ver.di*'s. The latter suggested that if problems arise in state-owned companies, the BMF could be given the task of controlling the observance of labor rights. In addition, it could ensure that companies implement the ILO standards and respect trade union freedom (Deutscher Bundestag - Petitionsausschuss 2015). An even better solution would be to entrust this task to the *Ministry of Labor*, as this is more familiar with labor rights.

Similar considerations also apply to numerous holdings of federal states such as *Volkswagen* because of its anti-union practices in Nigeria (Handelsblatt 2016; International Trade Union Confederation 2016f).

Ministry of Foreign Affairs (AA): German Embassies and Social Affairs Attachés

The *National Action Plan* (NAP), which has been developed under the leadership of the Federal Ministry of Foreign Affairs for the implementation of the UN Guiding Principles, was already discussed. This chapter will explore a further instrument under the jurisdiction of the same ministry, namely the German Embassies and their Social Affairs attachés.

German embassies can be instrumental in promoting co-determination abroad. They can serve as contact points and as advisory and exchange forums, which are accessible to a wide range of actors (Grabosch and Scheper 2015, 18). Ideally, embassies should possess a good knowledge of the German system of industrial relations and a good understanding of the political and economic situation and culture of the host country. This way information can be conveyed in an appropriate manner, and realistic assessments can be made regarding the best way to promote co-determination in the host country.

Social Affairs attachés, present in 21 embassies, could therefore be suitable to undertake this task. The attachés proposed by the DGB or the Ministry of Labor and Social Affairs (BMAS) have many responsibilities. Depending on the host country, their duties include exchanges with the ministries of labor and health of the host country, maintaining contact with trade unions, employers' associations and other civil society actors. Moreover, they are involved with the dissemination of information on regulations, institutions and associations in Germany and the support of foreigners interested in studying or training in Germany. Social Affairs attachés take on a report function towards Germany, an information function on Germany (which includes counseling host countries) and a linking function between governments, social administrations and associations (Botschaft der Bundesrepublik Deutschland Bratislava 2016; Schmidt, Link, and Wolf 2007, 301).

The exchange of information on co-determination and forms of industrial relations is considered a central task by many Social Affairs attachés. A survey, conducted in September 2016, among Social Affairs attachés of different German embassies shows that they are well informed about the German co-determination system and usually have scientific or practical expertise in the field.

This occurred particularly among those with a trade union background. Social Affairs attachés gave a positive evaluation to the German model. They pointed out, however, that a historically evolved model cannot be established blindly in another country. Other forms of relationship between management, employees and the government could be suitable. Many attachés reported a high interest in the German co-determination system in the host country of their embassy. As a result, they see great potential in their position to make employee participation widely known. They do so in part through lectures and workshops, but above all informally in exchange with trade unionists, employers' associations and politicians. For some countries of the Global South, however, it was noted that a co-determination system was not of great interest. These countries focused their effort in the enforcement of "fundamental labor rights as human rights". Trade unions and management representatives of some other countries reject a consensus-oriented system.

A proposal for the better dissemination of the topic within the context of embassy work is through foundations on-site (e.g. Friedrich Ebert Foundation). The latter could organize events about co-determination where social attachés could attend and offer their expertise. Organizing such events by themselves is rather unusual for embassies. Another starting point could be ILO conventions, which have already been ratified by the host country, but have not yet been translated into national policy. For example, Brazil has ratified Convention 135 on Workers' Representation, but has not yet transposed it into national law. In cases of common interest for the host country and the German government, workshops could be organized, where experiences and practical examples of best practice are exchanged.

In addition to the dialogue with the partners of the host country, embassies should provide a point of contact for German companies, which is responsible for co-determination in subsidiary companies or suppliers abroad. This way, German companies that have outsourced parts of their production chain to the country in question can receive relevant information on the risks of violating co-determination rights. They can therefore get assistance in developing strategies for securing these rights in the host country. Cooperation with the *Chambers of Commerce Abroad* could be a further step in this direction. Successful practical examples are already available from other European countries in the field of human rights protection in supply chains. For example, Danish embassies offer workshops on responsible supply chain management in countries with high risk and prepare the CSR reviews of local suppliers (Hadwinger et al. 2016).

An obstacle to dealing with co-determination in the host country is often the variety of tasks of social attachés. Thus, the work environment allows only a selective occupation with most of the topics, as long as no specific co-operations or projects exist. In addition, the distribution of social attachés between the individual embassies is, above all, bound to historical ties and is not necessarily helpful for the objective of supporting co-determination. For instance, no social attaché has been assigned to any of the five countries where, according the ILO, rights to freedom of association, collective bargaining and social dialogue are violated most often (International Labour Organisation 2012). The embassies' lack of a clearly communicated strategy directed to the support of labor rights reflects the Foreign Ministry's understanding of human rights. The latter focuses more on "general fundamental rights" or political freedoms and hardly on labor rights aspects. The *National Action Plan for Business and Human Rights* could be a fresh start for embassies towards a better treatment of workers' rights.

Federal Ministry for Economic Cooperation and Development (BMZ)

"One very important element of decent work is the freedom of workers to express their opinions, organize and engage in collective bargaining. Only then are the conditions in place for a functioning social dialogue, which is key to stable labor relations and productive development" (Bundesministerium für Wirtschaftliche Zusammenarbeit and Bundesministerium für Arbeit und Soziales 2015, translation: KK). This quote stems from a "vision paper" entitled "Good Work Worldwide" which was jointly published by BMZ and BMAS for the G7 presidency 2015. In the paper, the BMZ presents its different initiatives on the state level, the corporate and the consumer level to secure these rights.

In the following chapter, two of these BMZ initiatives will be explored. The *develoPPP.de* program, which supports private development cooperation, will be presented first. It is followed by the *Partnership for Sustainable Textiles*, which was launched in 2014 and aims to improve working conditions in textile production.

DeveloPPP.de

The budget of the BMZ in 2016 provided EUR 125 million to promote "development partnerships with business partners" (Bundesministerium für Finanzen 2016). The most important program for private development cooperation is develoPPP.de. Within the framework of Public Private Partnerships, develoPPP.de supports companies that invest in countries of the Global South, both financially and professionally.

The declared objective of the program is to combine "the innovative power of the economy with the resources, knowledge and experience of development policy" (Bundesministerium für wirtschaftliche Zusammenarbeit und Entwicklung 2016a, translation: KK). Thereby it seeks to mobilize additional resources for development policy processes and objectives According to the BMZ, in this way companies can "expand to new markets continuously and at the same time improve the living conditions of the local people", (Bundesministerium für wirtschaftliche Zusammenarbeit und Entwicklung 2016c, translation: KK).

Interested companies can apply for develoPPP.de with a project idea. Through the approval of a project, the BMZ supports simple projects with up to EUR 200,000. More elaborate projects also known as 'strategic development partnerships' are supported with higher sums. The projects are implemented in cooperation with the *German Investment and Development Company* (DEG), the *German Association for International Cooperation* (GIZ) and the development organization *sequa*, the members of which are the umbrella organizations of the German industry. Interested companies must be based in Germany and the EU in order to apply. For companies outside Europe, at least 25% of the shares must be owned by a European company (Bundesministerium für wirtschaftliche Zusammenarbeit und Entwicklung 2016f). As is customary in private-sector cooperation, *develoPPP.de* builds also an interface between development cooperation and foreign trade and investment promotion (Bundesministerium für wirtschaftliche Zusammenarbeit und Entwicklung 2016d; 2016f).

Companies can only reliably support the Federal Government in achieving development policy objectives, if clear requirements are placed on them. As mentioned in the beginning of this chapter, the BMZ has set itself the goal of complying with and promoting co-determination rights. The implication for *develoPPP.de* is that, on one hand, companies that receive subsidy should be prevented from violating co-determination rights. On the other hand, this chance should be used explicitly to strengthen co-determination rights through subsidized projects.

According to *develoPPP.de*, the selection of eligible projects is based on six criteria: Firstly, projects must be compatible with development policy objectives. This includes environmental and social compatibility. Secondly, projects should be "complementary". Public and private contributions should complement each other in such a way that the common goal is achieved as efficiently as possible. Thirdly, the principle of subsidiarity is intended to ensure that the approved projects could not be carried out by companies in the absence of the subsidy. Fourthly, applicant companies should have a financial interest in the project. Hence, charitable projects do not receive funding. Fifthly, the private partner must make a contribution of at least 50% of the costs. Sixthly, every project must be sustainable, thus leading to a long-term commitment of the company. Two of the criteria for sustainability are the *integration of local structures and organizations* and the *introduction and improvement of standards*. Trade unions or co-determination rights do not appear in the assessment criteria for funding (Bundesministerium für wirtschaftliche Zusammenarbeit und Entwicklung 2016f).

At first glance, the evaluation criteria for the protection of labor standards appear suitable. However, this would only be the case, if the above points were actually examined for each project. Actually, in the application form that a company must fill, labor rights are not mentioned at all. Instead, the focus of the application is put on strategies for solving a development policy problem, which the company itself chooses. If this problem is, for example, an ecological one, the question of respect for labor rights in general and of co-determination rights in particular is irrelevant in the application (Bundesministerium für wirtschaftliche Zusammenarbeit und Entwicklung 2016b). It is unclear whether these aspects are examined later in the application process, whether subsidized project are monitored and whether a violation of the principles leads to sanctions.

It is not surprising that under these, rather unclear, requirements also companies receive support which are already known for violations of co-determination rights. For example, *Shell* received EUR 473,500 from 2007 to 2011 to dispose of old pesticides in an environmentally friendly manner and to build up capacities for environmental management in Asia (Stabstelle Zusammenarbeit mit der Wirtschaft 2011). At the same time, *Shell* was responsible for spilling more than 200,000 barrels of oil into the Niger Delta, thereby destroying many of its livelihoods (Amnesty International 2012). In addition, the company has been accused for years for employing workers under inhumane conditions in

Pakistan and Nigeria and massive trade union suppression (IndustriALL 2016). The textile company *NKD*, which used to produce also at the Rana Plaza factory (collapsed in 2013), received EUR 175,000 between 2011 and 2013. *Deutsche Post* received EUR 161,500 between 2005 to 2011, while *Deutsche Telekom* received EUR 869,216 between 2010 to 2013 (Stabstelle Zusammenarbeit mit der Wirtschaft 2011).

Information on which companies are currently being supported is not available. However, a list of exemplary projects is available. For instance, through a *develoPPP.de* project, *Merck KGaA* is training companies and consumers on how to deal with special waste in Indonesia, the Philippines and Thailand. The same company was found guilty of oppressing trade unions and ignoring the freedom of association in Pakistan (Bundesministerium für wirtschaftliche Zusammenarbeit und Entwicklung 2016e; LabourNet 2012).

It is not clear how much money *Merck* received from the BMZ and whether existing allegations were taken into consideration during the evaluation of the project proposal. The BMZ provides neither the funding sum, nor information on compliance with social and ecological criteria. In addition, only some of the projects are published. It is thus impossible to understand which projects are currently being funded or how much money they receive. Thus it remains a mystery whether they lead to the expected results or if they pose environmental and social risks. By refusing to provide comprehensive information on supported projects, the BMZ can avoid unpleasant questions about the use of its funds, the selection of projects and the review of the social criteria.

If cooperation with the private sector is aimed at aiding the population of the host country, avoiding the negative impacts of projects does not suffice. Instead, it must also be shown that a project actually has the positive impact that the government expected when it granted the funds (Czornohus 2010). This is true in particular as the funds devoted to private development partnerships with industry are immense: As a matter of comparison, in 2016 they were more than three times as high as on the money spent on development education (Bundesministerium für Finanzen 2016). It would be particularly interesting to see whether the projects are actually carried forward after the grant. The web pages of *develoPPP.de* do not provide information on whether the effects of the projects are systematically evaluated. The NGO *VENRO* reports that impact analyzes have taken place, but the experience with *develoPPP.de* projects was rather sobering (VENRO 2011, 8).

Among the sample projects published this year, there are also projects that explicitly promote co-determination. Two out of the thirty-six sample projects published on the website are specifically intended to promote co-determination rights (and other labor rights). Both projects focus on the strengthening of labor rights in textile processing suppliers. However, the two projects represent a minority. The vast majority of the published samples deal with environmental aspects.

Even though the projects focusing on labor rights sound promising, it is questionable if the respect of fundamental labor rights should be rewarded with government subsidies as it is done in *develoPPP* projects. Although the ventures in this area might lead to partial improvements, they support an approach, which regards the respect of fundamental human rights as an act of charity. In fact, global corporations have the *duty* to respect the rights of their employees. Their respect is not a "good deed" for which the BMZ should pay for.

Furthermore, it is incomprehensible why only German and European companies can apply for funding. If the goal of *develoPPP.de* is the improvement of the living conditions of people in host countries, why should resident companies not push this improvement forward? Instead of consistently pursuing the objectives of "decent work" and the improvement of living conditions, *develoPPP.de* creates a competitive advantage for European companies. Thus it often strengthens already existing inequalities.

This was particularly evident in the case of the funding of *BAYER Crop Science*. The company received financial support to train Kenyan pesticide retailers in the sustainable and environmentally friendly use of pesticides. According to media reports, however, the participants in the training course were particularly trained on dealing with *Bayer* pesticides. They were subsequently awarded a *Bayer* seal of quality for their pesticide sales. The seminar seemed to have achieved what *Bayer* intended: Afterwards, participants evaluated the company as very positive (Norddeutscher Rundfunk 2013). *Bayer* was thus able to use German funds for development cooperation in order to expand its market power on site. In total, the group received more than EUR 1.1 million for "development partnerships" in various divisions from 2009 to 2013 (Stabstelle Zusammenarbeit mit der Wirtschaft 2011). The support of the competitive advantage of German companies may be reasonable from an economic point of view. However, from a developmental point of view it is counterproductive. Local businesses are being pressured by the unfair competition and higher costs could lead to the restriction of labor rights.

Public Private Partnerships in the field of development cooperation are justified on the basis of the fact that cooperation with the private sector provides more funds and projects are managed more efficiently. While this might be true, this leverage effect can be useful only if DEG, GIZ and *sequa* consistently use the funds towards the fulfillment of the objectives of development cooperation. For this purpose, it is not sufficient to rely on companies to set the right priorities themselves. Instead, clear criteria must be established that are verified during both the selection and the implementation of the project.

Since the projects are developed *together* with DEG, GIZ or *sequa*, these institutions could provide an effective support for the observance of rights in the host country. The experts of BMZ's ExperTS program could offer further support. In addition, the BMZ should provide transparency on which projects are funded, how much money they receive, as well as their expected impact. Further, it should be assessed to what extent the stated goals were reached after the project phase and the assessment should be published.

Partnership for Sustainable Textiles

The violation of freedom of association and the suppression of the trade unions of textile factories in Bangladesh, Pakistan, India, Cambodia and other countries is sufficiently documented (Bundesministerium für Wirtschaftliche Zusammenarbeit and Auswärtiges Amt 2015; Hall 2006; Köhnen and Scheidhauer 2002; Scheidhauer 2008). In response to these abuses and based on the shared responsibility of German textile companies, the BMZ, under Gerd Müller, launched in 2014 the *Partnership for Sustainable Textiles*. The aim of this partnership is to improve the ecological, social and economic sustainability along the entire production process together with the manufacturers and distributors of the textile and clothing industry.

Becoming part of the voluntary partnership involves a binding commitment to "comply with a mandatory process to realise [] joint measures, and thus achieve the objectives and standards of the Partnership", i.e. social, environmental and economic partnership standards for the entire value chain which have been agreed on (Partnership for Sustainable Textiles 2017) . The observance of the standards must be verifiable up to a certain date by an external supervisory body. As of mid-2016, the partnership has included 180 members, which in turn account for about half of the turnover in the German textile business. In 2017, the companies involved are expected to publish their targets in roadmaps. The deadline is set for the end of 2018. The steering committee of the partnership decides on concrete action based on the recommendations made by expert groups. In the steering committee, the following stakeholders are represented: business groups, development policy NGOs, the Federal Government, the DGB and a non-commercial standards organization (Bündnis für nachhaltige Textilien 2016).

The suppression of co-determination rights in textile production is part of the generally very problematic working conditions within the sector. A structural obstacle to the improvement of these conditions is the existence of various destructive conditions of competition. Competition, as in many other areas that use global supply chains, takes place on three levels: Firstly, between the textile companies in Northern countries who want to bind customers and secure market shares through low prices; secondly, between textile suppliers' factories in the South, which compete with the lowest possible sales prices for clinching purchase contracts; thirdly, between the various textile producing countries, which are competing for the lowest possible production conditions through weak environmental and social standards.

The suppression of co-determination rights is triggered on two of these levels, namely between the supplier factories and between textile producing countries. Supplier factories, which want to keep their production prices as low as possible due to competition, have an interest in curtailing the rights of their employees at the plant level. Textile-producing countries that want to attract buyers and investors through weak environmental and social standards, are doing so by suppressing trade unions and creating anti-union frameworks[12] (Anner 2015).

Against this background, two tasks are pivotal for the *Partnership for Sustainable Textiles* and similar initiatives. Firstly, 'downward competition' must be tackled at all three levels. Secondly, it must be acknowledged that the suppression of co-determination rights is both a plant-level and a national problem. Hence, conditions at both levels must be addressed to improve the situation. The following section provides an analysis of how these tasks could be performed. The existing potential is then compared with the current state of the partnership. The assessments on individual points are based on statements from various civil society actors.

The Partnership for Sustainable Textiles is explicitly designed to prevent a *competitive disadvantage at the level of northern textile firms*. As many companies as possible in the textile and clothing industry in Germany are supposed to join. The underlying assumption is that if all the important companies participate, no company can draw a disadvantage from the participation ('Level-Playing-Field'). Broad-based participation is also advantageous for responsible purchasers. In fact, joint issues such as co-determination rights can be tackled together and can be strengthened through the strategic purchase of products supplied under better conditions.

In order to prevent a *'downward competition' between suppliers*, binding minimum standards have to be established. At the same time, they should be counter-financed by higher purchasing prices. The focus on the establishment of co-determination rights throughout the entire supply chain is essential for a real and sustained improvement of the situation of textile workers. In practice, this must be reflected both in the precise elaboration of minimum standards and test criteria as well as in the review of these criteria.

The criteria under development should be based on social dialogue in production plants and a definition of human rights due diligence, which places co-

---

[12] This is particularly evident in 'special economic zones': in these zones, trade union activity is usually suppressed in order to create as favourable conditions as possible for foreign investors, together with other measures (Anner 2015, 7).

determination at the center as an "enabling right" of employees. This is the case for the first set of indicators already developed. The review criteria of the partnership are divided into two areas: company-specific criteria and "sector-wide commitment", i.e. criteria that must be jointly advanced by all companies. As explained above, addressing both areas is necessary. Criteria for the promotion of co-determination should therefore be anchored as a test criterion to both sector-wide as well as company-specific supply chains. In addition to ensuring rights in their own supply plants, individual companies could provide a positive impetus for strengthening union work on site. This can be done, for example, through offering trainings for local trade unions in cooperation with *IndustriALL*.

By reviewing the criteria, the partnership offers the opportunity to establish an alternative to the widely established auditing used in the context of *codes of conduct*. The latter practice has proved to be ineffective for the strengthening of labor rights, and in particular co-determination (Vogel 2005, 164). Instead of relying on the global audit industry, monitoring can be carried out through trade unions and NGOs on site in cooperation with the purchasing and supplying companies. In addition, a grievance mechanism, which is easily accessible to workers, should be set up in host countries in cooperation with trade unions.

In order to mitigate the *harmful competition between supplying countries*, the textile partnership can make use of two levers. Firstly, companies could pledge to pay higher purchase prices for better working conditions and refrain from shifting production to a country with lower production costs. Secondly, "partnership initiatives" could be used to strengthen co-determination. These initiatives bring together a number of partners to work out and promote a specific topic. An initiative in the field of co-determination, in conjunction with governments, trade unions and NGOs, could develop strategies for strengthening co-determination rights. Such an initiative would be particularly promising in cooperation of many textile firms because they can effectively put pressure on suppliers to respect rights. At the same time, the purchaser should be willing to support the establishment of rights through its own obligations, such as a higher purchasing price.

Partnership members from the German civil society argue that a meaningful design of the textile partnership can be achieved only in cooperation with trade unions in the producing countries. Similarly, central targets such as occupational safety and living wages can be achieved with support from local unions. The establishment of collective bargaining agreements on site could strengthen trade unions and their negotiating position in the producing countries. After all, rights such as freedom of association and unionization are anchored in the constitutions of most countries. The problem, however, is that trade unions are not accepted by business and government. A functioning social dialogue in plants of partnership members could strengthen local unions and their bargaining position. The potential is particularly high, if safeguarding co-determination rights in the context of the textile partnership is accompanied by a dialogue with government agencies and industry associations in the country of production. This can be achieved, for example, through the cooperation of German embassies or chambers of commerce as it was explained in more detail in the corresponding chapters.

Whether while setting criteria during the monitoring process or in alliance initiatives, the partnership should always take into account the role of the workers and the trade unions as co-determinants and carriers of the improvement process. This is the only way to avoid unintentional effects often reported in transnational campaign work. While the improvement of labor rights and necessary change are being discussed in purchasing countries, workers in production plants "are made sole witnesses of inhuman practices of companies without appearing as actors of change themselves" (Fütterer 2016, 210–11, translation: KK). For unions on site, this could mean that efforts to improve working conditions and to promote self-organization are put aside because of the necessity to scandalize conditions that are considered unacceptable (ibid., 210–11). In the worst-case scenario, co-determination on site could thus be weakened instead of strengthened

The *Partnership for Sustainable Textiles* is a pioneer project in Europe and worldwide. If it successfully leads to better working conditions and more co-determination practices, it could serve as a model for further, similar initiatives. In order to fulfill this role it should establish clear and binding minimum standards, ambitious corporate objectives and constructive cooperation with local unions. As a proof that improvements are possible in a highly competitive market and with all key players involved, numerous actors in other sectors and countries could borrow this initiative.

It remains unclear whether the textile partnership will be able to exploit its full potential. A watering down of the goals was feared when many big companies such as Kik, Aldi or Adidas and various large textile associations decided to join in the summer of 2015, after one and a half years of hesitation. Particularly indicative of the concerns was an often-cited newsletter of the *German Fashion Association* of April 2015. Among other things, it stated that "all the problematic points had been removed from the action plan", including its "binding character" (Dohmen 2015, translation: KK).

According to critics, the inclusion of the unanimity principle in the steering committee meant that nothing could be enforced against business interests (ibid.). Partnership partners, however, disagree with this assessment. Mandatory minimum standards remain in place and the common consensus principle for multi-stakeholder initiatives in the steering committee does not mean that firm interests do necessarily prevail. Unanimity instead also means that NGO representatives must likewise agree to any decision. The author of the *German Fashion* newsletter apologized for the misrepresentation.

The strategic decision, to shift away from a "frontrunner" approach, towards higher market coverage under somewhat less ambitious conditions, at the same time offers some potential. The relevant market power could be instrumental in the implementation of the mechanisms outlined above, if all partners are willing to go along.

In order to prevent the Partnership from becoming the often invoked *"Fig leave project"* (ibid., translation: KK), pressure must be exerted on companies, and in particular on the participating textile associations (which are described by many as far less constructive than single firms). This is currently possible due to the existing public interest in textile production. The loss of this momentum would complicate the build-up of the public pressure.

The government must therefore be consistent with its initial objectives and support civil society in the enforcement of binding and ambitious criteria, monitoring mechanisms and initiatives. This does not mean that the government should arbitrarily follow the views of trade unions and NGOs. However, the establishment of far-reaching labor rights can hardly be demanded from the companies alone, despite the constructive cooperation shown by some firms. In addition to civil society efforts, the government, which has committed itself to the goal of "Good Work Worldwide", must take its responsibilities (Bundesministerium für Wirtschaftliche Zusammenarbeit 2015).

The initial strong commitment to the Partnership demonstrated by civil society and business actors is hardly sustainable in the long term. A sustainable institutionalization, supported by the BMZ, is therefore important. In addition, the voluntary partnership should also be supplemented by binding government measures in order to maintain competition outside the initiative and implement a 'level playing field'. Potential measures have already been discussed in the section on the *National Action Plan* (Interviews with different civil society representatives, September - Oktober 2016; CIR - Christliche Initiative Romero e.V. 2015; Grabosch and Scheper 2015, 24; Kampagne für Saubere Kleidung 2014).

National approaches are influenced by policy at other levels. German co-determination rights are particularly affected by European policies. After having discussed the national government's potential to support these rights in the different ministries, the next part of this study examines the potential of trade and investment agreements negotiated at the European level to promote co-determination as well as their likely impact on co-determination.

Potential and Effects of Trade and Investment Agreements: Example of CETA

Trade and investment agreements can be an effective means of strengthening and expanding co-determination rights and other workers' rights. The European Commission, which is the lead negotiator for the upcoming trade agreements that will affect Germany, promises that: "The new approach also involves using trade agreements and trade preference programs as levers to promote, around the world, values like sustainable development human rights, fair and ethical trade and the fight against corruption. We will use future EU agreements to improve the responsibility of supply chains." (European Commission 2015, 5). The current chapter presents ways on how co-determination rights could be secured and promoted through trade policy, evaluating the effects of the *Comprehensive Economics and Trade Agreement (CETA)*, which has been negotiated between Canada and the EU and is about to be ratified, and the *Transatlantic Trade and Investment Partnership (TTIP)*, which is currently being negotiated by the US and the EU. Concretely, it is sought to analyze the extent to which these agreements can promote, or on the contrary, jeopardize co-determination rights.

A focus is placed on CETA, since its text is the only one available. It is to be assumed that many of the aspects of CETA are similar to TTIP, since even officially CETA is considered as a blueprint for TTIP (BMWi and Referat Öffentlichkeitsarbeit 2016b).

This chapter concentrates rather on the role of the European Commission than on the German government, since the former acts as the lead negotiator for the European states. However, the German government is indirectly involved, as its influence on European policy, and thus also on TTIP and CETA negotiations, is highly significant.

Social Clauses to Respect and Promote Co-determination

The inclusion of social clauses or social chapters has been proposed by various parties as a way to anchor the rights of employees, and thus also the right to co-determination, in trade agreements and to prevent their restriction (see for example Aaronson 2006; Greven 2012a; 2012b; Perulli 2014; Scherrer and Hänlein 2012). These clauses act as a safeguard against an anti-labor interpretation of the treaties. They also serve as a lever for the enforcement of social rights, since they can force governments involved in free trade to implement certain principles in their employment systems (Dombois 2006, 239–40).

The existing literature identifies various aspects that must be taken into account in an agreement so that social clauses can fulfill these tasks: Firstly, social clauses must include the *ILO's core labour standards*,[13] the obligation to ratify them, transpose them into national law, apply them effectively and to report regularly on the state of their implementation. Important for the maintenance and expansion of employee participation are, in particular, 'enabling rights'. Secondly, the social chapter should contain a clause, which prevents both a 'regulatory chill' (renouncement of improvements of standards in the future) and a 'race to the bottom' (reduction of standards due to competition). Moreover, in order to be able to correct negative unanticipated developments, safeguard and revision mechanisms should be established. Another important aspect is the existence of independent review and decision-making mechanisms accompanied by an effective sanctioning mechanism. Finally, the agreement should provide a forum for the exchange of information between governments and social partners, in which there is a clearly defined balance. In addition, the complaints and recommendations raised from the forum should be addressed by the respective governments (Dessewffy 2012, 62-64; 72-75; Greven 2012a, 91–93).

International working norms can be found in the CETA chapter on *Sustainable Development* under the subchapter *Trade and Labor*. In this subchapter, Europe and Canada reaffirm their commitment to "respect, promote and realise those principles and rights in accordance with the obligations of the members of the International Labour Organisation" (Council of the European Union 2016, art. 23.3(1)) and "effectively implement in its law and practices in its whole territory the fundamental ILO Conventions that Canada and the Member States of the European Union have ratified respectively " (ibid., art. 23.3(4)).

However, Canada has not signed ILO Convention 98, which contains the right of association and the right to collective bargaining and thus is fundamental to co-determination practice. Quite the contrary, Canada is the ILO member that has received the highest number of complaints in the *ILO Committee on Freedom of Association* (Development Solution 2011, 135).[14]

If the incorporation of the *ILO core labor standards* into CETA made Canada ratify the missing convention, it would indeed be a great advance for co-determination. In June 2016, a few months before CETA was signed, Canada ratified its second "missing" basic convention, the *Convention on the Minimum Age of Workers*. CETA supporters argue that this will soon be the case for Convention 98. This is however unlikely for reasons of domestic policy, since a consensus should be found in the provinces. Furthermore, the CETA text is vague regarding the convention's pending ratification and states only that the parties will make an ongoing and lasting effort to ratify the basic ILO

---

[13] And, according to the state of development of the country, the other priority agreements.

[14] From 1982-2008, 78 complaints, 90 per cent of which were regarded as a violation of the freedom of association (Development Solution 2011, 135).

Conventions, if they have not yet ratified them (Council of the European Union 2016, art. 23.3(4)). This does not imply any obligation on Canada to sign the missing convention (Fritz 2015, 27–28).

In addition to the core labor standards, the *OECD Guidelines for Multinational Enterprises* are referenced in the CETA text. However, they are mentioned only in the preamble which "encourage[s] enterprises operating within their territory or subject to their jurisdiction to respect internationally recognized guidelines and principles of corporate social responsibility, including the OECD Guidelines for Multinational Enterprises, and to pursue best practices of responsible business conduct " (Council of the European Union 2016, preamble). Although preambles often serve as interpreting aids, the wording of the guidelines is so vague that it cannot lead to any obligations (Waleson 2015, 172).

The chapter on *labor and trade* contains a clause in which contracting parties commit themselves not to lower labor standards for stimulating trade or investment (Council of the European Union 2016, art. 23.4). Even though this does not rule out 'regulatory chill', it could theoretically counteract a 'race to the bottom'. However, since the entire chapter on *sustainable development* and thus the sub-chapter on *labor and trade* are excluded from the general sanction mechanism, this clause has no effective impact (Fritz 2015, 29).

The labor chapter foresees its own dispute settlement mechanism, instead of accessing the general CETA dispute mechanism. Despite the "binding" character of the provisions in the labor chapter (Council of the European Union 2016, art. 23.11(3)) infringements are not punishable by trade sanctions (Fritz 2015, 28; Waleson 2015, 165). In the event of a conflict, bilateral government consultations are initially foreseen. If this is unsuccessful, a panel of experts may be requested to make recommendations. If an infringement is found, the parties agree on remedial measures or an action plan. However, what happens when there is no consensus, remains an open question (Council of the European Union 2016, art. 23.10; Fritz 2015, 28).

The non-enforceable character of the labor chapter is mainly due to the European Commission. Canada's negotiator wanted to compensate for violations at least by means of financial compensation (Fritz 2015, 28). The negative experiences of similar dispute settlement procedures under the *North American Free Trade Agreement* (NAFTA; Compa and Brooks 2008) suggest that CETA cannot effectively sanction the infringement of core labor standards and thus safeguard workers' rights.

The inclusion of stakeholders in a *civil society forum* is foreseen exclusively for the sustainability chapter in CETA. This forum is to be held annually in order to "conduct a dialogue on the sustainable development aspects of this Agreement " (Council of the European Union 2016, art. 22.5). Members should be "independent representative employers, unions, labor and business organisations, environmental groups, as well as other relevant civil society organisations as appropriate", which shall be in "balanced representation" (ibid., art. 22.5). Other chapters, and particularly the chapter on investment protection, which has an influence on the rights of workers and other stakeholders, do not stipulate similar exchanges between stakeholders.

Safeguard or revision mechanisms are neither foreseen in the CETA. Quite on the contrary, the agreement is a so-called 'living agreement', which can be interpreted and subsequently amended by bodies of representatives of the EU Commission and Canada, without necessarily obtaining authorization from the Member States or Parliaments (Scheytt 2016).

With regard to TTIP, a social chapter is also expected, since the US Senate established social clauses in 2002 as a condition for the approval of free trade agreements (Dombois 2006, 239). However, the likelihood of these provisions being more far-reaching or binding in the TTIP than in the CETA agreement is low.

Rights and Obligations of Investors

Social clauses serve to ensure that competition is not sought at the expense of the working population in international trade. They safeguard that states fulfill their obligation to protect citizens. However, modern agreements involve both trade and investment. The multilateral trade agreements overseen by the World Trade Organization (WTO) do not provide investors with a direct grievance procedure against the government of the host country. Investors must either take the normal legal route available in the host country or contact their own government, which can then put forward the complaint against the host country through the WTO dispute settlement procedure. New trade policy initiatives, such as CETA and TTIP, aim at strengthening the rights of the investors vis-a-vis the respective host country. In the case of alleged breaches of the equal treatment provisions stipulated in the agreements, the investor is to be given the right to appeal directly against the government of the host country before a private dispute settlement body (see below).

Against the background of this new form of agreement, there are claims that request the 'horizontal' effect of the social clauses to be supplemented by obligations of the investors, who enjoy special protection. These obligations could lead to a 'vertical' effect, which would enforce (new) investments to be made in a responsible way and ensure compliance with rights. While social clauses protect workers in the agreement's trade aspects ('horizontal effect'), investor obligations serve as a safeguard for labor rights in the context of the investment aspect of new agreements ('vertical effect') (Waleson 2015). Investment agreements offer the possibility to declare previously voluntary responsibilities of companies as binding. For this purpose, the obligations of the investors must be anchored in the investment chapters of comprehensive free trade agreements, in addition to their rights (Mückenberger 2015, 177; Waleson 2015, 168). This can be done, for example, by referring to the *Investment Policy Framework for Sustainable Development (IPFSD)* published by the UN *Conference on Trade and Development (UNCTAD)* in 2012, or by complying with the *OECD Guidelines* in the host country (Laskowski 2014, 3). This would ensure co-determination and other labor rights, regardless of the location of the investment.

The introduction of enforceable investor rights is not necessary in the case of an agreement between two constitutional states. Foreign companies can go before national courts in the case of expropriation or discrimination, just like domestic companies. If, however, investment clauses are included in the trade agreements, they must not hinder the governments of both countries from implementing new regulations such as higher labor standards. In addition to the investor and the accused state, other potentially concerned stakeholders should be included in the dispute resolution process (ibid., 19).

Apart from the obligation to comply with national law, CETA's investment chapter does not impose any obligation on investors. There are therefore no binding regulations regarding the responsibility of investors towards human rights, labor rights or an intact environment (Waleson 2015, 172).

Instead, investors are awarded with a broad range of rights. They are granted market access, non-discrimination, national treatment (foreign investors should not be treated worse than domestic ones) and most favorable treatment (investors from the country of the contracting party should not be treated worse than investors from other third countries) (Council of the European Union 2016, art. 8.4, 8.6 and 8.7; Fritz 2015, 10–11). In addition, investors enjoy the right to "fair and equitable treatment" and are protected from direct and indirect expropriation (Fritz 2015, 11). These rights are, in particular, very far-reaching because in CETA, "investment" means not only direct investments, but also assets which an investor directly or indirectly controls, including shares, bonds, business loans, concessions, production and turnover participation agreements as well as intellectual property rights (Council of the European Union 2016, art. 8.1).

The main problem arising from these investor rights is their ability to restrict the scope of state action. For instance, formally neutral state regulations, which (for whatever reason) have a particular effect on the investors of the contracting party, can be regarded as de facto discrimination and lead to lawsuits. Investors could go to court on the grounds of a violation of "fair and equitable treatment" if new legislations do not satisfy their "legitimate expectations"[15]. Such complaints are often associated with high compensation claims to the states and have been used frequently in the context of existing investor protection. For example, over 70 investor disputes are filed annually in arbitration courts (Eberhardt 2013; PowerShift and Canadian Centre for Policy Alternatives 2016, 12).

In order to settle disputes, investors have access to an *investor state dispute settlement mechanism* (ISDS) through CETA, which contains some reforms compared to existing arbitration courts. The judges of the "multilateral investment tribunal" are appointed by the contracting parties, the majority of the proceedings are public, there is the possibility of third-party submissions in proceedings, and an appellate body has been set up (Council of the European Union 2016, art. 8.23).

It is, however, still possible to go simultaneously before national courts and arbitration courts (although the reason must not be the same). Some documents are still inaccessible to the public (Fritz 2015, p. 13-14), and there is a lack of effective participatory rights for all parties (PowerShift and Canadian Centre for Policy Alternatives 2016, 17).

From a civil society perspective it is unclear as to why an arbitration court should be introduced at all. Through enforceable investor rights, the contracting state gives up on both legislative freedom and social responsibility. This applies in particular to areas that are important for the profitability of investments, but at the same time need state regulation most urgently: consumer, environmental and occupational protection (Broß 2015, 11). Correspondingly, a sustainability assessment commissioned by the EU Commission advises that investment protection should be abolished altogether (Development Solution 2011, p. 383) because of its possible restriction of political freedom, while not bringing any visible benefit (Development Solution 2011, 383).

According to the information published by the EU, a similar procedure is planned for TTIP. However, compared to the CETA text less attention is given to the improvements in the arbitration courts on the TTIP information pages. Contrary to the procedure in the agreement with Canada, the TTIP proposal on arbitration courts plans rights of participation for all parties concerned, i.e. citizens, NGOs, associations, competitors of the applicant etc. (European

---

[15] The contract text tries to avoid leeway by listing the facts that constitute an infringement and by accepting the investor's expectations as legitimate only if "a Party made a specific representation [] that created a legitimate expectation" (Council of the European Union 2016, art.8.10). It is precisely this "specific representation" that could provide companies with scope for complaints, because they could also refer to verbal commitments (Fritz 2015, 11)

Commission 2016a; PowerShift and Canadian Centre for Policy Alternatives 2016, 17).

When analyzing social clauses and investor protection in CETA and TTIP, the phenomenon of a 'dichotomy of legal norms', typical for international trade policy, is often encountered: While binding regulations protect the rights of companies, non-binding soft law is applied to regulate social issues (Hadwinger et al. 2016, 26). The chance to secure the participation of workers through social clauses and obligations of the investors in the CETA agreement (and probably also in TTIP), has been missed. In addition, other aspects of the agreement could further affect the German co-determination system. Potential dangers are dealt with in the next sections.

Liberalization of the Service Sector
According to the CETA text, the principles of national treatment and most favored nation also apply to trade in services, not just to trade in goods. Services provided by "in the exercise of governmental authority" are excluded, except for the numerous gray areas of public services, in which private enterprises also participate. Further exceptions are specific areas such as the cultural sector for Canada and the audiovisual sector for the EU, as well as financial and air transportation services for both contracting parties (Council of the European Union 2016, chapter 9).

In other sectors, the contracting parties or individual EU members can make exceptions, insofar as they include them in the so-called 'negative lists'. These lists determine which areas are excluded from liberalization. As a result, all other services as well as newly emerging services are generally declared open to the market (ibid., chapter 9).

As further liberalization drivers, both 'standstill' and 'ratchet' mechanisms are implicitly included. These obligate the contracting parties to keep the market at least as open as at the time of the agreement ('standstill'). Further liberalization is therefore permitted, while a withdrawal is only possible insofar the new situation is not more restrictive than that during the signature of the contract. 'Ratchet' mechanisms extend these obligations by allowing further liberalization measures under the condition that once granted concessions cannot be withdrawn. In order to preserve policy space, the chapter contains a list of reservations on future measures (Council of the European Union 2016, chapter 9; European Commission 2016b, 4). However, this is regarded as incomplete (Fritz 2015, 15–16).

The design of CETA leads to a widespread liberalization of the services sector, which in turn should result in increased competition. The pressure on German service companies and their workforce is likely to be exacerbated by the possible short-term labor migration foreseen in the agreement, which allows also the provision of services abroad "on site".

In order to ensure free trade in services and unlimited investment activity, the CETA agreement allows workers from Canada and the EU to stay temporarily in the other territory (Council of the European Union 2016, chapter 10). Specifically, it is envisaged that foreign employees may work for up to three years (with a possibility to extend for another 18 months) in each other's jurisdiction. This applies, for example, to Canadian employees, whose company offers services in Germany or opens a new company. According to CETA, Canadian employees would not be subject to the German labor law, thus complying only with the Canadian labor law. In other words, two companies that operate in the same country and sector are subject to different laws. Officially, this option should not concern labor law as well as social insurance, collective bargaining agreements or minimum wages of the host country. However, it can not be ruled out that unfair competition might arise, especially due to several consecutive short-term assignments (Fritz 2015, 25).

A further concern is that the burden of the consequential competitive pressure will be put on the shoulders of employees. The risk is that, similarly to the competitive pressure from privatization and deregulation (see e.g. Schulten, Brandt, and Hermann 2008), this leads to a fragmentation and individualization of the employees and thus to a weakening of trade unions and co-determination bodies. This is particularly problematic for employees in the service sector, whose rights are already often disrespected today. Even if companies are able to cope with the competitive pressure, new competitive constraints from CETA's increased competition in general or from short-term labor migration in particular, will strengthen the voices of those who claim that high labor standards are no longer affordable in the age of globalization.

Promotion of Co-determination through Public Procurement?

CETA entails the liberalization of goods and services also in the area of public procurement (above a certain contract value). On its CETA website, Canada's government is promoting access to one of the "world's largest public procurement markets" and the resulting benefits for Canadian businesses and the population (Government of Canada 2016). Similarly, the Commission's website advertising CETA mentions the possibility to submit bids for public tenders in Canada at all administrative levels.

As has been outlined above, the modernization of the German procurement law in April 2016 has strengthened the possibilities of setting environmental, social or innovative aspects in the contract awarding procedure. In addition, companies that benefit from publicly financed contracts are obliged to comply with the applicable environmental, social and labor obligations, in particular collective bargaining agreements (BMWi and Referat Öffentlichkeitsarbeit 2016f). This avoids the undermining of collective bargaining agreements and enables public contracting authorities to support companies, which respect co-determination rights across the entire supply chain. In a similar fashion, the sustainability impact assessment prepared before the signature for CETA suggested that setting social requirements for public procurement should be explicitly allowed (Development Solution 2011, 22).

Nevertheless, CETA's text does not include social and labor standards for public procurement. The allowed contract award conditions are solely measures necessary to protect public morals, order or safety, health, intellectual property or relating to production of persons with disabilities, philanthropic institutions or prison labor. The exclusion of companies is only possible on grounds of past professional misconduct: insufficient fulfillment of previous contracts, tax evasion or a final conviction sentence (Council of the European Union 2016, chapter 19). It is therefore questionable, whether binding the award of the contract to criteria such as the observance of labor rights is compatible with CETA and whether a prerequisite such as collective bargaining or the guarantee of fundamental co-determination rights falls under "public morality" (Dessewffy 2012, 62–64; Fritz 2015, 22). However, exactly these prerequisites would be of fundamental importance when trying to support co-determination rights by social procurement as explained above.

An Expansion of the Co-determination-free Zone
In addition to the aforementioned problems, CETA entails the danger of an expansion of spaces where no co-determination rights are granted within Germany. As has been stated above, the circumvention of corporate co-determination has already been possible before the concluding of CETA and TTIP. However, with increasing capital flows from Canada and, in particular, the USA it could arise more frequently. As has been explained, bypassing board-level co-determination is possible through the establishment of companies with a foreign legal form. In addition, co-determination could be further jeopardized by the new possibility of temporary entry and residence of natural persons for business purposes (Council of the European Union 2016, chapter 10).

The first possibility refers to corporate co-determination and has been frequently discussed in recent years (Biedenkopf, Streeck, and Wissmann 2006; Hans-Böckler-Stiftung 2010; Sick 2015a; 2015b; Sick and Pütz 2011). The establishment of companies of foreign legal form, made possible by European and German law, allows companies from the EU and Switzerland as well as US-American corporations to circumvent the laws on corporate co-determination (Sick 2015b, 3).

This right does not apply to companies from other countries, including Canada. A Canadian company, however, can use another strategy to bypass German regulations: By establishing a subsidiary, Canadian enterprises can likewise avoid the obligation to comply with corporate co-determination. In both cases, plant-level co-determination will continue to be governed by the *Works Constitution Act (Betriebsverfassungsgesetz)* (Sick and Pütz 2011, 34).

17 of the 94 companies with over 500 employees that in 2014 refused the participation of their employees in the supervisory board were US-American corporations (Sick 2015b). If TTIP brings more US investment and business start-ups into Germany, these figures could increase. CETA could simplify the establishment of Canadian subsidiaries,[16] which could also benefit under this loophole as soon as they have more than 500 employees.

A particular feature of the problem of short-term labor migration is that Canadian employees working in Germany for a short-term period (i.e. up to a maximum of four and a half years) are not guaranteed any co-determination rights. Therefore, within the German territory employment fields can arise which are exempted from both operational and corporate co-determination and instead are subject to regulations stipulated by Canada and the respective province.

Potential Impacts on Co-Determination Rights in Third Countries

The planned trade agreements have an impact not only on signatory countries, but also on other trade partners of Canada, the USA or the EU.

By weakening the economic position of third countries, a conclusion of the two agreements could ultimately lead to a restriction of labor rights in third countries. A damaging economic effect on countries other than the trading partners is estimated by studies on TTIP and CETA commissioned by the EU Commission and the Federal Government. They show that the agreements have a negative effect on third countries as opposed to the positive effects on growth and employment within the EU, the USA and Canada (Development Solution 2011; Ecorys 2016, 101; Felbermayr, Heid, and Lehwald 2013, 28-29; 39). These losses which are quantified from "negligible" to "drastic" depending on the study (Felbermayr, Heid, and Lehwald 2013, 28; regarding TTIP) are relativized in the studies as gains would be high enough to compensate losers (ibid., 29).

The identified losers are, above all, countries of the Global South (ibid., 29–30). Losses are explained by so-called trade diversion: imports from the South are replaced by products from the trading partner, which are not necessarily cheaper

---

[16] It should be noted that subsidiaries do not fall under investment protection, which gives them less rights than a CETA-protected investor (Council of the European Union 2016, art. 8.1).

to produce, but can be offered at a lower price due to better market access conditions (Balassa 1967; Viner 1950). This effect is particularly problematic for countries that have been in a preferential trade agreement with the EU due to their economic weakness. Declining income, higher unemployment and higher competitive pressures are conditions that make it more difficult to enforce better working conditions or more extensive co-determination rights (Berger and Brandi 2015). Experience shows that affected countries cannot realistically hope for compensation by the EU, Canada or the USA through CETA and TTIP.

CETA Labor Chapter Needs Strengthening

The European Commission could effectively use the new trade agreements to strengthen and expand co-determination rights in all participating countries. For this purpose, social clauses as horizontal and investor obligations as a vertical instrument would be suitable. However, the labor chapter provided in the CETA agreement (and, with greater uncertainty, also in TTIP) is neither sufficient nor binding. Moreover, investors are granted substantial enforceable rights but are not subject to binding obligations.

Like in many other occasions of global law, a "dichotomy of legal norms" is observed also in this case: while the rights of companies are bindingly secured and enforceable, social and labor standards (as well as environmental regulations) are based on unsanctionable soft law (Hadwinger et al. 2016, 26).

In addition to the lack of effective social clauses and investor obligations, the new trade agreements pose four other dangers. Firstly, the widespread liberalization of services, coupled with the possibility of short-term labor migration, puts further pressure on co-determination in the service sector. Secondly, the rules on public procurement in CETA could limit the promotion of co-determination rights due to the lack of clarity about the possibility to bind public procurement to social criteria. Thirdly, increasing US and Canadian capital inflows to Germany could further expand the spaces without co-determination within Germany. Finally, a conclusion of the trade agreements in its present form is expected to have negative economic effects on economically weak countries, thus increasing the pressure on their labor and social standards.

With the signing of CETA on 30 October 2016, the positive vote of the Trade Committee in January and of the EU Parliament in February 2017, the agreement can soon enter into force provisionally (as of March 2017). However, after the provisional application, the agreement has to be agreed upon by member states and selected regional parliaments. In view of the above considerations, the Federal Government should ensure that CETA is not implemented in its present form. Comprehensive reform proposals and concrete versions of new clauses, which could prevent the negative effects discussed, have been developed by the DGB (Deutscher Gewerkschaftsbund 2016a). They include, among other things, a sanctioning mechanism for the labor chapter and a limitation on investor protection. Moreover, future public services should be excluded from liberalization, while extensive participation and democratic control are to be introduced. It is also recommended that the objectives of sustainable development and climate protection should be anchored.

Against the background of the implementation of CETA and the possible signing of TTIP, the Federal Government should fill the legal gaps of corporate co-determination before its circumvention takes larger forms.

Summary and Recommendations

The German co-determination system, with its far-reaching rights to employee participation at the plant and board level, adheres to high democratic standards and brings numerous economic advantages. The German model is a historically developed special system. However, fundamental co-determination rights are anchored in the *ILO core labor standards* and are therefore to be respected worldwide. Co-determination rights as 'enabling rights' serve as goal and means at the same time: while they themselves constitute a fundamental right, they also bring people in the position to obtain further rights on their own. They should, therefore, be at the center of efforts to improve the working conditions worldwide.

The improvement of the situation of workers globally has also been set as a goal by the German Federal Government. It is, therefore, the government's responsibility to foster co-determination in Germany and, at the same time, ensure that basic co-determination rights are respected abroad, especially by German companies. This is particularly true against the backdrop of increasing uncertainty over the preservation of co-determination rights within Germany on the one hand, and the frequently occurring violation of co-determination rights abroad within the sphere of responsibility of German companies on the other.

In order to achieve these two objectives - the maintenance of the German co-determination system within Germany and its promotion abroad - the Federal Government can use its foreign economic policy strategically.

In this chapter, it was examined how various instruments of foreign economic policy can be used to protect and promote employee participation. According to an analysis by the World Bank, a government can effectively incentivize companies to comply with rights across the supply chain by demanding standards (*mandating*), facilitating their observance (*facilitating*), participating in the process (*partnering*) and by rewarding good behavior (*endorsing*). Hence, it was analyzed how these can be achieved by means of foreign economic policy instruments available to various federal ministries.

The chapter first examined the **export financing and export credit and investment guarantees** in the area of competence of the Federal Ministry of Economic Affairs and Energy (BMWi). The BMWi in cooperation with KfW-Bank offers these foreign trade and investment promotion instruments. In both areas, compliance with the right to co-determination in the supply chain of German companies and in financed projects abroad could be guaranteed by binding business to clear conditions. There is already a set of rules for export financing as well as for export credit and investment guarantees, which could provide these conditions. Despite the fact that co-determination rights are enclosed in these rules, they are completely ignored in the review procedure. This happens firstly because only a minimal part of the projects has to carry out an environmental and social impact assessment. For example, companies from OECD countries are exempted from assessment requirements when requesting export financing. Further, a review is only required for "high risk" projects. However, the risk of violating the rights of employees does not lead to a classification of "high risk". Secondly, co-determination is not taken into account by the environmental and social impact assessments. Thirdly, if a project is actually reviewed and does not meet the requirements, it can nevertheless be approved if the inter-ministerial committee, supported by business consultants, wishes so. There are several reasons for the disproportion between high ambitions regarding ecological and social standards and their weak practical implementation. Firstly, their procedures are extremely confusing. Secondly, the lack of transparency on financed projects, particularly on their ecological and social impact hinders civil society when trying to push through more responsible procedures. This lack of clarity and transparency thirdly leads to the ineffectiveness of the established grievance procedures. This imbalance could be resolved by setting enforceable human rights due diligence obligations across the supply chain as a condition for **all** financing and guarantees coupled with transparency on projects and their impacts. Moreover, projects that do not fulfill the set requirements should be consistently excluded. Monitoring mechanisms and a uniform, unbiased and freely accessible grievance procedure should be established and representatives of civil society should be involved.

Public procurement also offers great potential for the promotion of co-determination rights. If the award of contracts is linked to the observance of rights, the increased segmentation of the labor market within Germany can be counteracted. Concurrently, this would prevent the associated loss of co-determination rights in secondary labor markets. This is particularly necessary because of the increased privatization and outsourcing of public services. In addition, rights can be guaranteed worldwide, if contractors are obliged to ensure standards across their entire supply chain.

The new procurement law introduces collective bargaining and compliance with the minimum wage as fixed criteria for the award of contracts. Contracting authorities may also include other ecological and social criteria in the selection of contractors. In order to use the award as an effective tool, the inclusion of standards should be explicitly requested, in particular the compliance with *ILO core labor standards* across the supply chain. The social and ecological criteria should be clear and ambitious and supplemented with a review and monitoring mechanism. The existing support for socially responsible procurement by the *Competence Center for Sustainable Procurement* is to be welcomed. However, the institution should be expanded and civil society groups should be firmly involved.

In order to make it easier for German companies to meet ambitious goals concerning their activity abroad, the **German Chambers of Commerce Abroad**, for example, could support them locally through workshops on responsible supply chain management. The *German Trade and Invest* portal should also provide information on the risk of violating the right to co-determination and its effective prevention.

A tool explicitly used to promote co-determination rights and other labor rights across the supply chain of global corporations are the **OECD Guidelines for Multinational Enterprises**. The latter and the work of the **National Contact Point (NCP)** located in the BMWi were examined in this study. Although the *OECD Guidelines* are a very well thought-out instrument and contain co-determination as a central concept, their voluntary nature renders them almost ineffective in practice. For example, an investigation of various cases of complaints about the violation of co-determination rights shows that the mediation of the NCP mainly results in vague and company-friendly conclusions. It can thus not be assumed that incentives for better behavior are being given. The potential of the *OECD Guidelines* could be developed particularly, if their observance was compulsory. Binding compliance could be requested for public procurement or for the use of foreign trade and investment promotion instruments. A reformed, independent NCP with a quadri-partite organizational structure could serve as a complaint and exchange forum.

The **UN Principles for Responsible Investment (PRI)** network could also lead to an improvement in co-determination rights across the entire supply chain. The credo of rewarding employee-friendly management practices with financial investment and punishing anti-employee companies by excluding them from the portfolio can incentivize companies to engage in safeguarding co-determination rights. This approach is particularly promising if, in addition to social and environmental investment strategies, the influencing capacities of investors such as votes and supervisory positions are put to use. The German PRI network, founded by KfW-Bank, could contribute to this if it applies clear standards and at the same time tries to involve as many investors as possible.

Subsequently, it was explored whether the Federal Government itself could guarantee co-determination rights in companies with state participation as a shareholder. **State-owned companies** were covered within the areas of responsibility of the Ministry of Finance (BMF), which is responsible for almost all of the globally operating companies in public hands. Two of the six companies concerned - *Deutsche Post,* of which the Federal Government owns 21% and *Deutsche Telekom*, with almost 32% - have received massive complaints for violations of co-determination rights in subsidiary companies abroad. The government has ignored these cases and argued that it was not its responsibility to claim the respect of rights such as freedom of trade unions in companies with German participation. This is unacceptable considering the obligation to manage companies with state participation ethically. The Federal Government should provide clear and binding requirements for companies that it co-manages and help clarify the existing legal infringements.

In addition to the duty of companies to respect co-determination rights, the German government should also bear in mind the duty of the states to protect rights. It should therefore exchange with governments that have so far neglected this duty in their economic activities. In this context, **embassies and their Social Affairs attachés** were examined in the area of responsibility of the Ministry of Foreign Affairs (AA). The social affairs attachés have often reported of great interest in the German co-determination system from their countries of duty. There is already an exchange in many places about its possible design. These efforts could be strengthened with a larger capacity of Social Affairs offices and their strategic use. Furthermore, German embassies, similarly to the *Chambers of Commerce Abroad*, could support German companies abroad in complying with rights in subsidiaries and supplying companies. To this end, it would be useful to establish Social Affairs offices in embassies in countries where violations of co-determination rights occur frequently but which have no such institution so far.

Furthermore, **develoPPP.de** was analyzed since it is the most important program of private development cooperation under the jurisdiction of the German Federal Ministry for Economic Cooperation and Development (BMZ). *DeveloPPP.de* partially finances projects that are initiated by companies in countries of the Global South. The program does not present a clear way of how to prevent the exclusion of labor rights in the projects it finances, nor does it contribute systematically to the promotion of certain rights of employees. Another problem is the lack of transparency concerning financed projects and their potential (positive or negative) impacts. In order to ensure co-determination rights through *develoPPP.de*, clear requirements must be placed on the subsidized projects. Corporations that have repeatedly violated their due diligence should be excluded from funding. Demands on companies should be supported by the advisory services of the accompanying institutions and experts on site. Moreover, the policy of promoting only European companies should be reconsidered because of its negative impact on the economy and possibly on the working conditions of the host country.

The second instrument of the BMZ, which was considered, is the **Partnership for Sustainable Textiles** launched in 2014. It was examined as to what extent the Partnership has been able to contribute to the guarantee of co-determination rights in textile production. The partnership offers the potential to counteract various forms of 'downward competition'. The large market coverage of the alliance partners can prevent competitive disadvantages for German companies that support better conditions along their supply chain and thus pay higher prices to their suppliers. In order to counter the competition between suppliers to produce as cheap as possible at the expense of good working conditions, clear minimum standards must be applied to supplier companies of the alliance partners. These can be financed by higher customer prices. A dialogue between alliances, local governments and trade unions, and the development of joint solutions can alleviate the problematic competition between textile producing countries, which leads to lower social standards for securing investment and production in their territory. The task of the BMZ in this process should be to ensure that trade unions and employees of the textile-producing countries work together. In addition, dilution of the alliance must be prevented through ambitious criteria, monitoring and sanction mechanisms.

An instrument that could have significantly combined all the above initiatives and contributed to the shaping of a coherent government policy is the **National Action Plan on Business and Human Rights (NAP)** adopted by the government in 2016. The inclusion of binding and enforceable human rights due diligence for companies across the supply chain would have made the NAP an instrument for the promotion of co-determination. Unfortunately, the existing NAP does not contain binding due diligence obligations, nor does it provide a definition of human rights due diligence, which would place 'enabling rights' at the forefront. Instead, the NAP continues to focus on voluntary measures. It thus prevents neither the impunity of corporations that suppress fundamental co-determination rights, nor does it lead to the creation of a 'level playing field'. It is to be hoped that the government and other stakeholders will at least implement the existing plan ambitiously, and binding measures will be taken if targets are not met.

The guarantee of co-determination rights by globally operating companies as foreseen by the *UN Guiding Principles* is above all a human rights and democratic obligation. After a period of upheaval, however, German companies could also benefit from the economic advantages of involving all employees.

Finally, this work analyzed the extent to which the German co-determination system could be affected by the conclusion of new **trade agreements**. The examination of the CETA text shows that the agreement does not meet the necessary criteria for ensuring co-determination and its promotion. The agreement does not contain sanctionable social clauses to provide 'horizontal protection' in terms of minimum security in the participant countries and thus prevent social dumping in free trade. It neither includes investor obligations, which could 'vertically' ensure compliance with rights in all investment projects and thus leverage the investment aspects of the agreement. The liberalization of the service sector, particularly in combination with "short-term labor migration", is expected to increase the competitive pressure within the sector. This could put pressure on co-determination rights in a sector where fundamental rights are already often violated today. It is further questionable whether socially responsible public procurement, similarly to the new procurement regulations in Germany, is compatible with CETA. Corporate co-determination could also come under pressure by CETA and TTIP, if existing circumvention possibilities are reinforced through the agreements. Finally, the negative economic effects to be expected by the agreements on countries of the Global South could lead to a worsening of the situation of workers and thus a weakening of co-determination rights.

In summary, foreign economic policy has considerable potential to promote co-determination rights. A clear commitment by the government to fundamental labor rights and its rigorous integration into external instruments and planning is required. A first important step in this direction would have been the implementation of an ambitious National Action Plan.

References

Aachener Stiftung Kathy Beys, and Industrie und Handelskammer Nürnberg für Mittelfranken. 2015. "Prinzipien für verantwortliches Investieren (UNPRI)." In *Lexikon der Nachhaltigkeit*, eds. Aachener Stiftung Kathy Beys and Industrie und Handelskammer Nürnberg für Mittelfranken.

Aaronson, Susan A. 2006. "Reality Bites: The Myth of Labor Rights as a Non-trade Issue." *Unpublished paper (used with permission)*.

Agaportal. 2016a. "Exportkreditgarantien: A-Projekte vor Entscheidung 2016." http://www.agaportal.de/pages/aga/projektinformationen/a-projekte.html#mexiko_duengemittelwerk (November 2, 2016).

———. 2016b. "Investitionsgarantien." http://www.agaportal.de/pages/dia/index.html (September 29, 2016).

———. 2016c. "UFK-Garantien." http://www.agaportal.de/pages/ufk/index.html (November 5, 2016).

Amnesty International. 2012. "Shell's wildly inaccurate reporting of Niger Delta oil spill exposed." https://www.amnesty.org/en/latest/news/2012/04/shell-s-wildly-inaccurate-reporting-niger-delta-oil-spill-exposed/ (November 21, 2016).

Andersen, Uwe. 2013. "Mitbestimmung." In *Handwörterbuch des politischen Systems der Bundesrepublik Deutschland*, eds. Uwe Andersen and Wichard Woyke. Heidelberg: Springer VS.

Anner, Mark S. 2012. "Corporate Social Responsibility and Freedom of Association Rights: The Precarious Quest for Legitimacy and Control in Global Supply Chains." *Politics & Society* 40 (4): 609–44.

———. 2015. *Stopping the race to the bottom: Challenges for workers' rights in supply chains in Asia*. Berlin: Friedrich-Ebert-Stiftung, Department for Asia and the Pacific.

Balassa, Bela. 1967. "Trade Creation and Trade Diversion in the European Common Market." *The Economic Journal* 77 (305): 1.

Banerjee, Subhabrata B. 2014. "A critical perspective on corporate social responsibility." *Critical perspectives on international business* 10 (1/2): 84–95.

Barrientos, Stephanie, Gary Gereffi, and Arianna Rossi. 2010. *Economic and Social Upgrading in Global Production Networks: Developing a Framework for Analysis*. Capturing the Gains Working Paper, 3.

Berger, Axel, and Clara Brandi. 2015. *What Should Development Policy Actors Do About the Transatlantic Trade and Investment Partnership (TTIP)?* Deutsches Institut für Entwicklung. Briefing Paper, 1.

Bermig, Andreas, and Bernd Frick. 2011. "Mitbestimmung und Unternehmensperformance: Der Einfluss von Arbeitnehmervertretern im Aufsichtsrat auf den Unternehmenswert." *Die Betriebswirtschaft : DBW* 71 (3, (5/6)): 281–304.

Biedenkopf, Kurt, Wolfgang Streeck, and Hellmut Wissmann. 2006. *Kommission zur Modernisierung der deutschen Unternehmensmitbestimmung*.

Biedenkopf, Kurt, Kurt Ballerstadt, Erich Gutenberg, Harald Jürgensen, Wilhelm Krelle, Hans-Joachim Mestmäcker, Rudolph Reinhardt, Fritz Voigt, and Hans Willgerodt. 1970. *Mitbestimmung im Unternehmen: Bericht der Sachverständigenkommission zur Auswertung der bisherigen Erfahrungen bei der Mitbestimmung*. Stuttgart.

Bierbaum, Heinz, and Marion Houben. 2005. "Kosten und Nutzen der Mitbestimmung in KMU." *Expertise des INFO Institut für Organisationsentwicklung und Unternehmenspolitik*. Saarbrücken.

Botschaft der Bundesrepublik Deutschland Bratislava. 2016. "Botschaft der Bundesrepublik Deutschland Bratislava: Sozialreferent." http://www.pressburg.diplo.de/Vertretung/pressburg/de/02/Botschafter__und__Abteilungen/seite__sozialreferat.html (September 13, 2016).

Broß, Siegfried. 2015. *Freihandelsabkommen, einige Anmerkungen zur Problematik der privaten Schiedsgerichtsbarkeit* [ger]. Düsseldorf. 4. http://hdl.handle.net/10419/126127.

Bundesministerium der Finanzen. 2013. "Die Beteiligungen des Bundes - Beteiligungsbericht 2013." http://www.bundesfinanzministerium.de/Content/DE/Standardartikel/Themen/Bundesve

rmoegen/Privatisierungs_und_Beteiligungspolitik/Beteiligungspolitik/Beteiligungsberic hte/beteiligungsbericht-des-bundes-2013.pdf?__blob=publicationFile&v=3 (Accessed November 15, 2016).

———. 2014. "Beteiligungsbericht 2014." http://www.bundesfinanzministerium.de/Content/DE/Standardartikel/Themen/Bundesve rmoegen/Privatisierungs_und_Beteiligungspolitik/Beteiligungspolitik/Beteiligungsberic hte/beteiligungsbericht-des-bundes-2014.pdf?__blob=publicationFile&v=3 (Accessed November 15, 2016).

———. 2015a. "Bundeshaushalt-Info.de: Einzelpläne." February 19. https://www.bundeshaushalt-info.de/#/2015/soll/ausgaben/einzelplan.html (November 4, 2016).

———. 2015b. *Die Beteiligungen des Bundes: Beteiligungsbericht 2015*. https://www.bundesfinanzministerium.de/Content/DE/Standardartikel/Themen/Bundesv ermoegen/Privatisierungs_und_Beteiligungspolitik/Beteiligungspolitik/Beteiligungsberi chte/beteiligungsbericht-des-bundes-2015.pdf?__blob=publicationFile&v=6 (Accessed November 7, 2016).

Bundesministerium für Finanzen. 2016. "Bundeshaushalt-Info.de: Ausgaben Entwicklungspartnerschaft mit der Wirtschaft." February 19. https://www.bundeshaushalt-info.de/#/2016/soll/ausgaben/einzelplan/230268701.html (November 21, 2016).

Bundesministerium für Umwelt, Naturschutz und Reaktorsicherheit. 2012. *Nachhaltig und verantwortlich investieren - ein Leitfaden: Die UN Principles for Responsible Investment*. Berlin.

BMWi - Bundesministerium für Wirtschaft und Energie. 2004. "Erklärung der deutschen Nationalen Kontaktstelle für die ‚OECD-Leitsätze für multinationale Unternehmen' zu einer Beschwerde der deutschen Kampagne für Saubere Kleidung (CCC) gegen adidas-Salomon." http://www.bmwi.de/BMWi/Redaktion/PDF/E/erklaerung-der-deutschen-nationalen-kontaktstelle-fuer-die-oecd-leitsaetze-fuer-multinationale-unternehmen-zu-einer-beschwerde,property=pdf,bereich=bmwi2012,sprache=de,rwb=true.pdf (Accessed September 29, 2016).

———. 2007. "Erklärung der deutschen Nationalen Kontaktstelle für di e ‚OECD-Leitsätze für multinationale Unternehmen' zu einer Beschwerde des DGB gegenüber Bayer AG." http://www.bmwi.de/BMWi/Redaktion/PDF/E/erklaerung-der-deutschen-nationalen-kontaktstelle-fuer-oecd-leitsaetze,property=pdf,bereich=bmwi2012,sprache=de,rwb=true.pdf (Accessed September 29, 2016).

———. 2014a. "Abschlusserklärung der deutschen Nationalen Kontaktstelle für die Beschwerde der Metro Habib Employee Union, Karachi, Pakistan gegen METRO Cash & Carry." http://www.bmwi.de/BMWi/Redaktion/PDF/A/abschlusserklaerung-deutsche-nationale-kontaktstelle-inoffizielle-uebersetzung,property=pdf,bereich=bmwi2012,sprache=de,rwb=true.pdf (Accessed September 29, 2016).

———. 2014b. "Gemeinsame Abschlusserklärung der deutschen Nationalen Kontaktstelle (NKS) für die OECD-Leitsätze für multinationale Unternehmen, der Gewerkschaft UNI Global Union (UNI) und der internationalen Transportarbeiter-Föderation (ITF) sowie der Deutschen Post DHL (DP-DHL) zu der von UNI/ITF gegen DP-DHL/Bonn vorgebrachten Beschwerde." http://www.bmwi.de/BMWi/Redaktion/PDF/G/ gemeinsame-abschlusserklaerung-deutsche-nationale-kontaktstelle,property=pdf, bereich=bmwi2012,sprache=de,rwb=true.pdf (Accessed September 29, 2016).

———. 2014c. "Gemeinsame Erklärung der deutschen Nationalen Kontaktstelle für die „OECD- Leitsätze für multinationale Unternehmen" zu einer Beschwerde der Indocement Union, SP-ITP, der Federation of Indonesian Cement Industry (FSP-ISI), der Confederation of IndonesianTrade Unions (CITU-KSPI) und der IndustriALL Global Union gegen PT Indocement Tunggal Prakarsa, Indonesien, und HeidelbergCement AG, Deutschland." http://www.bmwi.de/BMWi/Redaktion/PDF/G/gemeinsame-abschlusserklaerung-nks-indonesien-deutschland,property=pdf,bereich=bmwi2012,sprache=de,rwb=true.pdf (Accessed September 29, 2016).

———. 2014d. "Gemeinsame Erklärung der deutschen Nationalen Kontaktstelle für die „OECD-Leitsätze für multinationale Unternehmen" zu einer Beschwerde der Indocement Union, SP-ITP, der Federation of Indonesian Cement Industry (FSP-ISI), der Confederation of Indonesian Trade Unions (CITU-KSPI) und der IndustriALL Global Union gegen PT Indocement Tunggal Prakarsa, Indonesien, und HeidelbergCement AG, Deutschland." http://www.bmwi.de/BMWi/Redaktion/PDF/G/gemeinsame-abschlusserklaerung-nks-indonesien-deutschland,property=pdf,bereich=bmwi2012,sprache=de,rwb=true.pdf (Accessed September 29, 2016).

———. 2014e. *OECD-Leitsätze für multinationale Unternehmen: Empfehlungen für verantwortungsvolles unternehmerisches Handeln in einem globalen Kontext und Nationale Kontaktstellen.*

———. 2015. "Abschließende Erklärung der deutschen Nationalen Kontaktstelle für die „OECD-Leitsätze für multinationale Unternehmen" anlässlich einer Beschwerde der Industriegewerkschaft Metall (IG Metall) gegen Hyundai Motor Europe Technical Center GmbH (HMETC) in Rüsselsheim." http://www.bmwi.de/BMWi/Redaktion/PDF/A/abschlusserklaerung-ig-metall,property=pdf,bereich=bmwi2012,sprache=de,rwb=true.pdf (Accessed September 29, 2016).

———. 2016a. "Abgeschlossene Beschwerdefälle bei der deutschen Nationalen Kontaktstelle." http://www.bmwi.de/DE/Themen/Aussenwirtschaft/Internationale-Gremien/oecd-leitsaetze,did=429912.html.

———. 2016b. *Neue Impulse für den internationalen Wettbewerb um strategische Großprojekte: Chancen für Deutschland verbessern.* Strategiepapier (Accessed November 5, 2016).

———. 2016c. "UFK-Garantien." http://www.agaportal.de/pages/ufk/index.html (September 29, 2016).

———. 2016d. "Weiterentwicklung der Garantieinstrumente des Bundes zur Außenwirtschaftsförderung." Schlaglichter der Wirtschaftspolitik - Monatsbericht, August 2016. http://www.bmwi.de/Dateien/BMWi/PDF/Monatsbericht/Auszuege/2016-08-

aussenwirtschaftsfoerderung,property=pdf,bereich=bmwi2012,sprache=de,rwb=true.pdf (October 24, 2016).

———. 2016e. *Im Dialog mit der Wirtschaft: Protokoll Workshop V: "UFK-Garantien imUmfeld der aktuellen Rohstoffmärkte"*. Berlin (Accessed November 5, 2016).

BMWi - Bundesministerium für Wirtschaft und Energie, Euler Hermes, and PricewaterhouseCoopers. 2016a. "Home | AGA-Portal - AuslandsGeschäftsAbsicherung der Bundesrepublik Deutschland." http://www.agaportal.de/index.html (October 9, 2016).

———. 2016b. "UFK-Garantien." http://www.agaportal.de/pages/ufk/index.html (September 29, 2016).

BMWi - Bundesministerium für Wirtschaft und Energie, and Referat Öffentlichkeitsarbeit. 2015a. "Nationale Kontaktstelle (NKS)." http://www.bmwi.de/DE/Themen/Aussenwirtschaft/Internationale-Gremien/oecd-leitsaetze,did=429916.html (September 13, 2016).

———. 2015b. "BMWi - Übersicht und Rechtsgrundlagen." https://www.bmwi.de/DE/Themen/Wirtschaft/Oeffentliche-Auftraege-und-Vergabe/uebersicht-und-rechtsgrundlagen.html (November 13, 2016).

———. 2016a. "BMWi - Finanzierung und Absicherung von Auslandsgeschäften." http://www.bmwi.de/DE/Themen/Aussenwirtschaft/Aussenwirtschaftsfoerderung/finanzierung-und-absicherung-von-auslandsgeschaeften.html (October 24, 2016).

———. 2016b. "CETA: Häufig gestellte Fragen." https://www.bmwi.de/DE/Themen/Aussenwirtschaft/Freihandelsabkommen/CETA/faqs.html (October 2, 2016).

———. 2016c. "Export- und Investitionsfinanzierung." http://www.bmwi.de/DE/Themen/Aussenwirtschaft/Aussenwirtschaftsfoerderung/finanzierung-und-absicherung-von-auslandsgeschaeften,did=190886.html (October 24, 2016).

———. 2016d. "Investitionsgarantien." http://www.bmwi.de/DE/Themen/Aussenwirtschaft/Aussenwirtschaftsfoerderung/finanzierung-und-absicherung-von-auslandsgeschaeften,did=190896.html (October 25, 2016).

———. 2016e. "Kabinett verabschiedet Eckpunkte für Exportstrategie: Neue Impulse für den internationalen Wettbewerb um strategische Großprojekte." http://www.bmwi.de/DE/Presse/pressemitteilungen,did=782046.html (October 24, 2016).

———. 2016f. "Reform des Vergaberechts." http://www.bmwi.de/DE/Themen/Wirtschaft/Oeffentliche-Auftraege-und-Vergabe/reform-des-vergaberechts.html (October 3, 2016).

BMWi & BMAS - Bundesministerium für Wirtschaftliche Zusammenarbeit, and Bundesministerium für Arbeit und Soziales. 2015. "Gute Arbeit weltweit: Zukunftspapier." https://www.bmas.de/SharedDocs/Downloads/DE/PDF-Publikationen/zukunftspapier-gute-arbeit-weltweit.pdf?__blob=publicationFile (September 30, 2016). English: *Good Work Worldwide: Vision Paper by Federal Minister Dr Gerd Müller and Federal Minister Andrea Nahles*. Berlin.

BMZ - Bundesministerium für wirtschaftliche Zusammenarbeit und Entwicklung. 2015. "Für globale Nachhaltigkeit und faires Wirtschaften: Menschenrechte und Unternehmensverantwortung in Deutschland und weltweit." Bundesministerium für wirtschaftliche Zusammenarbeit und Entwicklung, BMZ. December 3. http://www.bmz.de/de/presse/aktuelleMeldungen/2015/dezember/20151203_pm_096_F uer-globale-Nachhaltigkeit-und-faires-Wirtschaften-Menschenrechte-und-Unternehmensverantwortung-in-Deutschland-und-weltweit/index.html (February 7, 2017).

———. 2016a. "Angebote für Unternehmen." Bundesministerium für wirtschaftliche Zusammenarbeit und Entwicklung, BMZ. July 12. http://www.bmz.de/de/themen/privatwirtschaft/entwicklungspartnerschaften/index.html (November 21, 2016).

———. 2016b. "Bewerbungsunterlagen | developpp.de." https://www.developpp.de/de/content/bewerbungsunterlagen (November 21, 2016).

———. 2016c. "Chancen für Unternehmen | developpp.de." https://www.developpp.de/de/content/chancen-f%C3%BCr-unternehmen (November 21, 2016).

———. 2016d. "develoPPP.de." Bundesministerium für wirtschaftliche Zusammenarbeit und Entwicklung, BMZ. April 20. http://www.bmz.de/de/themen/privatwirtschaft/entwicklungspartnerschaften/develoPPP/index.html (November 21, 2016).

———. 2016e. "Laborchemikalien sicher entsorgen | developpp.de." https://www.developpp.de/de/content/laborchemikalien-sicher-entsorgen (November 21, 2016).

———. 2016f. "Teilnahmekriterien | developpp.de." https://www.developpp.de/de/content/teilnahmekriterien (November 21, 2016).

Bundesministerium für wirtschaftliche Zusammenarbeit und Entwicklung, and Auswärtiges Amt. 2015. "Dokumentation 3. Plenumskonferenz Nationaler Aktionsplan für Wirtschaft und Menschenrechte: 3. Dezember 2015 im BMZ in Berlin." http://www.auswaertiges-amt.de/cae/servlet/contentblob/723080/publicationFile/212351/151203_Plenumskonferenz3-Dokumentation.pdf (Accessed February 7, 2017).

Bündnis für nachhaltige Textilien. 2016. "Bündnis für nachhaltige Textilien: Frequently Asked Questions." September 30. https://www.textilbuendnis.com/de/faq (September 30, 2016).

CDU Deutschland, and S. P. CSU-Landesleitung. 2013. "Deutschlands Zukunft gestalten: Koalitionsvertrag zwischen CDU, CSUund SPD. 18. Legislaturperiode." Berlin: Eigenverlag.

Christliche Initiative Romero, and Arbeitsgemeinschaft der Eine-Welt-Landesnetzwerke in Deutschland. 2015. *Synopse zum Stand der Tariftreue- und Vergabegesetze in den Bundesländern: Stand: Frühjahr 2015* (Accessed November 13, 2016).

CIR - Christliche Initiative Romero e.V. 2015. "Position der Clean Clothes Campaign – Kampagne für Saubere Kleidung (CCC-D): Stellungnahme zur Teilnahme im Bündnis für nachhaltige Textilien und Umsetzung öko-sozialer Standards in der globalen Lieferkette." http://www.ci-romero.de/de/textilbuendnis/ (September 30, 2016).

Compa, Lance A., and Tequila Brooks. 2008. "The North American Free Trade agreement (NAFTA) and the North American Agreement on Labor Cooperation (NAALC)." In *Labour law and industrial relations*, ed. R. Blanpain. Köln: Kluwer.

CoRA-Netzwerk für Unternehmensverantwortung. 2015. *Öffentliche Beschaffung mit der neuen EU-Vergaberichtlinie 2014/24/EU*. Briefing Paper. http://www.cora-netz.de/cora/wp-content/uploads/2015/07/CorA_Beschaffung-mit-EU-Richtlinie_2014.pdf (Accessed November 13, 2016).

CoRA-Netzwerk für Unternehmensverantwortung, Forum Menschenrechte, VENRO - Verband Entwicklungspolitik und humanitäre Hilfe, Amnesty International, Brot für die Welt, Germanwatch, and Misereor. 2016. "Kein Mut zu mehr Verbindlichkeit: Kommentar deutscher Nichtregierungsorganisationen zum Nationalen Aktionsplan Wirtschaft und Menschenrechte der Bundesregierung."

Council of the European Union. 2016. *Comprehensive economic and trade agreement (CETA) between Canada, of the one part, and the European Union and its members states, of the other part*.

Czornohus, Sascha. 2010. *Unternehmerisches Engagement für nachhaltige Entwicklung: Public Private Partnerships in der deutschen Entwicklungszusammenarbeit*. Bd. 9 of *Bonner Studien zum globalen Wandel*. Marburg: Tectum-Verl.

Demirovic, Alex. 2008. "Mitbestimmung und Perspektiven der Wirtschaftsdemokratie." *WSI-Mitteilungen* 7 (2008): 387–93.

Dessewffy, E. 2012. "EU-Handelspolitik: Verankerung von Sozialnormen in Freihandelsabkommen." *WISO. wirtschafts-und sozialpolitische Zeitschrift* 33 (3): 57–77.

Detje, Richard, WOlfgang Menz, Sarah Nies, Günther Sanne, and Dieter Sauer. 2008. "Gewerkschaftliche Kämpfe gegen Betriebsschließungen: Ein Anachronismus?" *WSI-Mitteilungen* 61 (5): 238–45.

Deutsche Bundesregierung. 2016. "Nationaler Aktionsplan: Umsetzung der VN-Leitprinzipien für Wirtschaft und Menschenrechte 2016-2020." Berlin.

Deutsche Investitions- und Entwicklungsgesellschaft. 2015. "Jahresabschlussbericht." (Accessed November 3, 2016).

———. 2016a. "DEG-Umwelt- und Sozialrichtlinie." [de]. October 21. https://www.deginvest.de/Internationale-Finanzierung/DEG/%C3%9Cber-uns/Was-wir-tun/DEG-Umwelt-und-Sozialrichtlinie/ (November 3, 2016).

———. 2016b. "Was wir tun." [de]. October 21. https://www.deginvest.de/Internationale-Finanzierung/DEG/%C3%9Cber-uns/Was-wir-tun/ (October 25, 2016).

Deutsche Rohstoffagentur. 2016. "BGR - Rohstoffinformationen." http://www.deutsche-rohstoffagentur.de/DERA/DE/Rohstoffinformationen/rohstoffinformationen_node.html (November 11, 2016).

Deutscher Bundestag. 2013a. "Antwort der Bundesregierung auf die Kleine Anfrage der Abgeordneten Josip Juratovic, Anette Kramme, Hubertus Heil (Peine), weiterer Abgeordneter und der Fraktion der SPD: Vereinigungsfreiheit auch bei Tochterunternehmen deutscher Unternehmen sicherstellen." Drucksache 17/12588. http://dipbt.bundestag.de/dip21/btd/17/128/1712808.pdf (November 8, 2016).

———. 2013b. *Betriebsverfassungsgesetz: BetrVG*.

———. 2015a. *Gesetz über die Drittelbeteiligung der Arbeitnehmer im Aufsichtsrat: Drittelbeteiligungsgesetz - DrittelbG*.

———. 2015b. *Gesetz über die Mitbestimmung der Arbeitnehmer: MitbestG*.

———. 2015c. *Gesetz über die Mitbestimmung der Arbeitnehmer in den Aufsichtsräten und Vorständen der Unternehmen des Bergbaus und der Eisen und Stahl erzeugenden Industrie: MontanMitbestG*.

———. 2015d. *Kleine Anfrage der Fraktion DIE LINKE: Drucksache 18/5139* (Accessed November 1, 2016).

Deutscher Bundestag - Petitionsausschuss. 2015. "Petition an den deutschen Bundestag Nr. 59803." https://epetitionen.bundestag.de/petitionen/_2015/_07/_06/Petition_59803.nc.html (November 8, 2016).

Deutscher Gewerkschaftsbund. 2009. *Stellungnahme zum letzten Report des UN-Sonderbeauftragten für Wirtschaft und Menschenrechte, John Ruggie*. Berlin.

———. 2016a. "Assessment of SPD Party Congress Decision and the Current Debates on Protocols in CETA from the Perspective of the DGB." www.labournet.de/wp-content/uploads/2016/09/dgb-zu-ceta-leak.pdf (October 1, 2016).

———. 2016b. "Menschenrechte in der Wirtschaft brauchen eine ambitionierte Umsetzung: Stellungnahme des Deutschen Gewerkschaftsbundes zum Entwurf des Nationalen Aktionsplanes Umsetzung der VN-Leitprinzipien für Wirtschaft und Menschenrechte." Berlin.

Deutsches Institut für Menschenrechte. 2015. *National Baseline Assessment*. Berlin.

———. 2016. "»Zögerliche Umsetzung«: Der politische Wille reichte nicht weiter: Deutschland setzt die UN-Leitprinzipien um - mit kleinen Schritten."

Development Solution. 2011. *A Trade SIA relating to the Negotiation of a Comprehensive Economic and Trade Agreement (CETA) between the EU and Canada*. Trans. Colin Kirkpatrick, Selim Raihan, Adam Bleser, Dan Prud'homme, Karel Mayrand, Jean-Frédéric Morin, Hector Pollitt, Leonith Hinojosa and Michael Williams (Accessed October 1, 2016).

Dilger, Alexander. 1999. *Betriebsratstypen und Personalfluktuation: Eine empirische Untersuchung mit Daten des NIFA-Panels* [deu]. Greifswald : Univ., Rechts- und Staatswiss. Fak.

Dohmen, Caspar. 2015. "Textilbündnis: "Feigenblattprojekt"." *Süddeutsche.de,* October 15. http://www.sueddeutsche.de/wirtschaft/textilbuendnis-feigenblattprojekt-1.2693534 (Accessed September 29, 2016).

Dombois, Rainer. 2006. "Sozialklauseln in US-Freihandelsabkommen — ein wirksames Mittel internationaler Arbeitsregulierung?" *Industrielle Beziehungen / The German Journal of Industrial Relations* 13 (3): 238–52.

Eberhardt, Pia. 2013. "Politikbekämpfung als Geschäftsmodell: Die Rolle der Rechtsbranche im internationalen Investitionsrecht." *juridikum* 2013 (3): 386–91.

Ebert, Franz C., and Anne Posthuma. 2015. *Labour Standards and Development Finance Institutions: A Review of Current Policies and Activities*. International Labour

Organisation. http://www.ilo.org/wcmsp5/groups/public/---dgreports/---inst/documents/publication/wcms_192837.pdf (Accessed November 3, 2016).

Ecorys. 2016. *Trade SIA on the Transatlantic Trade and Investment Partnership (TTIP) between the EU and the USA: Interim Technical Report* (Accessed October 2, 2016).

Ellguth, Peter, and Elke Ahlers. 2003. *Betriebsräte und betriebliche Personalpolitik*. IAB Nürnberg und WSI Düsseldorf. Abschlussbericht.

Ellguth, Peter, and Susanne Kohaut. 2016. "Tarifbindung und betriebliche Interessenvertretung: Ergebnisse aus dem IAB-Betriebspanel 2015." *WSI-Mitteilungen* (4): 283–91. http://www.boeckler.de/pdf/wsimit_2005_07_ellguth.pdf (Accessed November 13, 2016).

Emmenegger, Patrick, Silja Häusermann, Bruno Palier, and Martin Seeleib-Kaiser, eds. 2012. *The age of dualization: The changing face of inequality in deindustrializing societies. International policy exchange series*. Oxford, New York: Oxford University Press.

Erklärung von Bern, Südwind Institut, and Clean Clothes Campaign. 2012. *Made in Europe: Deutsche, Österreichische und Schweizerische Berufsbekleidungfirmen profitieren von Armut und Angst unter mazedonischen Arbeiterinnen* (Accessed November 12, 2016).

Euler Hermes Aktiengesellschaft. 2013. "Umwelt- und Sozialprüfung von Exportgeschäften: Die Common Approaches, Exportkreditgarantien des Bundes." http://www.agaportal.de/pdf/hds/hds_umweltpruefung.pdf (November 4, 2016).

———. 2015. *Jahresbericht über die Exportkreditgarantien der Bundesrepublik Deutschland* (Accessed November 4, 2016).

European Commission. 2015. *Trade For All: Towards a More Responsible Trade and Investment Policy*. Brüssel.

———. 2016a. "Questions and answers (TTIP)." March 16. http://ec.europa.eu/trade/policy/in-focus/ttip/about-ttip/questions-and-answers/index_en.htm (March 30, 2017).

———. 2016b. "Services and investment in EU trade deals: Using 'positive' and 'negative' lists." http://trade.ec.europa.eu/doclib/docs/2016/april/tradoc_154427.pdf (Accessed October 3, 2016).

Felbermayr, G., B. Heid, and S. Lehwald. 2013. *Transatlantic Trade and Investment Partnership (TTIP): Who benefits from a free trade deal?* Gütersloh.

Fichter, Michael. 2005. "The German Way: Still Treading the Path of Institutionalized Labor Relations?" In *Surviving Globalisation?: Perspectives for the German Economic Model*, eds. Stefan Beck, Frank Klobes and Christoph Scherrer. Springer, 93–109.

Figueroa Clark, Victor. 2016. *Den Code brechen: Verletzung internationaler Normen durch die DHL*. International Transport Worker's Federation (Accessed November 8, 2016).

Fox, Tom, Halina Ward, and Bruce Howard. 2002. *Public sector roles in strengthening corporate social responsibility: A baseline study*. Washington, D.C.: World Bank.

Fritz, Thomas. 2015. "Analyse und Bewertung des EU-Kanada Freihandelsabkommens CETA." (October 1, 2016).

Fütterer, Michael. 2016. "Gewerkschaft als internationale soziale Bewegung: Das ExChains-Netzwerk in der Bekleidungsindustrie." [de]. *PERIPHERIE – Politik • Ökonomie •*

Kultur 36 (142-143). http://budrich-journals.de/index.php/peripherie/article/view/24677/21527.

Ganguly, Meenakshi, ed. 2015. *Whoever Raises their Head Suffers the Most: Workers' Rights in Bangladesh's Garment Factories.* New York N.Y.: Human Rights Watch.

German Chambers of Commerce - Worldwide Network. 2017. "The German Chambers of Commerce Abroad."

Germanwatch, and Brot für die Welt. 2016. "Unternehmensverantwortung im europäischen Vergleich: Der deutsche Aktionsplan Wirtschaft und Menschenrechte gemessen an Rahmensetzungen in anderen Ländern." https://www.brot-fuer-die-welt.de/fileadmin/mediapool/user_upload/Kurzpapier_NAP.pdf (Accessed February 7, 2017).

Germany Trade and Invest GmbH. 2015. "Bangladeschs Textilproduzenten müssen Fertigung verbessern." April 3. http://www.gtai.de/GTAI/Navigation/DE/Trade/Maerkte/suche,t=bangladeschs-textilproduzenten-muessen-fertigung-verbessern,did=1212506.html (Accessed September 27, 2016).

———. 2016a. "GTAI - Startseite." http://www.gtai.de/GTAI/Navigation/DE/welcome.html (November 14, 2016).

———. 2016b. "Lohn- und Lohnnebenkosten: Kolumbien." July 20. http://www.gtai.de/GTAI/Navigation/DE/Trade/Maerkte/Geschaeftspraxis/lohn-und-lohnnebenkosten,t=lohn-und-lohnnebenkosten--kolumbien,did=1495990.html (Accessed September 27, 2016).

Golder Associates Inc. 2016. "Environmental and Social Due Diligence Review: Topolobampo 2200 MTPD Ammonia Plant, State of Sinaloa, Mexico." http://www.agaportal.de/pdf/nachhaltigkeit/eia/esdd_mexiko_duengemittelwerk.pdf (Accessed November 2, 2016).

Government of Canada. 2016. "Federal labour standards and equity: Information on rights, termination and severance pay, minimum wage, hours of work, vacation and leave and pay equity." http://www.esdc.gc.ca/en/jobs/workplace/employment_standards/index.page (October 2, 2016).

Grabosch, Robert, and Christian Scheper. 2015. *Die menschenrechtliche Sorgfaltspflicht von Unternehmen.* Berlin.

Greifenstein, Ralph, and Leo Kissler. 2010. *Mitbestimmung im Spiegel der Forschung: Eine Bilanz der empirischen Untersuchungen 1952-2010.* Vol. 123 of *Forschung aus der Hans-Böckler-Stiftung.* Berlin: Ed. Sigma.

Greven, Thomas. 2012a. "Anforderungen an Legitimität und Effektivität von Sozialkapiteln in Handelsverträgen." In *Sozialkapitel in Handelsabkommen: Begründungen und Vorschläge aus juristischer, ökonomischer und politologischer Sicht.* 1st ed. Vol. 38 of *Integration Europas und Ordnung der Weltwirtschaft*, eds. Christoph Scherrer and Andreas Hänlein. Baden-Baden: Nomos, 83–99.

———. 2012b. "Stand der politischen Debatte zur Verknüpfung von Sozialstandards und Handel." In *Sozialkapitel in Handelsabkommen: Begründungen und Vorschläge aus juristischer, ökonomischer und politologischer Sicht.* 1st ed. Vol. 38 of *Integration*

Europas und Ordnung der Weltwirtschaft, eds. Christoph Scherrer and Andreas Hänlein. Baden-Baden: Nomos, 71–82.

Hadwinger, Felix, Brigitte Hamm, Katrin Vitols, and Peter Wilke. 2016. *Unternehmensverantwortung für Menschenrechte und Arbeitnehmerrechte: Die UN-Leitprinzipien für Wirtschaft und Menschenrechte als Thema für Betriebsräte und Gewerkschaften*. Hamburg, Duisburg.

Hall, John A. 2006. "Human Rights and the Garment Industry in Contemporary Cambodia." August 25.

Hamm, Brigitte. 2005. *Die OECD-Leitsätze für multinationale Unternehmen: Ihr Einsatz durch zivilgesellschaftliche Organisationen in Deutschland*. Trans. Friedrich-Ebert-Stiftung. Bonn.

Hamm, Brigitte, Christian Scheper, and Maike Schölmerich. 2011. *Menschenrechtsschutz und deutsche Außenwirtschaftsförderung: Ein Pladoyer für konsequente Reformen*. Duisburg: Institut für Entwicklung und Frieden. INEF Policy Brief, 08. https://inef.uni-due.de/cms/files/policybrief08.pdf (Accessed October 11, 2016).

Handelsblatt. 2016. "Volkswagen in den USA: Gewerkschaft gewinnt Streit um Werk Chattanooga." http://www.handelsblatt.com/unternehmen/industrie/volkswagen-in-den-usa-gewerkschaft-gewinnt-streit-um-werk-chattanooga/13445598.html?nlayer=Organisation_11804700 (November 7, 2016).

Hans-Böckler-Stiftung. 2010. "Ltd. und Co. KG fehlt die Mitbestimmung." *Böckler Impuls* (5): 6–7.

———. 2016. "Wie Firmen die Mitbestimmung aushebeln." *Böckler Impuls* (6). http://www.boeckler.de/64443_64474.htm (Accessed November 13, 2016).

Haufe. 2016. "Vergaberecht 2016: Was ändert sich mit der Reform?" https://www.haufe.de/recht/weitere-rechtsgebiete/wirtschaftsrecht/was-aendert-sich-mit-der-reform-des-vergaberechts_210_333806.html (November 12, 2016).

Heydenreich, Cornelia. 2004. "Die OECD-Leitsätze für multinationale Unternehmen-Erfahrungen und Bewertungen." *Menschenrechts-, Arbeits-und Umweltstandards bei multinationalen Unternehmen. Kontext Globalisierung* 1: 41–48.

———. 2014. *Globales Wirtschaften und Menschenrechte: Deutschland auf dem Prüfstand*. Berlin: Germanwatch [u.a.].

Höpner, Martin. 2003. *Wer beherrscht die Unternehmen?: Shareholder Value, Managerherrschaft und Mitbestimmung in Deutschland*. Bd. 46 of *Schriften aus dem Max-Planck-Institut für Gesellschaftsforschung, Köln*. Frankfurt, New York: Campus Verlag.

Hübler, Olaf. 2003. "Zum Einfluss des Betriebsrates in mittelgroßen Unternehmen auf Investitionen, Löhne, Produktivität und Renten - empirische Befunde." *Wunderbare WirtschaftsWelt : die New Economy und ihre Herausforderungen ; 4. Freiburger Wirtschaftssymposium*: 77–94.

IndustriALL. 2016. "Survey reveals abusive use of precarious work at Shell." http://www.industriall-union.org/survey-reveals-abusive-use-of-precarious-work-at-shell (November 21, 2016).

International Finance Corporation. 2012. "Performance Standards on Environmental and Social Sustainability." http://www.ifc.org/wps/wcm/connect/115482804a0255db96fbffd1a5d13d27/PS_Englis h_2012_Full-Document.pdf?MOD=AJPERES (Accessed November 21, 2016).

International Labour Organisation. 2012. "ILO nennt fünf Länder wegen ernsthafter Verletzung des Rechts auf Vereinigungsfreiheit." [de]. August 12. http://www.ilo.org/berlin/presseinformationen/WCMS_193592/lang--de/index.htm (September 27, 2016).

International Trade Union Confederation. 2016a. "Global Rights Index." http://survey.ituc-csi.org/ (November 5, 2016).

———. 2016b. "Global Rights Index: Brazil." http://survey.ituc-csi.org/Brazil.html#tabs-3 (November 5, 2016).

———. 2016c. "Global Rights Index: Egypt." http://survey.ituc-csi.org/Egypt.html?lang=en (November 5, 2016).

———. 2016d. "Global Rights Index: Mozambique." November 5. http://survey.ituc-csi.org/Mozambique.html?lang=en#tabs-3 (November 5, 2016).

———. 2016e. "Global Rights Index: Nigeria." November 5. http://survey.ituc-csi.org/Nigeria.html?lang=en#tabs-3 (November 5, 2016).

———. 2016f. "Global Rights Index: Nigeria." November 5. http://survey.ituc-csi.org/Nigeria.html?lang=en#tabs-3 (November 5, 2016).

———. 2016g. "Global Rights Index: Peru." http://survey.ituc-csi.org/Peru.html#tabs-3 (November 5, 2016).

———. 2016h. "Global Rights Index: South Africa." http://survey.ituc-csi.org/South-Africa.html?lang=en (November 5, 2016).

———. 2016i. "Global Rights Index: Tanzania." http://survey.ituc-csi.org/Tanzania.html#tabs-3 (November 5, 2016).

Jaehrling, K. 2015. "The state as a 'socially responsible customer'?: Public procurement between market-making and market-embedding." *European Journal of Industrial Relations* 21 (2): 149–64.

Jirjahn, Uwe. 2011. "Ökonomische Wirkungen der Mitbestimmung in Deutschland: Ein Update." *Schmollers Jahrbuch* 131 (1): 3–57.

Kampagne für Saubere Kleidung. 2014. "Stellungnahme der Kampagne für Saubere Kleidung zum geplanten Textilbündnis des BMZ." http://www.saubere-kleidung.de/index.php/2-uncategorised/416-stellungnahme-der-kampagne-fuer-saubere-kleidung-zum-geplanten-textilbuendnis-des-bmz (September 29, 2016).

Keller, Berndt, and Frank Werner. 2007. "Arbeitnehmerbeteiligung in der Europäischen Aktiengesellschaft (SE)-Eine empirische Analyse der ersten Fälle."

KfW Bank. 2013. "Verantwortungsbewusste Kapitalanlage: Treffen des Deutschen PRI-Netzwerks 2013 bei der KfW." [de]. Frankfurt am Main. September 13. https://www.kfw.de/KfW-Konzern/Newsroom/Aktuelles/Pressemitteilungen/Pressemitteilungen-Details_175169.html (September 14, 2016).

———. 2014. "Neuer PRI-Leitfaden: ESG-Kriterien unterstützen Anleiheinvestoren beim Risikomanagement." [de]. September 30. https://www.kfw.de/KfW-Konzern/Newsroom/Aktuelles/News/News-Details_228480.html (October 1, 2016).

———. 2016a. "Der nachhaltige Investmentansatz der KfW: ESG Kriterien." https://www.kfw.de/nachhaltigkeit/PDF/Nachhaltiges-Investment/2016_ESG-Kriterien-Unternehmen.pdf.

———. 2016b. "Principles for Responsible Investment (PRI)." [de]. Frankfurt am Main. September 14. https://www.kfw.de/nachhaltigkeit/KfW-Konzern/Nachhaltigkeit/Nachhaltige-Unternehmensprozesse/Nachhaltiges-Investment/Principles-for-Responsible-Investment-(PRI)/index.html (September 14, 2016).

KfW IPEX Bank. 2016. "Geschäftsbericht der KfW IPEX-Bank 2016." [de]. October 31. https://www.kfw-ipex-bank.de/Internationale-Finanzierung/KfW-IPEX-Bank/Presse/Download-Center/Gesch%C3%A4ftsbericht/ (October 31, 2016).

KfW IPEX-Bank. 2015a. *Geschäftsbericht 2015*. 2 (Accessed October 31, 2016).

———. 2015b. *Nachhaltigkeitsrichtlinie: Richtlinie der KfW IPEX-Bank GmbH für ein umwelt- und sozialgerechtes Finanzieren* (Accessed November 1, 2016).

Kirner, Eva, Ute Weißfloch, and Angela Jäger. 2010. "Beteiligungsorientierte Organisation und Innovation." *WSI-Mitteilungen* (2): 87–94.

Kleinschmidt, Christian, Wilfried Kruse, Rainer Lichte, Wolfgang Hindrchs, Uwe Jürgenhake, and Helmut Martens. 1997. *Sozialer Umbruch in der Stahlindustrie: Das Ende des "Malochers" und die Rolle der Betriebsräte 1960 bis heute*. Sozialforschungsstelle Dortmund. Abschlussbericht.

Kocka, Jürgen. 2006. "Geschichte und Zukunft der Mitbestimmung." *Magazin Mitbestimmung* 4: 2006.

Köhnen, Heiner, and Anne Scheidhauer. 2002. "Organising the Battlefield: Arbeiterinnen in den Freihandelszonen Sri Lankas." Ränkeschmiede - Texte zur internationalen ArbeiterInnenbewegung. Offenbach: tie - Internationales Bildungswerk e.V. http://www.tie-germany.org/publications/tie_publications/RS_18_TIE.pdf (September 30, 2016).

Koller, Lena, Claus Schnabel, and Joachim Wagner. 2008. "Freistellung von Betriebsräten: Eine Beschäftigungsbremse?" *Zeitschrift für ArbeitsmarktForschung* 41 (2/3): 305-326.

Kompass Nachhaltigkeit. 2016. "Willkommen beim Kompass Nachhaltigkeit." [de]. http://www.kompass-nachhaltigkeit.de/ (November 13, 2016).

Kompetenzstelle für nachhaltige Beschaffung. 2016. "Kompetenzstelle für nachhaltige Beschaffung: Allgemeines." November 11. http://www.nachhaltige-beschaffung.info/DE/Allgemeines/allgemeines_node.html;jsessionid=55464700AC804 E1CB5B1224EF36B4EC2.2_cid362 (November 11, 2016).

Kraft, Kornelius, and Jörg Stank. 2004. "Die Auswirkungen der gesetzlichen Mitbestimmung auf die Innova-tionsaktivität deutscher Unternehmen." *Schmollers Jahrbuch: Journal of Applied Social Science Studies/Zeitschrift für Wirtschafts-und Sozialwissenschaften* 124 (3): 421–49.

Kriegesmann, Bernd, Th Kley, and Sebastian Kublik. 2010. "Innovationstreiber betriebliche Mitbestimmung." *WSI-Mitteilungen* (2): 71–78.

LabourNet. 2012. "Gewerkschaften und Arbeitskämpfe in Pakistan." December 19. http://archiv.labournet.de/internationales/pk/arbeitskampf.html (November 21, 2016).

Laskowski, Silke. 2014. *Rechtliche Expertise im Rahmen der öffentlichen Konsultationen der EU zum Investitionsschutzkapitel des geplanten TTIP-Freihandelsabkommens zwischen der EU und den USA*. Ver.di. Öffentliche Konsultation zum Investitionskapitel TTIP.

Legge, Karen. 2005. *Human resource management: Rhetorics and realities. Management, work and organisations*. Houndmills, Basingstoke, Hampshire, New York, N.Y.: Palgrave Macmillan.

Martens, Helmut, and Uwe Dechmann. 2010. "Am Ende der Deutschland AG: Standortkonflikte im Kontext einer neuen Politik der Arbeit."

McCrudden, Christopher. 2004. "Using public procurement to achieve social outcomes." *Natural Resources Forum* 28 (4): 257–67.

———. 2007. "Corporate social responsibility and public procurement."

Mey, Stefan. 2015. "Gewerkschafter gehen gegen T-Mobile in den USA vor." *heise online*, August 1. http://www.heise.de/newsticker/meldung/Gewerkschafter-gehen-gegen-T-Mobile-in-den-USA-vor-2725903.html (Accessed November 8, 2016).

Mückenberger, Ulrich. 2015. "Can International Investment Agreements support labour standards?" In *Long-term investment and the Sustainable Company: A stakeholder perspective*. Vol. 3 of *Sustainable Company book series*, ed. Sigurt Vitols. ETUI, 177–205.

Müller-Wrede, Malte. 2015. *Vergaberechtsreform 2016: Die wichtigsten Eckpfeiler. WISO direkt*. Bonn: Friedrich-Ebert-Stiftung, Abt. Wirtschafts- und Sozialpolitik.

Norddeutscher Rundfunk. 2013. "Billigproduktion im Ausland: Staat fördert Firmen." [de]. http://daserste.ndr.de/panorama/archiv/2013/Billigproduktion-im-Ausland-Staat-foerdert-Firmen,greenwashing109.html (November 21, 2016).

OECD. 2016. "OECD Recommendations: Common Approaches." http://www.oecd.org/officialdocuments/publicdisplaydocumentpdf/?cote=TAD/ECG%282016%293&doclanguage=en (Accessed September 29, 2016).

oecom research. 2013. *Der Einfluss nachhaltiger Kapitalanlagen auf Unternehmen: Eine empirische Analyse*.

Office of the Compliance Advisor Ombudsman. 2012. *CAO Audit of a Sample of IFC Investments in Third-Party Financial Intermediaries*. http://www.cao-ombudsman.org/newsroom/documents/Audit_Report_C-I-R9-Y10-135.pdf.

Organisation for Economic Co-operation and Development. 2011. "OECD Guidelines for Multinational Enterprises." (Accessed April 2, 2017).

Partnership for Sustainable Textiles. 2017. "Plan of Action Partnership for Sustainable Textiles." https://www.textilbuendnis.com/en/home/plan-of-action.

Perulli, Adalberto. 2014. "Fundamental Social Rights, Market Regulation and EU External Action." *International Journal of Comparative Labour Law and Industrial Relations* 30 (1): 27–47.

Portz, Norbert. 2016. *Das neue Vergaberecht: Darstellung und Bewertung aus kommunaler Sicht.* Deutscher Städte- und Gemeindebund.

PowerShift, and Canadian Centre for Policy Alternatives. 2016. "Investitionsschutz und Streitbeilegung in CETA." In *CETA lesen und verstehen: Analyse des EU-Kanada Freihandelsabkommens.*, eds. PowerShift and Canadian Centre for Policy Alternatives. Berlin, Ottawa, 11–18.

PRI Associations, UNEP Finance Initiative, and UN Global Compact. 2015. "PRI Reporting Framework 2016: Main Definitions." (Accessed September 14, 2016).

PricewaterhouseCoopers. 2015. *Jahresbericht über die Investitionsgarantien der Bundesrepublik Deutschland* (Accessed November 4, 2016).

Renaud, Simon. 2008. *Arbeitnehmermitbestimmung im Strukturwandel.* Metropolis-Verlag GmbH.

Rüb, Stefan. 2000. *Weltbetriebsräte und andere Formen weltweiter Arbeitnehmervertretungsstrukturen in transnationalen Kozernen.* Arbeitspapier. http://www.boeckler.de/pdf/p_arbp_027.pdf (Accessed November 13, 2016).

Rudolph, Wolfgang, and Wolfram Wassermann. 2001. *Betriebsräte zwischen Erosion und neuer Beweglichkeit: Eine empirische Studie zu den Konsequenzen der Auflösung und Umwandlung von Betriebs- und Unternehmensstrukturen.* Bfs Kassel. Abschlussbericht.

Scheidhauer, Anne. 2008. "Schuften für unsere Kleider: Und sonst nichts?" Ränkeschmiede - Texte zur internationalen ArbeiterInnenbewegung. Frankfurt: tie - Internationales Bildungswerk e.V. http://www.tie-germany.org/publications/tie_publications/RS_18_TIE.pdf (September 30, 2016).

Scherrer, Christoph, and Andreas Hänlein, eds. 2012. *Sozialkapitel in Handelsabkommen: Begründungen und Vorschläge aus juristischer, ökonomischer und politologischer Sicht.* 1st ed. Vol. 38 of *Integration Europas und Ordnung der Weltwirtschaft.* Baden-Baden: Nomos.

Scheytt, Stefan. 2016. ""Da werden die roten Linien überschritten"." *Magazin Mitbestimmung* (15.9.2016).

Schmidt, S., W. Link, and R. Wolf. 2007. *Handbuch zur deutschen Außenpolitik.* VS Verlag für Sozialwissenschaften.

Schulten, T., T. Brandt, and C. Hermann. 2008. "Liberalisation and privatisation of public services and strategic options for European trade unions." *Transfer: European Review of Labour and Research* 14 (2): 295–311. http://www.boeckler.de/pdf/p_wsi_schulten_brandt_hermann_transfer.pdf (Accessed October 2, 2016).

Schulten, Thorsten, Kristin Alsos, Pete Burgess, and Klaus Pedersen. 2012. "Pay and other social clauses in European public procurement. An overview on regulation and practices with a focus on Denmark, Germany, Norway, Switzerland and the United Kingdom." *Euro pean Federation on Public Service Unions [cited 13 August 2014]. Available from Internet: http://www. epsu. org/IMG/pdf/EPSU_Report_final. pdf.*

Seibold, Bettina, Martin Schwarz-Kocher, Jürgen Dispan, and Ursula Richter. 2010. "Betriebsratshandeln im Modus arbeitsorientierter Innovationsprozesse." *WSI-Mitteilungen* (2): 95–102.

Seyboth, Marie, and Rainald Thannisch. 2008. "Zukunftsfaktor Mitbestimmung." *WSI-Mitteilungen* 9: 519–22.

Sick, Sebastian. 2015a. *Mitbestimmungsfeindlicheres Klima: Unternehmen nutzen ihre Freiheiten-Arbeitnehmer werden um ihre Mitbestimmungsrechte gebracht.* Mitbestimmungsförderung Report.

———. 2015b. *Der deutschen Mitbestimmung entzogen: Unternehmen mit ausländischer Rechtsform nehmen zu.* Mitbestimmungsförderung Report, 8. http://www.boeckler.de/pdf/p_mbf_report_2015_8.pdf (Accessed October 1, 2016).

Sick, Sebastian, and Lasse Pütz. 2011. "Der deutschen Unternehmensmitbestimmung entzogen: Die Zahl der Unternehmen mit ausländischer Rechtsform wächst." *WSI-Mitteilungen* (1): 34–40 (Accessed October 2, 2016).

Sperling, Hans J., and Harald Wolf. 2010. "Zwischen Sicherung und Gestaltung-Varianten mitbestimmter Innovation in der Industrie." *WSI-Mitteilungen* (2): 79–86.

Stabstelle Zusammenarbeit mit der Wirtschaft. 2011. "Entwicklungspartnerschaften mit der Wirtschaft: Laufende Projekte 2010/2011." http://daserste.ndr.de/panorama/archiv/2013/panorama4521.pdf (November 21, 2016).

Stettes, Oliver. 2007. "Die Arbeitnehmermitbestimmung im Aufsichtsrat: Ergebnisse einer Unternehmensbefragung." *IW-Trends-Vierteljahresschrift zur empirischen Wirtschaftsforschung aus dem Institut der deutschen Wirtschaft Köln* 34 (1): 1–15.

Streeck, Wolfgang, Karl-Heinz Briam, Klaus Murmann, Dieter Schulte, Frank von Auer, and Reinhardt Mohn. 1998. *Mitbestimmung und neue Unternehmenskulturen, Bilanz und Perspektiven: Bericht der Kommission Mitbestimmung. Mitbestimmung und neue Unternehmenskulturen.* Gütersloh: Verlag Bertelsmann Stiftung.

The Equator Principles Association. 2011. "The Equator Principles." [en-GB]. http://www.equator-principles.com/ (November 21, 2016).

the public eyes awards. 2016. "Hall of Shame." http://publiceyeawards.ch/de/hall-of-shame/ (November 4, 2016).

The World Bank Group. 2007. "Environmental, Health, and Safety Guidelines." http://www.ifc.org/wps/wcm/connect/topics_ext_content/ifc_external_corporate_site/ifc+sustainability/our+approach/risk+management/ehsguidelines (November 21, 2016).

———. 2016. "Safeguard Policies." http://web.worldbank.org/WBSITE/EXTERNAL/PROJECTS/EXTPOLICIES/EXTSAFEPOL/0,,menuPK:584441~pagePK:64168427~piPK:64168435~theSitePK:584435,00.html (November 21, 2016).

Umweltbundesamt. 2016. "Umweltfreundliche Beschaffung." November 6. http://www.umweltbundesamt.de/themen/wirtschaft-konsum/umweltfreundliche-beschaffung (November 7, 2016).

United Nations Human Rights - Office of the High Commissioner. 2011. "Implementing the United Nations "Protect", "Respect" and "Remedy" Framework." New York, Geneva: United Nations Organization. http://www.ohchr.org/Documents/Publications/GuidingPrinciplesBusinessHR_EN.pdf.

United Nations Principles for Responsible Investment. 2016. "The Six Principles." https://www.unpri.org/about/the-six-principles (September 13, 2016).

urgewald. 2015. *Die Schattenseite der KfW: Finanzierung zu Lasten von Mensch und Umwelt* (Accessed November 1, 2016).

VENRO. 2011. "VENRO Positionspapier zum G20-Gipfel in Cannes." http://www.venro.org/fileadmin/Presse-Downloads/2011/November/VENRO_Positionspapier_G20.pdf (November 21, 2016).

Verfassung des deutschen Reiches (Weimarer Reichsverfassung). 1919. In *documentarchiv.de*.

Vilmar, Fritz. 1973. *Strategien der Demokratisierung.* Vol. 53 of *Sammlung Luchterhand.* Darmstadt, Neuwied: H. Luchterhand.

Viner, J. 1950. *The customs union issue.* Carnegie Endowment for International Peace.

Vitols, Sigurt, ed. 2015. *Long-term investment and the Sustainable Company: A stakeholder perspective.* Vol. 3 of *Sustainable Company book series.* ETUI.

Vogel, David. 2005. *The market for virtue: The potential and limits of corporate social responsibility.* Washington, D.C.: Brookings Institution Press.

Waleson, Joshua. 2015. "Corporate Social Responsibility in EU Comprehensive Free Trade Agreements: Towards Sustainable Trade and Investment." *Legal Issues of Economic Integration* 42 (2): 143–74.

Waring, Peter, and John Lewer. 2004. "The Impact of Socially Responsible Investment on Human Resource Management: A Conceptual Framework." *Journal of Business Ethics* 52 (1): 99–108.

We Expect Better. 2016. "Petition - We Expect Better." http://www.weexpectbetter.org/petition (November 8, 2016).

Werner, Jörg-Richard, and Jochen Zimmermann. 2005. "Unternehmerische Mitbestimmung in Deutschland: Eine empirische Analyse der Auswirkungen von Gewerkschaftsmacht in Aufsichtsräten." *Industrielle Beziehungen / The German Journal of Industrial Relations* 12 (3): 339–54.

Ziegler, Astrid, and Frank Gerlach. 2010. "Das deutsche Modell auf dem Prüfstand: Innovationen in der Krise." *WSI-Mitteilungen* (2): 63–70.

Zugehör, Rainer. 2003. *Die Zukunft des rheinischen Kapitalismus: Unternehmen zwischen Kapitalmarkt und Mitbestimmung.* Vol. 180 of *Forschung Soziologie.* Wiesbaden: VS Verlag für Sozialwissenschaften.

Zwick, Thomas. 2003. *Works councils and the productivity impact of direct employee participation.* Mannheim.

5. The Enforcement of Workers' Rights through Conditional or Promotional Trade Agreements: A Comparison of US and EU Social Chapters

Madelaine Moore

Since the North American Free Trade Agreement (NAFTA) and the stalling of the Doha round of the World Trade Organization (WTO) negotiations, there has been an increase in the number of free trade agreements (FTAs) that include some form of social chapter[1] that specifically deals with labour rights. Although there is no multilateral resolution on the inclusion of such standards, this appears to be a new norm in unilateral, bilateral, and regional trade agreements. Yet despite the inclusion of such chapters – which shows some positive discursive shift – there have been very few cases of enforcement, and in the rare case that enforcement has occurred, the impact this has had on labour standards is in dispute. The studies that have attempted to explore the impact of social chapters on labour rights have been largely inconclusive, with most suggesting that there is some positive impact in certain case-specific circumstances when such chapters work in partnership with, or build up, other conditions necessary for enforcement. In this way, the inclusion of social chapters signifies a necessary discursive shift in regards to the trade-labour linkage, but has fallen short on implementation and enforceability.

This study focuses primarily on the question of *enforcement* of International Labour Standards (ILS) in social chapters. Enforcement goes beyond ratification, requiring certain necessary conditions of which other parts of the FTA may be affected, thus some points will be flagged regarding the integration of social chapters within the rest of the agreement and the global trade regime. Building on the existing research, which is rather unclear about whether existing social chapters have had, and from this could have, any positive impact on labour rights, this study asks a slightly different question: Why aren't these existing social clauses being enforced? And what external conditions, partnered with a specific chapter design, could enable more consistent enforcement? This study firstly unpacks some of the reasons for a lack of enforcement, situating FTAs into the broader development of ILS including the ongoing debate over the trade-labour linkage. This then leads to a normative description of what the necessary conditions are that would tackle enforcement issues. The second part of the paper unpacks the current designs of social chapters: Specifically the differences between the European Union (EU) and United States (US) (promotional/conditional) approaches and issues that each raise particularly

---

[1] Across agreements some refer to social clauses and some to chapters, there is some difference between the two (normally around how comprehensive they are), however for this study the term social chapter will be used.

around: monitoring, content, sanctions/incentives, inclusion of social partners, coherence and dispute settlement mechanisms. The concluding section of the paper puts forward some policy recommendations regarding the ongoing inclusion of labour rights within trade agreements.

The Trade-Labor Linkage: an Uneasy Partnership?

The inclusion of social chapters within trade agreements needs to be understood in the wider context – and debate – over the relationship between trade and development, and labour rights in particular. The trade-labour linkage has had a rocky relationship, and there is still no universal consensus that such a relationship should exist. There were failed attempts to cement the trade-labour linkage multilaterally in the WTO framework in the 1996 and 1999 WTO meetings. These failed in part due to push back from developing countries that claimed that it was a form of protectionism. The prevailing argument was that labour rights would occur once a certain developmental level had been reached, which itself was dependent on increased liberalization. Ever since, trade and labour rights have existed in separate bodies (the International Labour Organization (ILO) and WTO) and regulation has diverged, with only the WTO holding enforcement capabilities (Scherrer and Beck 2016, 9). Thus, as Ewing-Chow describes, the two regimes have developed 'in splendid isolation' from one another with many WTO principles working against the promotion of labour rights (Ewing-Chow 2007, 171-2). [2] Some authors argue that there is space for labor rights clauses within the GATT rules, although it remains unclear whether social chapters or ILS in bilateral FTAs can work around existing WTO frameworks as few cases have ever been tested (Marceau 2009, 549).[3] The failure of the Doha round of negotiations, where these issues were once again on the agenda, meant that any deepening of the institutional connection between trade and labour at the multilateral level further stagnated (Scherrer and Beck 2016).

Underpinning this debate is the heated question of whether further liberalization can ever lead to ILS or sustainable development. There are those who claim a

---

[2] For example, Article I (most favour nation) and Article III (National Treatment Principles) can have a damaging effect on domestic legislation that aims to promote ILS. The potential GATT legal frameworks that could help protect ILS are limited to the Anti-Dumping GATT Article VI (limited to price not social dumping), Countervailing Duties (Article XVI), Nullification and Impairment Provisions (Article XXII) but none of these can be explicitly linked to ILS (Scherrer and Beck 2016, 9–10). The GATT 1994 does allow for legitimate government policies that may be contrary to the GATT agreement if they aim to protect 'public morals, health or the environment' notably this does not mention labour rights (Marceau 2009, 545).

[3] The unilateral GSP approaches have been able to get around the GATT or WTO limitations by utilizing the enabling clause (Ebert and Posthuma 2011, 1)

direct link between increasing economic growth through liberalization and ILS (trickle down economics), there are those that state that liberalization will always negatively impact ILS, and those with a somewhat more pragmatic position that trade exists, and therefore we must guard against the negative repercussions that are inherent to it. The general consensus of trickle down economics has come under increased criticism (Brown 2007, 56–7), particularly following the financial and debt crises that resulted in stagnating wages and a demand for a fairer Globalization (Ebert and Posthuma 2011, v). It is widely recognized that the benefits of trade liberalization have failed to reach those most in need – especially in developing countries – and that fairer economic rules are not enough in themselves to promote social justice (Doumbia-Henry and Gravel 2006, 187). As Giumelli and van Roozendaal conclude in their 2017 study, 'FTAs by their very nature might undermine the protection of workers. Therefore, it is worth exploring whether adding labour standards to FTAs can really make a difference at all.' (2017, 57).

Despite the ongoing debate, the inclusion of social chapters in bilateral FTAs has increased rapidly over recent years, suggesting a new global norm. The North American Agreement on Labor Cooperation (NAALC) chapter of NAFTA was the first example within a US led agreement (Cabin 2009, 1057–8). By the early 2000s the EU also began to include social chapters into bilateral agreements, and in recent years this has become more explicit. There are, however, some key differences between the two approaches; the US employs a conditional design and the EU uses FTAs in a promotional way, underpinned by ongoing dialogue rather than pressure. There is a common argument that because the US social chapters tend to include sanctions and have pre-conditions they are more effective. However, these sanctions are rarely, if ever, applied making this causality link less clear. Since 2008, it is estimated that over 80% of FTAs have included some form of labour provision; this is also the case between south-south trading partners and agreements between smaller states. The 1998 ILO Declaration is often used as the baseline for these provisions (Bakvis and McCoy 2008, 1; ILO 2016, 6).

The New Generation of FTAs

The so-called new generation of trade agreements (in particular TTIP, TPP, CETA and TISA)[4] raises new questions over the feasibility of the trade-labour linkage in FTAs. As tariffs have been reduced to record lows these agreements focus on the reduction of non-tariff barriers (NTBs), as well as strengthening investor rights. Conversely, many of them also contain relatively detailed and

---

[4] I acknowledge that it looks like TTIP and TPP may no longer be ratified by the US and thus may not survive, however, I suggest that they signify the dominant and probably ongoing shifts within FTAs, so are worth analyzing for this reason.

progressive social chapters, perhaps as an attempt to claw back lost trust from the general public and social partners (Schillinger 2016). NTBs may appear fairly innocuous but usually refer to domestic regulations established by governments in the national interest; these can include environment or Occupational Health and Safety (OHS) standards, and labour regulation. They also include more protections for investors such as investor-state dispute settlement (ISDS) clauses. For example, TTIP targeted public ownership, as well as the public provision of services where they might impinge upon investor rights (Scherrer 2014, 1). The erosion of socially agreed to norms and regulations within the domestic sphere, teamed with the secrecy that most negotiations are carried out in, has led to a loss of trust and support for this new generation of FTAs within the general public (Schillinger 2016, 1). As the IUF, an international union federation has argued:

'...at the heart of these projects is the drive to further expand the already considerable power of transnational investors by restricting the regulatory power of governments and locking the system into place to prevent new regulatory initiatives or reverse privatizations.' (IUF 2014, 160).

What has come under particular public scrutiny is the growing inclusion of investor rights and ISDS clauses. ISDS clauses allow for investors to sue governments, setting up arbitration courts run by the business community. These courts act outside the normal legal process and can decide whether new regulations such as worker protection, minimum wage laws, or environmental protection, for example, may harm projected investment returns.[5] As Eberhardt describes (2014, 100), 'no ordinary court in the world has as much power'; the independence of the arbitrators is not guaranteed, meetings are often closed to the public, and rulings are often secret. This in effect puts investor's rights at the same level as national governments, weakening local level democracy and policy space, whilst locking in liberalization (Scherrer 2014, 3). What comes into question is the ability to democratically set and pursue social and environmental policy aims – undermining the ability for ILS to be enforced even if a separate labour chapter is included as they contradict one another and usually economic considerations win (Scherrer and Beck 2016, 32–3; Beck 2014, 11). Although some have argued that this clause could also be accessed by trade unions (i.e. in the CETA agreement), access issues need to be thought through. When we understand that lawyer fees can cost up to $1000 an hour for those schooled in investor-state proceedings, and the existing lack of knowledge of how these proceedings work in most states – let alone civil society groups –

---

[5] For a detailed discussion of cases where this has already occurred see Eberhardt (2014).

the stage is set against this ever being used as a tool for the protection of social and labour rights (Eberhardt 2014, 106).[6]

It is a logical assumption that civil society groups would be monetarily excluded from participation in these forums even if they were opened up to include more than investor rights (Eberhardt 2014, 107). This undermines any case for ISDS clauses to be seen as useful for the social interest. The new generation of agreements are thus incoherent in relation to ILS; there is an increased inclusion of often non-binding (or unenforced) social chapters and increased (and enforced) investor rights through ISDS clauses and reductions in NTBs (ETUC n.d, 3). This problematizes the goal of these new FTAs; is it further trade liberalization through an attack on public services and NTBs, or does it aim to re-socialize FTAs? I suggest that the deep trade agenda (i.e. NTBs) is not coherent with the promotion of ILS.

Why Are Existing Labour Rights Chapters Not Being Enforced?

The increasing inclusion of ILS in trade agreements is a step in the right direction. However, there is no conclusive evidence that social clauses have had a marked positive impact on ILS and it is hard to measure their effectiveness; many argue this is in part due to a lack of enforcement. Critically it is very hard to show or develop any model that can prove a level of direct causality between labour provisions in FTAs and lived working conditions – there is a gap between what is written in the agreement and enforcement. When social chapters do have sanctioning potential it is rarely utilized, suggesting a lack of political will or capacity to do so. I suggest this comes down to numerous factors at the macro and micro level including legislation, institutions, culture, politics and so on that impact upon how, and what, enforcement entails (ILO 2016, 72).

A direct issue here is that the enforcement of ILS requires strong institutional input, however liberalization can weaken institutions and regulatory ability (note NTBs)(ILO 2016, 67). The areas where FTAs may have the most potential for impact are around pre-ratification measures including institutional and legal reforms, and technical cooperation and capacity building, during the monitoring and implementation stages (ILO 2016, 73). FTAs, as legal documents, can do no more than develop legal frameworks and institutional foundations (i.e. pushing for ratification of standards or on-paper reforms); it comes down to states to actually push forward the reforms and attitudinal shift necessary for enforcement (Schmieg 2015, 28). However, where some improvements in labour standards have occurred through the implementation of FTAs, it tends to be in very case-specific contexts that are dependent upon 'the interplay between a variety of

---

[6] Notably the case between Germany and Vattenfall (against the phase-out of nuclear energy) has cost the country 6.5million euros to date just in legal costs (Eberhardt 2014).

political, social and economic factors' (Ebert and Posthuma 2011, 29). Somewhat reflecting these claims, Sengenberger in his 2005 study, proposed that the necessary conditions for ILS to be respected include; regulatory and policy coherence (national and international level), understanding and respect for ILS at the political and institutional setting, political will, strong labour institutions, government and institutional capacity, and strong economic performance (Sengenberger 2005, 100). The repetition of these necessary criteria informs the conditions outlined in this study; regulatory reform, political will on both sides, and the capacity and presence of strong social partners – especially independent trade unions.

Enforcement should be thought of as having two sides, the ratification of standards *and* their successful implementation. As a first step, enforcement requires the implementation of certain standards into national law. The second side of enforcement is the *response* of the government/s when a violation occurs. Thus the effective enforcement of social chapters, particularly around ILS, requires certain conditions that could foster labour rights but also the *political will* of both actors to uphold what they have agreed to. Political will can be linked to capacity issues within developing states regarding labour legislation, labour courts, inspections, weak trade unions, and sometimes the overlapping interests between government and business.

Within developed states/regions political will can be lacking because of competing economic or political concerns, or issues around their own legitimacy on such issues (i.e. the US hasn't ratified certain ILO conventions) to name a few. Central to questions of political will is the power and role of civil society, especially independent trade unions, to force their respective governments to take this seriously – to both *implement and enforce* the chapters that they have signed up to. As such, a lack of enforcement is directly related to trade union capacity: Sheer membership but also specifically their knowledge of, and access to, remedy mechanisms including social chapters. Problematically, due to the perceived lack of enforcement of existing social chapters and the lengthy and inefficient process when enforcement has occurred, trade unions and other civil society organizations can be put off from accessing this enforcement route as it is seen as time consuming, costly, and impossibly stacked against them. This can be exacerbated by the 'spaghetti bowl' of regulation and the lack of coherence between the multiple ILS regimes, as well as access (both monetary and knowledge) issues. As such, strong domestic social partners – particularly independent trade unions – are central to any ILS scheme and the enforcement of ILS in social chapters. They can push for political will and act as monitoring institutions, they also, if correctly engaged, can add much needed social legitimacy to FTAs, legitimacy that has rightly been questioned through the growing secrecy and unequal power balance that FTAs tend to institutionalize.

In summary, the necessary conditions for the effective enforcement of ILS including social chapters, comprise of; the ratification of certain ILS (i.e. ILO conventions), supportive national legal frameworks and labour regulatory regimes, national labour courts, freedom of association, collective bargaining rights, and the *capacity* for enforcement (i.e. inspectors, training, and clear legislation). There would also need to be a strong civil society and respected role for trade unions to act as whistle blowers, key bargaining actors, and also exert continued pressure globally to push enforcement. Related specifically back to FTAs, what this then requires is that there is an *effective* and *accessible* enforcement mechanism or dispute settlement process in the agreement that states and civil society groups can utilize. As a recent ILO report points out, the successful implementation of labour provisions crucially relies upon the extent that social partners are involved in the process of both negotiating, and implementing, the trade agreement (ILO 2016, 7–8). Critically, the weakening of necessary public institutions pushed for in the new generation of FTAs that take aim at public services could directly undermine this (Scherrer 2014, 3). Thus social chapters in FTAs need to be both understood in relation to the role they play in ILS and trade regimes, as well as how coherent they are across the whole trade or investment agreement.

An Overview of Existing Approaches to Social Chapters in Trade Agreements

Social chapters can be grouped as either promotional or conditional in design. A promotional chapter relies on dialogue; including monitoring or bilateral dialogue, or is cooperation based; employing mostly knowledge sharing and development assistance, and does not normally include sanctions or prescriptive enforcement processes. EU led agreements tends to fall into this camp. US agreements tend to follow conditional designs and, at least on paper, rely on incentives or sanction-based compliance either ex-ante; where certain standards must be met before ratification of the agreement, or ex-post; where these conditions will be met through the life of the agreement through continued monitoring and capacity building (Ebert and Posthuma 2011, 4). Although FTAs can be loosely categorized into these two camps, each agreement tends to differ in their content and form. However, the 1998 ILO Declaration is increasingly becoming the basis for such chapters (Ebert and Posthuma 2011, 7). EU and US-led agreements form the basis of this study, however, it is important to note that South-South agreements are also beginning to include social clauses and tend to prefer promotional labour provisions such as knowledge sharing, rather than the conditional approach (Ebert and Posthuma 2011, 6). Alongside these bilateral/regional agreements there are also unilateral designs such as the GSP schemes, which will be briefly mentioned below.

There is a common belief that because conditional agreements include the possibility for sanctions they are more effective at enforcing ILS than promotional chapters.[7] Recent research suggests that this argument needs to be critically assessed, as it seems to be much more dependent on context and political will rather than a blanket design (Van den Putte 2016, 31). Furthermore, this claim may be valid for ex-ante chapters in regards to pushing for ratification of ILS (i.e. changes on paper), but is much less clear in relation to enforcement of both the agreed to ILS and dispute processes outlined in the chapter.[8] Interestingly, although much of the literature tends to focus on the differences between promotional and conditional chapters, Ebert and Posthuma (2011) in their detailed analysis of the impact of social chapters, argue that in practice most labour provisions are actually promotional, as they tend to favour dialogue and cooperation before very rarely leading to sanctions, thus the presence of underutilized sanctions may have little actual impact. Although it is important to recognize that this split is less explicit in practice, there are some key differences between the design and implementation of the US and EU approaches that will be outlined below.

Promotional Chapters: The EU

The EU has been integrating social chapters into FTAs since 2001. Since the Treaty of Lisbon these chapters have been further merged into broader sustainable development chapters integrating free and fair trade, environmental protection and the protection of human rights (Van den Putte 2016, 24). Overall, the promotional approach can be characterized as follows; it directly references ILO standards (usually the 1998 Declaration), the trade-labour linkage is fostered through cooperation and dialogue, there is little pressure to improve standards beyond what the partners have already agreed to, and that labour norms are regarded as non-trade issues (Van den Putte 2016, 70–1). Since the 1990s there has been a deepening and widening of the content of social chapters, linking labour rights to human rights, and becoming more binding and prescriptive. Governance has also deepened meaning that more actors are involved at more levels, such as the inclusion of business and civil society consultation through Domestic Advisory Groups (DAGs) or Expert Panels (see the EU-Korea agreement) (Van den Putte and Orbie 2015, 268–9).

An important thing to consider with the EU approach is the history and role of social dialogue as a means to promote ILS through trade. This model is at the heart of the design and implementation of EU promotional social chapters. The lack of sanctions or pre-ratification conditions may be more connected to this

---

[7] It is suggested that within trade agreements the US approach is seen to be more effective in promoting labor rights through trade whereas the EU is seen to have more legitimacy on this issue (Van den Putte, Orbie, and Bossuyt unpub., 1).

[8] This can be seen in the recent side letters of the TPP agreement, especially in Vietnam.

belief in the value of dialogue, rather than because of a lack of commitment to the enforcement of ILS, as some have suggested. The reliance upon cooperation and dialogue to enforce ILS highlights how critical *political will* is in the case of promotional provisions, as real power rests with governments rather than other institutions or civil society. Many have argued that because there is no recourse if dialogue fails, the EU approach has been less effective (Bull, 2007). Thus, even if there is political will, there is no space to enforce that will.

The EU Korea agreement is representative of this; content wise it is relatively comprehensive, and stipulates engagement with social partners through the DAGs and Panel of Expert meetings (Lukas and Steinkellner 2010). However, in practice, there is no process beyond continued dialogue (there are no provisions if dialogue fails) and the broad language used around the DAGs has allowed for the Korean government to cherry pick the participants of those committees (FES Korea 2016). Yet, some studies have suggested that although there is less regulatory impact,[9] there may be some improvement through the knowledge and capacity building that can occur through dialogue between state and non-state actors during the negotiation and implementation of the agreement (Van den Putte 2016, 30). Thus, there may be little direct impact, but indirectly the use of dialogue may improve "respect" for labour rights as it provides spaces – or institutions – for learning and policy exchange.

Nevertheless, the institutional confusion and incoherence across the EU in regards to social chapters has allowed for the possible to be sidestepped. Across the EU-led agreements there is little coherence or standard language used, creating a multiplicity of requirements with little common ground. It has been shown that the way that the EU pursues social clauses tends to differ between each agreement; they have broadened over time in their normative content and scope, but are inconsistent between trading partners (Ebert and Posthuma 2011, 13-14). This can lead to competition between different chapters and a lack of detailed knowledge of each agreement across EU departments. There has also been a shift away from including ILS as human rights towards sustainable development – a much less defined and enforceable concept. The shift away from more-politicized labour or human rights terminology towards sustainable development, reflects the highly charged and ongoing debate over the relationship between FTAs and ILS (Schmieg 2014, 8). This has had problematic repercussions regarding who the right department is for managing

---

[9] Within the EU Korea agreement there is only mention of the *intention* to ratify conventions not the *need* to ratify, meaning that Korea has made little move towards ratification. The Korean government has signaled that it is *considering* ratifying conventions 95 and 118 and some changes may be made regarding the Trade Union and Labour Relations Adjustment Act, however, these actions, if they come to pass, cannot be solely attributed to the agreement as form part of a larger policy framework (Van den Putte 2016, 88–9).

these complaints and negotiations; should it be DG Trade or DG Development or a mix of departments?

The growing importance of the EU parliament in the ratification of FTAs – a good thing in itself – has often further put the content of ILS at odds with the interests of the Commission and other specific departments in charge of overseeing the actual implementation of agreements. As such, there has been a lack of institutional ownership of labour issues, allowing for ILS to fall into the cracks between trade and development. As Van den Putte succinctly describes the lack of coordination between EU functions and policies can mean that the trade-labour linkage remains 'conveniently conflicted' and the EU can avoid doing anything on the issue (2016, 33).

Conditional Chapters: The US
Unlike the EU, the US has not ratified many key ILO conventions and thus has less international legitimacy on the issue of ILS, leading to some suspicion of an underlying protectionism. Despite these contradictions there seems to be more measureable impact of the US agreements, in part, because they have been largely following the same content and process since NAFTA. Research highlights that this impact is largely connected to: the public submissions process, regulatory change through pre-ratification conditionality, the dialogue forums which allow labour issues to be on the agenda in intergovernmental meetings, and the aid directed at targeted programs (Van den Putte 2016, 103).

There seems to be more coherence and policy coordination within the US approach compared to the EU, bringing together aid programs, policy development, and a common institutional framework. For example, the 2004 CAFTA-DR (Dominican Republic, Central America, and USA) agreement targeted the gap between law and enforcement through strengthening the capacity of labour institutions with specific target goals before ratification. After ratification this was followed up with development cooperation, monitoring, dialogue and $170million in capacity building aid (ILO 2016, 94). Increased coherence may be linked to the fact that all social chapters come under the ownership of the Department of Labour. Procedurally, there is an office within the labour ministry or a Joint Committee set up to oversee the chapter and a clear procedural guarantee with obligations for coordination. Also, unlike the EU approach, civil society groups can file public submissions when they believe violations have occurred, and there is the option for sanctions to be applied when all else fails (Anuradha and Dutta 2017, 21–2).

Critically, and differing from the EU approach, labour norms are regarded as trade issues and the dispute settlement mechanism is often applicable to the whole agreement including the labour chapter (Van den Putte 2016, 78). However, US agreements remain conservative in content by rarely going beyond original ILO commitments or existing domestic labour legislation; increasingly the 1998 ILO Declaration is referenced, although rarely specific conventions, furthermore the ILO tends to be excluded from any monitoring or advisory role (Anuradha and Dutta 2017, 18). In the most recent generation of US agreements (Peru onwards), the content has begun to go beyond already existing domestic labour law (Giumelli and van Roozendaal 2017, 41–2). However, in their 2017 study, Giumelli and van Roozendaal claim that despite being stronger in content and enforcement mechanisms, the recent generation of agreements have not been any more effective in improving ILS in trading partner countries, with only Colombia showing any measureable improvement (2017, 52).

When compared to the EU design, much noise is made over the ability of the US agreements to apply sanctions, yet these clauses are largely theoretical and rarely applied (they are usually fines rather than trade sanctions with amicable dispute resolution such as dialogue, preferred) (Ebert and Posthuma 2011, 10–11). For example, the NAALC chapter of NAFTA has had limited results, with many studies suggesting that this is because although sanctions can be employed, there is a lack of political will to use them, thus the impact was episodic rather than systematic (Greven 2005). This suggests that the US "conditional" approach is rarely fully employed, and instead, in practice both the EU and US tend to follow a soft approach, shying away from sanctions when they could be applied (Oehri 2015).

South-South Agreements
Many of the south-south agreements especially those negotiated between Asian counties tend to be in the form of side arrangements, and emphasize cooperation based on knowledge sharing and joint projects. They also tend to include provisions against the weakening of labour law for trade and investment purposes. Those that reference ILS as side arrangements usually do not have any legal consequences if they are breached, whereas those that are included in the main body tend to include a mix of promotional and conditional provisions, may be submitted to the regular dispute settlement mechanism, and can result in trade sanctions, although this is less common (Ebert and Posthuma 2011, 17).

Unilateral Approaches
The Generalized System of Preferences (GSP) is the dominant unilateral approach pursued by the EU and US in regards to ILS. The US GSP program was instituted in 1974, and currently 94 countries benefit from preferential trade arrangements (ILO 2016, 24). The EU has two unilateral programs – the Everything but Arms scheme open to Least Developing Countries (LDCs) and GSP+ scheme (ILO 2016, 25). A main difference between the EU and US design is that the EU labour provisions directly build on the ILO Conventions, and the US defines a list of internationally recognized workers' rights separate from the ILO Declaration (ILO 2016, 30). The US has suspended its GSP

program on four occasions – Belarus, Myanmar, Bangladesh and Swaziland. Whereas the EU has suspended its scheme three times: Myanmar (1996-2012), Belarus (2006 – ongoing), and in 2010 they downgraded Sri Lanka from GSP+ to the regular GSP scheme (ILO 2016, 33–4). The application of the GSP process has not been uniform across both the EU and US, instead it has been applied selectively and tends to reflect broader foreign policy objectives, again highlighting the conflicting role of the trade-labour linkage and often lack of political will in this area. For example, although Myanmar (then Burma) was removed by the EU, Colombia and Georgia both states with very poor ILS records (especially during this period) were given GSP+ status (Bakvis and McCoy 2008, 5). The recent case of Bangladesh within the EU GSP scheme is another case in point; where the US has removed Bangladesh from the scheme, the EU commission has not taken sufficient action to hold the government to account or investigate reported violations (Burrow and Visentini 2017).

In regards to improving working conditions, studies have shown that several countries have ratified ILO conventions in order to comply with the EU GSP scheme, however there has been no clear improvements in labour standards (Ebert and Posthuma 2011, 25). Although ratification of conventions has increased in GSP partner countries, so has criticism that 'ratification is cheap' and little real progress on the ground has been made (Orbie 2011, 171). The conditions that have increased the impact of the GSP scheme – especially in the US where civil society can make submissions – is the presence of strong domestic actors such as unions, who can add external pressure (as in the case of Burma). Yet, as Greven points out, the absence of strong domestic partners is often what has led to the violation in the first place (2005, 15). Furthermore, many are beginning to argue that the GSP system (especially in the US) is loosing its relevance as tariffs are becoming so low, and there has been a proliferation of bilateral trade agreements with previous GSP recipients undermining the benefits of preferential treatment through the scheme (Greven 2005, 11). Furthermore, in regards to the more hardline US approach, initial evidence suggests that after preferences are removed there is a scramble to show that improvements have been made, but whether they are long term – and sustainable – is up for debate (Brown 2007, 55). Critically the mid-term review of the EU GSP+ regime has found that there is no consensus on how effective the GSP regime has been in promoting human and labour rights (Development Solutions 2017, 31).

Chapter Design and Enforcement

As stated previously there is little conclusive evidence that social chapters in trade agreements have had any substantive impact on the enforcement of labour rights. This absence of enforcement of existing ILS and social chapters is linked to a lack of political will on both sides, coherence issues, capacity of government and institutions, regulation and legal frameworks, and perhaps most critically strong domestic civil society and social partners, in particular independent trade unions. Despite this, the specific design of social chapters – both promotional and conditional – in regards to content, institutional and social partner involvement, dispute settlement mechanisms, the use of sanctions, and monitoring, could contribute to the potential for these chapters to be enforced.

Content

Most agreements (both the US and EU) do not go beyond existing national regulation or norms. They can thus be considered conservative; pushing for the acceptance of already existing regulation, rather than improving the situation.

Previously the US had shied away from referencing the ILO, however there is a growing convergence between the EU and US agreements around content, with most now referencing the 1998 ILO Declaration, and at times, specific ILO conventions. This is a good shift for two key reasons, firstly, increasing international policy coherence will make the requirements more streamlined and easier for states to understand, follow up, and potentially enforce, what they have agreed to (Ebert and Posthuma 2011, 30). Critically, and why many criticize the EU "spaghetti bowl of tariffs" approach (Greven 2005, 41), multiple regimes with multiple demands puts both extra pressure on labour (or other respective) departments to keep on top of what is demanded, but also on social partners who do not necessarily have the capacity (knowledge, legal or monetary) to keep track of what is available to them.

Secondly, the deepening of commitments shows that there is a growing discursive shift towards recognizing the trade-labour linkage and importance of ILS. However, as Cabin (2009, 1081) asserts the ILO declaration is necessarily ambiguous and flexible, which can readily allow for the trade-labour linkage to be sidestepped in practice. For example, mentioning the 1998 ILO Declaration, although an important first step, does not provide any specific prescription on how these commitments are to occur, what they mean for the country in question, timetables, or repercussions (Cabin 2009, 1081). Within the EU agreements, the CARIFORUM EPA has been the most explicit in having an overarching goal of sustainable development with many parts of the agreement working together to push for this; it was not just an "add-on" social chapter but stipulated aid, capacity building, and an explicit goal of fighting poverty (Schmieg 2015, 21–3). Tensions over content and language can be seen in the EU-Korea agreement where it was agreed by the parties that Korea should move towards commitment to, and continuous improvement of, labour standards, but there are no repercussions for non-improvement, or specification on what "improvement" actually entails, meaning there was no space to move beyond dialogue (FES Korea 2016).

Another key element of the content of social chapters that feeds into enforcement is whether they are promotional or conditional. Those that are more promotional tend also to be more ambiguous, or less prescriptive in both content, and on how enforcement is to occur (as there is less to directly enforce). Whereas conditional chapters have more detail regarding processes, dispute settlement mechanisms, commitments and monitoring – although this is also not always the case. This raises a point over the type of language chapters' employ; the more direct and less ambiguous a chapter is, the less open to interpretation and thus dependent upon political will, they are (Greven 2005, 28). Interestingly, social chapters in bilateral agreements tend to be more aspirational, whereas unilateral programs (i.e. GSP scheme) are much more explicit in what they demand, how, and the repercussions for non-compliance (Polaski 2003).

Overall, conditional agreements are more likely to be enforced when they are ex-ante, demanding pre-ratification changes before the FTA comes into effect. Ex-ante conditionality aims at changing the law before ratification, whereas post-ratification (ex-post) aims more at the enforcement of existing law; thus, if the goal is to force a country to ratify new conventions, pre-ratification would be more applicable, and if it was more about the enforcement of existing laws vice versa. US chapters tend to follow this model, and there is some evidence to show that significant regulatory changes have occurred through their use in the US-Bahrain and Oman agreements; although the actual enforcement of these newly agreed to regulations is debatable (Giumelli and van Roozendaal 2017, 45). The TPP-Vietnam side letter was one recent example of ex-ante demands pushing for *increased* ILS, rather than the normal conservative commitment to uphold what already exists.

Institutional Design and Monitoring

The agreements that are more likely to be enforced seem to have either an ongoing and permanent institutional framework such as the Labour department in the US, or have the ILO as some sort of advisory or monitoring body. This is critically linked back to political will, coherence and legitimacy issues. Following on from the issues of ambiguity and interpretation, the ILO can have a neutralizing or de-politicizing role necessary to counter the at times competing political, economic or diplomatic interests. Across the board, the enforcement of social chapters seems to be dependent on the political constellation at the time, for example, in the case of the Korea-US FTA (KORUS) the vague wording of the clause means that Republican or Democratic governments can interpret it as they will, leading to inconsistent enforcement (Van den Putte 2015b, 227).

Research suggests that monitoring mechanisms that apply across multiple agreements tend to be more permanent and consistently enforced than those only applicable to single agreements. The US appears to be the leader in this with the most established and permanent advisory committees, however representation tends to be skewed towards the private sector (ILO 2016, 134). What is critical in the US approach is that monitoring is almost always housed within the Labour Department. This allows for more consistency across agreements, but also the creation of more permanent institutional frameworks, specific knowledge about labour issues, and coordination between other programs within the labour department such as aid and capacity building. However, this process is still heavily reliant on political will for complaints and issues to be taken any further. Because, despite the central and consistent role of the Department of Labor in monitoring social chapters, the President has the power to make the ultimate decision on whether the dispute process should be utilized, making the process politically vulnerable.

The EU does not have this consistency across each agreement; instead they tend to specify different monitoring or institutional frameworks depending on the trading partner. Becoming more common is some form of Domestic Advisory Group (DAG), where there is an allocated role for civil society groups within the monitoring process; however, these are more often temporary advisory committees around specific agreements such as TTIP where public interest is high. The DAGs are more formalized, but so far only the EU Korea DAG meets regularly, and not without some criticism (see below) (ILO 2016). EU monitoring mostly relies upon the designated office, or contact point, with less formalized access channels and processes beyond consultation. These consultation forums are heavily reliant on the political will of the EU to bring up labour issues in these meetings (Van den Putte, Orbie, and Bossuyt unpub.). The CARIFORUM EPA provided a somewhat novel mechanism for monitoring[10] that allowed for modifications of the agreement to occur if issues arose in the implementation process, and an annual meeting between the relevant authorities and consultative committee including civil society. However, the infrequent meetings (annually), and inadequate funding for these meetings seem to counter their effectiveness (Schmieg 2015, 26).

This suggests that there may be a need for an outside monitoring institution, such as the ILO, to remove part of this "political will" dependency. Most studies suggest that it is beneficial to have the ILO in some form of monitoring role as it takes away some of the "politics" attached to enforcement. However, the necessary pre-requisites for social dialogue (independent and relatively strong social partners and accountable institutions) is a big obstacle to the ILO and EU approaches, as it is far from reality or feasible in some regions and sectors. The lack of enforceability beyond the soft approach within the ILO is also a limitation (Sengenberger 2005, 101). Yet coherence with ILO conventions or an

---

[10] What is monitored through these mechanisms goes beyond labour rights including human rights and the environment through a broad sustainable development agenda.

ILO monitoring role may still have use; as although the US cases tend to have more notable impact, the lack of input from the ILO and the separation of the chapters from ILO jurisprudence can be problematic, especially when they are worded ambiguously, removing neutral oversight (Cabin 2009, 1047). Linking back to the use of social chapters in pushing for the ratification of new conventions, an interesting point is that following ratification the ILO supervisory mechanism can be applied to those states under those conventions, indirectly increasing the monitoring role of the ILO (Doumbia-Henry and Gravel 2006, 198).

Studies have also shown that the inclusion of the ILO as some sort of advisory body can be useful as they can provide technical assistance, monitoring, and coherence through the development of cooperation programs (ILO 2016, 9). However, within the US Cambodia Textile Agreement (1999-2005) and the subsequent Better Work Program, the centrality of the ILO at the expense of local NGOs and trade unions has come under some criticism for increasing dependence, and possibly hindering the development of such groups (Berik and Rodgers 2010, 25).

Dispute Settlement Mechanism

A key difference between the US and EU is the way that the dispute settlement mechanism is designed – underpinned by either pressure or dialogue. Most US labour chapters, due to the explicit relationship between trade and labour, extends the normal mechanism to the labour chapters. This has been the case since NAFTA, where findings of the dispute settlement procedure are binding, and if the recommendations are not adhered to a monetary fine and then sanctions can be applied. However what was covered by NAALC is very narrow, limited to child labour, OHS and minimum wage standards and to date no case has reached the point of sanctions (ILO 2016, 44). Yet, as previously mentioned the US enforcement process is not judicial but rather political, for example, the labour office came under increased pressure to close under the Bush administration, showing that the power – and interpretation – of labour chapters are vulnerable to the politics of those in power (Greven 2005, 35–6). Interestingly, the US-Peru agreement was the first example where through the inclusion of specific ILO conventions in the labour chapter, and the extension of the dispute settlement mechanism to the labour provisions, there was 'an enforceable obligation to adopt and maintain the principles recognized in the ILO declaration within domestic law.' (Cabin 2009, 1073). This highlights how the different ILS systems such as the ILO and social chapters can work in tandem potentially complementing each other.

Conversely, the EU approach has been more promotional, employing dialogue and cooperation when violations occur. Apart from the EU-CARIFORUM agreement there is no option for sanctions or suspension of trade benefits, and the dispute process goes no further than necessary dialogue. Since the EU-CARIFORUM agreement the dispute settlement mechanism has got more substantial, shifting from government consultation to a Panel of Experts, but there still remains no provisions for enforcement, meaning only soft pressure can be applied (Schmieg 2014, 6). Across most agreements, when disputes arise the parties are required to consult with one another and take the ILO's activities/recommendations into consideration. If all else fails, they can request that the Trade and Sustainable Development Sub-Committee be convened where recommendations will be made, and from which the parties need to then take adequate steps. However, the current issues plaguing the EU-Korea dispute process suggest that continued dialogue is not always enough (ILO 2016, 42). This may also be tied to the ambiguous wording of "improvements" and the contradictory claims by Korea and the EU over how much improvement has been made in reference to the ratification of ILO conventions (FES Korea 2016). The Colombia EU agreement has also come under fire, as although it is quite good on content, the only enforcement avenues available are dialogue and cooperation and thus there is no legal enforceability (Orbie 2011, 175).

The inclusion of some form of public submissions process such as that in the US-Guatemala agreement, which allows for civil society groups to participate and lodge complaints, tend to result in more enforcement as there is a designated role for social partners to push political will. This is directly connected to how the institutional and dispute settlement mechanism are designed to allow for social partners to have an unambiguous role in proceedings. Critically, outside pressure can help enforce the political will of trading partners who may be unwilling to pursue these issues otherwise. However, such a submission process relies on strong domestic social partners, especially trade unions, being able to access these channels; having the necessary knowledge, capacity, and faith in the process to do so. In best practice examples, this has resulted in transnational linkages occurring between trading partner trade unions, strengthening solidarity, dialogue, and knowledge sharing (although this is not the norm!). For example, within the US-Guatemala agreement the AFL-CIO and Guatemalan trade unions lodged a shared complaint against Guatemala over their failure to comply with their labour rights obligations (ILO 2016, 45). This led to increased transnational advocacy networks.

However, as most submissions continue to fail and are not adequately followed up, submissions can begin to tail off due to "submission fatigue" (Greven 2005, 35). As Greven concludes; 'if unions and NGOs stop using it (submissions process) because it is too expensive and ineffective, cooperative activities may also end altogether' (Greven 2005, 38). There is hope that the proposed civil society forums in the new round of EU FTAs may lead to increased respect for labor rights through knowledge transfer and indirect transnational linkages, as has occasionally occurred through the US public submissions process (Van den Putte and Orbie 2015, 271).

Engagement of Social Partners

It is argued that the inclusion of civil society groups in both the development and implementation of social chapters will give much needed legitimacy to future agreements and trade-labour linkages (Van den Putte 2016, 36). There has been a steady increase in mechanisms that could lead to more involvement of civil society stakeholders in the design and implementation of FTAs across both EU and US agreements (ILO 2016, 127). However, these mechanisms have been rarely used in practice. This is connected to the issues that affect enforceability in the first place, such as the accessibility of the mechanism, or the absence of independent trade unions or civil society groups making any mechanism somewhat redundant. Enforcement relies upon strong unions at all levels; local, national and global (Bakvis and McCoy 2008, 11), and when social partners and civil society groups are included in an unambiguous and meaningful way, enforcement is much more likely to occur. However, inclusion must be meaningful, as social partners need to see value in participating; yet the interests involved in the negotiation of FTAs tends to mean that the cards are stacked against them (i.e. ISDS clauses and accessibility) (Scherrer and Beck 2016).

To date, no FTA has significantly involved civil society groups in the negotiation process. The way that social partners have been included in the social chapter after ratification differs slightly between the EU and US. The public submissions process in the US approach, is an important channel not available in EU agreements, meaning there is a lack of formal feedback mechanisms (ILO 2016, 137-8). Another difference is that the EU stipulates regular meetings with civil society, whereas the US enters into dialogue only once a problem arises (Van den Putte 2016, 75–6). The EU-CARIFORUM EPA signaled a shift in European policy around civil society engagement (Schmieg 2015, 28). However, to date, civil society forums in European led FTAs have only been fully implemented and meet regularly in the EU-Korea agreement, and not without significant controversy (Van den Putte 2015b, 222). Notably, in the case of the EU-Korea civil society forum, the forum has been plagued with issues as the Korean government has been accused of handpicking government friendly NGOs and civil society groups to participate, as a response there has been a seemingly never ending dialogue process between the two governments with little tangible results (FES Korea 2016; ILO 2016, 147). The failure of the governments or mechanisms to fully address civil society concerns in the EU Korea agreement may limit its ongoing efficacy, as civil society groups loose faith, or develop dialogue fatigue, and cannot see any tangible benefits in continuing the process.

The EU-Peru and Colombia agreements have also had disputes over civil society participants, questioning the legitimacy of these dialogue forums as little policy space has actually been given to social partners, and the specificities of the issues are rarely addressed (Van den Putte 2016, 91).[11] The problems surrounding this obviously relate to a lack of political will within trading partners, but also the ambiguity in the wording of the clause that left these decisions somewhat up to interpretation. Furthermore, where trading partners either do not have a tradition of dialogue, or hold a different conception of what social dialogue is, the focus on such processes can lead to ineffectiveness (i.e. in Korea) (FES Korea 2016). This highlights the constraints of such a model when strong social partners and independent trade unions, not least to say, this tradition of cooperation, is not in place.[12] Ultimately the effectiveness of these forums rely upon them meeting regularly, with key labour groups in attendance, government consultations where labour rights issues can be raised, and the capacity of transnational advocacy networks developing outside these forums (Van den Putte and Orbie 2015, 272).

Because there has been little recognized benefits from participation in these forums, there is growing civil society fatigue (especially in regards to EU Korea or the NAALC process) (Lukas and Steinkellner 2010, 4). The more often that suggestions and complaints from civil society groups are not taken up, the less likely these actors will be to participate in the future (Van den Putte 2016, 93). That the negotiation of agreements takes place behind closed doors, and trade unions and other civil society groups are often unable to participate in forums or implementation processes post-ratification due to limited access and capacity, further weakens any social footing that such agreements purport to hold (Lukas and Steinkellner 2010, 3). In regards to the EU-Korea, EU-Colombia and EU-Peru agreements, dialogue fatigue has set in with little realized change. This is exacerbated by the ineffective DAG process, little connection between the domestic and transnational bodies, the government oversight of these forums (for example in Colombia civil society groups participated in forums where government bodies were present and thus had little real ability for open and transparent discussion), selective selection of civil society participants in the case of Korea, little trade union faith in the process, and finally a lack of financing that has made them inaccessible to trade union and civil society

---

[11] The CARIFORUM Civil society forum has also not taken place for many years because of an ongoing dispute over who should participate.

[12] This is also reflected in the EU-Peru and EU- Colombia agreements where dialogue has not been effective because the necessary pre-conditions (strong social partners and experience with social dialogue) were not in place, creating an ineffective policy design for the context-specific conditions of those countries, as well as forums where trade unionists felt threatened by the presence of government bodies who had been instrumental in their persecution (Van den Putte 2016, 94).

groups (Van den Putte 2016, 94–5). This is an access issue tied both to knowledge of how the processes work within base level union membership, and what their rights are, but also the cost of participating in endless negotiations.

Studies suggest that those where the design is complex, hard to navigate, lengthy, and costly, dissuade social partners from participating, and thus limit their effectiveness (Ebert and Posthuma 2011, 24). Critically and poignantly Van den Putte notes that none of the civil society groups perceive the EUs trade-labour linkage as 'providing them with a strong tool to improve their labour situation.' And very few civil society groups are even aware of the obligations their governments have agreed to, or the tools available to them in the agreements (Van den Putte 2016, 101).[13]

Furthermore, within European civil society organizations there is also a reluctance to take part in a mechanism that would oversee the implementation of a trade agreement that they do not agree with; there is a continuous insider-outsider dilemma for civil society groups with the possibility of giving legitimacy to bad agreements. This can mean that those that do participate may not actually be representative. Exacerbating this is the limited access of stakeholders to texts under negotiation. Where some access has occurred, most still see this as lacking transparency, with many meetings such as the Civil Society Dialogue on Trade within the EU, acting more as an information session rather than real dialogue or two-way discussion. The secrecy surrounding the negotiation of the recent TTIP agreement is a case in point (Scherrer 2014, 1). The inclusion of social partners in TTIP perhaps warrants a specific mention as it represents the new generation of regional/bilateral FTAs including CETA, TPP, and TISA and many have hailed its social chapter as progressive. Importantly, and as stated previously, in most of these analyses the social chapter is considered in isolation from the rest of the agreement that undermines the capacity of public institutions, and gives more power to capital at the expense of labour around issues of accessibility. Yet, when looking specifically at the social chapter, although maybe more extensive content-wise than previous agreements, the proposals around monitoring and implementation are vague, and the inclusion of civil society is limited to the right to be 'informed' and 'heard', as such there is no explicit mention of influence, prescriptive dispute processes, or sanctions (Beck 2014, 20).

Sanctions or Incentives

There is an ongoing debate over whether, and if so what type of, sanctions should be used in regards to ILS in social chapters. The lack of sanctions within EU agreements has often been cited as the reason behind their lack of

---

[13] Notably EU based trade unions are an exception to this, highlighting the uneven power dynamics across trade unions within trading partners.

enforcement, but the reality is more complex (Giumelli and van Roozendaal 2017, 45). Although sanctions are never explicitly outlined in the EU chapters there is one avenue open to sanctions being utilized; because social rights can be included in the essential elements clause this can also mean that once the non-enforceable dispute mechanism has been exhausted, this clause could be utilized possible resulting in the suspension of trade benefits (Van den Putte and Orbie 2015, 270). Nonetheless this is probably not likely to ever occur.

Some argue that sanctions are likely to do more harm than good to developing economies (Maskus, n.d., 1) and thus wind back ILS gains; as punitive trade restrictions for non-compliance or enforcement can lead to job losses in developing countries, hurting those that ILS are aiming to benefit (Singh and Zammit 2000, xv). Citing another extensive study on the effectiveness of sanctions, Michael Ewing-Chow states that in over 100 cases economic sanctions have only worked about a third of the time (although even this may be overstated), and that sanctions often impact citizens more than those in power (Ewing-Chow 2007, 153–4). A way around this would be to 'emphasize incentives for labour standards compliance,' rather than punitive action for violations (Berik and Rodgers 2010, 4). In Singh and Zammit's study (2000, xv) on the promotion of ILS in developing economies, they suggest that adherence is more likely to occur through the provision of technical and financial assistance, alongside cooperation with domestic and international civil society groups, rather than through punitive or sanction-based mechanisms. This is also backed up by Greven (2005), and Lukas and Steinkellner's (2010) reports, that show that the presence of sanctions is not as critical, rather, it is the capacity of local trade unions, labor inspectorates and programs targeted at specific labour rights issues, which have the most impact for the enforcement of ILS. Consistently, incentives rather than sanctions appear to be most effective, as instead of shaming countries into action, which can have political fallout (and thus limit political will to enforce) this could also be linked to capacity building and development aid around country-specific goals (Ebert and Posthuma 2011, 29).

The US approach has aid and institutional frameworks for capacity building around labour issues built into their social chapters to a much larger degree (content and monetary wise) than EU FTAs (Doumbia-Henry and Gravel 2006, 194). Thus, although sanctions are on offer, what is actually more utilized are the aid or capacity building projects, which may be the most effective part of the agreements (Doumbia-Henry and Gravel 2006, 194). The US-Chile (2004) agreement falls somewhere in the middle, and has been cited as potential best practice; it includes the payment of fines into a fund for improving the specific labour rights violations that occurred, alongside the removal of trade preferences as a last resort (Lukas and Steinkellner 2010, 7). The US-Cambodia textile agreement (1999-2005) is another fairly successful example of this; incentives in the form of increased quotas for Cambodian textile imports into the US were directly linked to the improvement of factory safety and labour rights in the sector (Scherrer and Beck 2016, 14). The small positive steps seen in Cambodia in respect to labour rights in the garment industry, may be attributed to Better Factories Cambodia which grew out of this project (Berik and Rodgers 2010, 3).

Despite these critiques, the presence of sanctions may have a role to play. Firstly, their presence can act as a deterrent (although this is hard to measure or prove) and they can also do reputational damage for the country in question, providing political leverage beyond the economic scope of the agreement (Ebert and Posthuma 2011, 21). Any direct causality is hard to show, but this idea that they may act as a disincentive is commonly held (Anuradha and Dutta 2017, 26). Yet, even when sanctions are available most disputes never reach this point, suggesting that in reality there is not as much difference between the promotional and conditional approaches when it comes to enforcement through sanctions. Furthermore, there is an inconsistent application of the sanctions process undermining the perceived threat of their presence. The removal of trade preferences under the unilateral approach of both the EU and US GSP system has been employed much more than any FTA process (Ebert and Posthuma 2011, 21). There is some evidence that the use of sanctions under the GSP scheme did improve the political situation in the target states by weakening business support for the regimes (Giumelli and van Roozendaal 2017, 46). However, until 2011 none of the labor provisions in US trade agreements (where sanctions are available) had resulted in their use (Ebert and Posthuma 2011, 23–4). This highlights the necessary (and currently lacking) political will of trading partners to follow through on what they have agreed to, and potential lack of social partner capacity – or faith – in pursuing this process.

Reflecting the debate over dialogue versus pre-ratification conditionality, economic sanctions can have effect in pushing forward legislative changes, but may have little impact on pushing through changes in attitudes, behaviors and beliefs. This backs up the claim that although you can force ratification, this doesn't work in the case of enforcement, which is more complex. Whether or not sanctions do act as a deterrent, what does limit their effectiveness is their inconsistent application (both through the GSP and FTA approach). What is more important is that there are clear unambiguous directives about what happens when violations occur, a well devised process, and consistent application, otherwise – as we see with the current US sanctions system that is rarely utilized – it becomes somewhat meaningless. If sanctions exist they must be consistently and quickly applied to have affect and act as a deterrent to others (Giumelli and van Roozendaal 2017, 45).

Recommendations

In suggesting possible ways forward, what is critical to keep in mind is that there is little conclusive evidence that social chapters in trade agreements have been effective in promoting and enforcing labour rights. This can be down to numerous factors, the first being the problematic relationship of liberalization and ILS especially when NTBs are becoming the target of trade agreements. Secondly, there is a lack of *enforcement* of the existing provisions in social chapters. So, putting aside whether or not liberalization can benefit ILS, there may be certain issues and designs of social chapters that can best encourage enforcement. Enforcement comes down to political will, attitudinal change and the presence of strong independent trade unions; it is more complex than whether or not sanctions are included. What is clear is that there is no one size fits all policy prescription, and that each condition (political will, capacity, regulation, independent social partners...) is dependent on the other, meaning that for successful policy each must be addressed rather than seen as isolated or independent variables; isolating and directing impact towards only one issue will most likely open up a Pandora's box of other limitations. For example, an effective labour chapter needs a clear dispute resolution system beyond mere dialogue, yet even dialogue requires the participation of civil society groups such as trade unions, however trade unions may well be unlikely to want to participate and give legitimacy to firstly, an agreement that undermines key rights and issues in the public good (i.e. new generation of FTAs tackling NTBs), and furthermore, dialogue fatigue will set in if their concerns are not addressed, or the processes outlined for participation are seen as rubber stamping, or lacking bite. Starting from this, it appears that the design of an agreement needs to comprehensively address all these concerns to have the most potential for success. Despite these restraints some recommendations can be made around the design of any future social chapter:

- *The design, monitoring and implementation of the chapter must be accessible to social partners; this includes meaningful engagement, and consideration of capacity constraints.*

In pushing governments to enforce these agreements political will is often forced upon them either through external pressure from civil society – requiring knowledge of the agreement and capacity from such groups – or internally through dispute processes and channels, again requiring certain knowledge, time and faith in such processes. Issues of access plague most agreements, raising broader questions around what types of resources (knowledge or monetary) are required to access the dispute or monitoring processes? Is it prohibitive to workers and their organizations? And do the necessary social partners firstly exist, and secondly, have the capacity to use these tools? The cost and time of dispute procedures must also be taken into account as being normally prohibitive to under-resourced and time-poor trade unions that do not have the capacity to pursue such avenues when there is at least historically little evidence of success. The further ingraining of these mechanisms into ISDS clauses and the language of investment rights rather than human rights, further excludes such groups from the necessary background knowledge required to comprehend and make use of these tools. Funding to finance participation is key to allow for diverse and representative participation in numerous civil society forums (Van den Putte 2015a). A public submissions process such as in the US, teamed with strict monitoring and timely procedures could help. What might also abet some of these issues could be the US approach of holding one meeting for discussion with civil society groups regarding all trade agreements rather than requiring civil society to participate in separate and frequent meetings on all agreements (how the EU chapters are designed), stretching already low resources.[14]

- *Social chapters need to be coherent across and within agreements.*

Coherence is the other key issue that severely limits the enforcement of ILS. Currently there is a lack of coherence across multiple levels; the relationship between the social chapter and the motivations of the rest of agreement, the lack of coherent application of existing procedures and specifically in relation to the EU, a lack of coherence across EU institutions and policy "ownership". Does the procedure relate to one or more agreement? Or are civil society groups and government bodies required to understand the nuances of each social chapter within each FTA? If it is a case-by-case basis this increases the workload of civil society groups and thus probably decreases their ability to participate, as well as the capacity of governments to monitor commitments. Furthermore, the impact of labour provisions is dependent on their relationship with the other provisions in the agreement (Gravel, Kohiyama, and Tsotroudi 2011, 11). The EU's move towards subsuming ILS into much broader and less defined sustainable development chapters further facilitates the lack of ownership of these issues across departments, taking them further away from a core human rights agenda. There is little substantive or prescriptive definition of what sustainable development in relation to labour rights should mean in practice, as such 'if trade agreements lack concrete strategic goals, it becomes hard to design concrete policy.' (Van den Putte 2015a, 80). Critically, on a more macro level there is also a lack of coherence between the US and EU, muddling the field for trading partners over what is demanded of them, returning to this idea of a spaghetti bowl of regulation straining the already limited capacity of labor and

---

[14] However the US approach is not without complaint, where criticism has been leveled at the meeting structure that certain agreements are not discussed or examples of labour rights violations being "ranked" meaning those considered of less importance not discussed due to time constraints (For example the focus was on Colombia rather than Korea) (Van Den Putte 2015b, 230).

trade departments and civil society groups, such as trade unions. Transnational cooperation could be improved through collaboration between governments when trade agreements are being negotiated at the same time.[15] Furthermore, regular Human Rights Impact Assessments would be beneficial to explore how the rest of the agreement and social chapter are compatible and the impact that they will have/are having. A standard social chapter design might also be useful.

- *The 1998 ILO Declaration and key conventions should form the basis of what is included in social chapters. The ILO could also act in a consultative capacity or in a third party monitoring role.*

The move towards the inclusion of ILO standards is a good step towards increased coherence and convergence of the multiple ILS regimes and should be encouraged. Although there are obvious weaknesses of the ILO (due mostly to lack of enforcement), these limitations and the content/coherence limitations of existing agreements could be overcome if the ILO conventions as well as 1998 Declaration formed the basis of social chapters, and were directly linked to explicit mechanisms in the agreement (Cabin 2009, 1068). The ILO also offers an important monitoring opportunity, countering to some degree the politics of enforcement[16]. The use of the ILO as an independent body to monitor this alongside a transparent public submissions process (i.e. that complaints will be listened to and addressed) may alleviate some of these limitations. This in turn will require that ILO reports be credible, timely and transparent.

- *Pre-ratification conditions should be employed to push for regulatory changes beyond existing ILS commitments*

Where social chapters may have the most tangible and to some extent more pragmatic impact may be in pushing for regulative change through pre-ratification conditionality. The pressure that FTAs can exert onto countries during negotiations has been shown in the recent side letter of the TPP between Vietnam and the US. This extra pressure from the trade negotiations, alongside lengthy dialogue and pressure campaigns may result in Vietnam ratifying some new ILO conventions, and altering their domestic legislation to allow for increased freedom of association. Critically, these shifts cannot be put down solely to the TPP, as it formed one tool in the diplomatic toolbox of the US, and added extra pressure to negotiations with the EU during recent years, but it does

---

[15] Increased cooperation may be hard to facilitate through agreements that have increased competition at their heart – highlighting the conflicting nature of trade (competition) and labour (cooperation).

[16] It must be noted that the ILO is not at all free from politics. As we have seen in the recent protracted stalemate over the right to strike the tripartite body is often highly political, yet what is meant here is that it removes the domestic (and potentially competing) economic or diplomatic concerns from overriding violations of ILS; the ILO can act as the mediator or watchdog.

show that when working in partnership with other policies, social chapters in FTAs may facilitate regulative change. Pre-ratification commitments have also been shown to be useful in pushing regulative changes in the US-Oman, and US-Bahrain agreements.

Pre-ratification conditions are most likely to be enforced (or carried out) as they provide a clear prescription for what is demanded, when, and how. They are measureable, allowing them to sidestep some of the issues plaguing other areas of enforcement; as such they should be fully embraced and extended to as many regulatory areas as is feasible. FTAs can demand that certain conventions or regulatory changes are made prior to the agreement coming into force. These conditions could be extended to the building up of labour inspectorates or capacity building programs to assist trading partners to meet these demands. Potentially such demands could also work with the promotion of a living wage or be used in regional agreements to work with domestic campaigners to legislate for a regional living wage such as the Asian Floor wage campaign.

- *The monitoring and institutional design of the chapter must be clearly defined. This should include regular and consistent department meetings and social partners and civil society groups must be meaningfully included in the process.*

Regarding the inclusion of civil society, Van den Putte suggests that this must be obligatory and specific in how this is to work – it cannot be left up to government discretion to consult civil society as the 'more precise the formulation, the higher the level of institutionalization.' (Van den Putte 2015b, 225). Such a process could use the current DAGs format as a starting point, teamed with public submissions and some formalized role for civil society in the dispute settlement process. However, these processes must be open and safe; the main purpose of civil society meetings or forums need to be addressed on a case by case basis dependent on how much experience the trading partner has in regards to their experience of social dialogue procedures, as well as the matureness of the mechanism, or even how viable/safe dialogue between these groups may be (Van den Putte, Orbie, and Bossuyt unpub.). Replicating the US approach where the Department of Labor is responsible for all social chapters seems to be the most effective institutional design if it is paired with regular and locked-in meetings with civil society groups. There is also space for the ILO to play a role either as a last resort in disputes or in a consultative or chairing capacity. A panel of experts made of a mix of the social partners from both trading partners could also be beneficial. Meetings and consultative forums should meet more than annually and funding and access issues addressed (Lukas and Steinkellner 2010, 12).

- *The Dispute Settlement Mechanisms must be timely, transparent, include social partners and be accessible. This same mechanism should apply across the whole agreement.*

Including the social chapter under the same mechanism as the rest of the agreement aids in coherence as well as reinforces the trade-labour linkage, further integrating ILS into economic trade concerns. As stated previously, the success of the social chapter resides on social partners seeing that it is useful to them and enforced. The direct and meaningful involvement of social partners through public submissions or a seat at the table would help this, as would making the process more transparent and accountable. In practice this could include stakeholders in some form of tripartite committee and the possibility for a third party chairperson (i.e. maybe the ILO) to act if resolution is not possible. The speed of such processes should be at the forefront to avoid ongoing delays, with space for public submissions and time stipulations on how quickly such problems or submissions should be addressed. This could include national contact points and individual petitions (Bartels 2014, 17). In their draft social chapter, Lukas and Steinkellner suggest that submissions should be addressed within 90 days (2010, 20–22).

- *Sanctions should be available but should work alongside incentives, capacity building programs and aid.*

Sanctions should be considered as a last resort and act as some form of deterrent. If teamed with a prescriptive and non-negotiable dispute settlement mechanism the application of sanctions may become more consistent. This should work in three steps; firstly, consultation, secondly, a monetary fine if the violation is not resolved before finally, resorting to the removal of trading preferences. Ideally, and following the model of many Canadian FTAs (Peru (2009) and Chile (2004)), the monetary fine should go into a fund that would specifically target the labour violation under consideration (Lukas and Steinkellner 2010, 7). Where this fine is not paid within the given time frame then there could be a suspension of trade benefits, but this would be the last resort. Working alongside these more punitive measures could be some form of incentive scheme with increasing market access or aid when certain ILS markers are reached; a form of post-ratification conditionality. The US agreements that link aid programs and capacity building training to country-specific issues that arise through the negotiation and monitoring stages of the agreement seem to be best practice, and have measurable impact. If these programs could be developed in partnership with independent domestic trade unions, this would be especially beneficial and may also counter some of the pushback from such groups.

Conclusion: Smart Design and Mobilization

Ultimately, the enforcement of social clauses relies on smart design but also the more macro level confluence between legal, political and development cooperation, and the need for legal resources to be combined with political pressure (ILO 2016, 128). Civil society and social partners play a crucial role in the functioning of labour provisions. For this reason, they must be involved from the early stages, allowing for better implementation and increasing transparency of the procedures (Ebert and Posthuma 2011, 30). As Greven describes, labour rights mechanisms will only work when there are domestic actors who can make use of them and where these processes can act as extra pressure points for transnational campaigns; they are not an end in themselves finishing at ratification (Greven 2005, 38).

The agreements need to be coherent on numerous levels – building on the ILO CLSs would be a starting point. This could allow for both civil society groups and governments with limited resources to have some better understanding of what they need to implement; otherwise this can be a repetition of the numerous and largely ineffective MSI regimes. There must also be coherence amongst relevant EU agencies, as although the trade-labour linkage is accepted in a normative way, how this is to be actualized is not clear, and seems to differ across agencies. The US approach where one department (Labor) has responsibility and plays an active and, to some extent, coherent role should be replicated. This will also counter any lack of political will, by limiting opportunities for the buck to be passed. Linked to this, is the need for agreements and labour chapters to be clear on what is required throughout the dispute settlement procedures or the makeup of DAGs (i.e. see the issues that have plagued the EU Korea agreement).

Furthermore, timeframes and outcomes need to be prescribed in the agreement in as clear and direct language as possible to avoid miscommunication or different interpretations (on both sides). Following this, sanctions do not seem to be the determining factor of enforcement, instead it is consistency across the procedures and use of incentives such as increased trade access, aid or capacity building programs that appear most effective. As such, some sort of mix of the three teamed with an unequivocal dispute procedure where the concerns of civil society groups, such as trade unions, are given *real* space may be most effective.

Critically for any social clause to work or have impact there needs to be buy-in from civil society, which on a larger scale requires the re-building of trust in, and legitimacy of, the power of trade agreements to benefit workers and not just the wealthy few. This will require a re-socialization of trade agreements, more transparent negotiation and opportunities for independent civil society to participate, and have power, in the negotiation, implementation, and enforcement of the agreement. It will also require more detailed and compulsory impact assessments including human rights, the environment, and labour (Schillinger 2016, 3). The corporate agenda cannot be the driving force behind such agreements, rather they must allow for policy space for states to regulate in the public interest, irreversibility clauses must be blocked, compensation schemes outlined, and participation mechanisms and accessibility issues addressed (Schillinger 2016, 5). As Ebert and Posthuma summarize in their detailed study of social clauses 'given that challenges in the promotion of labour standards often have multiple roots, an integrated and multi-faceted approach seems most promising,' (Ebert and Posthuma 2011, 29). Social chapters need to be understood as one part of a policy mix rather than a solution in themselves.

References

Anuradha, R, and Nimisha Singh Dutta. 2017. 'Trade and Labour under the WTO and FTAs'. Centre for WTO Studies. Accessed January 14. http://wtocentre.iift.ac.in/Papers/Trade%20Labour%20Study.pdf.

Bakvis, Peter, and Molly McCoy. 2008. 'Core Labour Standards And International Organizations: What Inroads Has Labour Made?' Briefing papers 6. Global Trade Union Porgram. Friedrich Ebert Stiftung. http://library.fes.de/pdf-files/iez/05431.pdf.

Bartels, Lorand. 2014. 'The European Parliament's Role in Relation to Human Rights in Trade and Investment Agreements'. Directorate-General for Extrernal Policies of the Union. Policy Department Study. European Parliament. http://www.europarl.europa.eu/RegData/etudes/etudes/join/2014/433751/EXPO-JOIN_ET(2014)433751_EN.pdf.

Beck, Stefan. 2014. 'Assessing TTIP and Its Supporting Studies'. In *The Transatlantic Trade and Investment Partnership (TTIP): Implications for Labor*, edited by Christoph Scherrer. Vol. 5. Labor and Globalization. München: Rainer Hampp Verlag.

Berik, Günseli, and Yana Van Der Meulen Rodgers. 2010. 'Options for Enforcing Labour Standards: Lessons from Bangladesh And Cambodia'. *Journal of International Development* 22 (1): 56–85. doi:10.1002/jid.1534.

Brown, Drusila. 2007. 'Globailization and Employment Conditions Study'. Tufts University.

Burrow, Sharon, and Luca Visentini. 2017. 'GSP Eligibility for Bangladesh. Addressed to the European Parliament, EU International Trade Committee and EU Human Rights Committee', January 18.

Cabin, Michael A. 2009. 'Labor Rights in the Peru Agreement: Can Vague Principles Yield Concrete Change?' *Columbia Law Review* 109 (5): 1047–93.

Development Solutions. 2017. 'Interim Evaluation of the EU's Generalized Scheme of Preferences (GSP): Draft Inception Report'. European Commision. http://www.gspevaluation.com/wp-content/uploads/2016/12/Draft-Inception-Report-GSP-Evaluation-09-01-2016-clean.pdf.

Doumbia-Henry, Cleopatra, and Eric Gravel. 2006. 'Free Trade Agreements and Labour Rights: Recent Developments'. *International Labour Review* 145 (3).

Eberhardt, Pia. 2014. 'Assymetry: Investor and Labor Rights, Investment Protection at a Crossroads'. In *The Transatlantic Trade and Investment Partnership (TTIP):*

Implications for Labor, edited by Christoph Scherrer. Vol. 5. Labor and Globalization. München: Rainer Hampp Verlag.

Ebert, Franz, and Anne Posthuma. 2011. 'Labour Provisions in Trade Arrangements: Current Trends and Perspectives'. Discussion Paper Series. Geneva: International Institute for Labour Studies.

ETUC. n.d. 'TTIP Sustainable Development Chapter: Labour Issues'. ETUC.

Ewing-Chow, Michael. 2007. 'First Do No Harm: Myanmar Trade Sanctions and Human Rights'. *Northwestern Journal of Human Rights* 5 (2): 153.

FES Korea. 2016. 'Evaluation of the Korea-EU FTA's Labor Standards Provisions and Their Implementation Status'. Interim Report. Friedrich Ebert Stiftung.

Giumelli, Francesco, and Gerda van Roozendaal. 2017. 'Trade Agreements and Labour Standards Clauses: Explaining Labour Standards Developments through a Qualitative Comparative Analysis of US Free Trade Agreements'. *Global Social Policy* 17 (1): 38–61. doi:10.1177/1468018116637209.

Gravel, Eric, Tomi Kohiyama, and Katerina Tsotroudi. 2011. 'A Legal Perspective on the Role of International Labour Standards in Rebalancing Globalization'. In *The Role of International Labour Standards in Rebalancing Globalization*. ILO, Geneva: International Labour Office.

Greven, Thomas. 2005. 'Social Standards in Bilateral and Regional Trade and Investment Agreements: Instruments, Ebforcement, and Policy Options for Trade Unions'. 16. Dialogue on Globalization. Geneva: Friedrich Ebert Stiftung.

ILO. 2016. 'Assessment of Labour Provisions in Trade and Investment Arrangements'. Report. International Labour Organization. http://www.ilo.org/global/publications/books/WCMS_498944/lang--en/index.htm.

IUF. 2014. 'Trade Deals That Threaten Democracy'. In *The Transatlantic Trade and Investment Partnership (TTIP): Implications for Labor*, edited by Christoph Scherrer. Vol. 5. Labor and Globalization. München: Rainer Hampp Verlag.

Lukas, Karin, and Astrid Steinkellner. 2010. 'Social Standards in Sustainability Chapters of Bilateral Free Trade Agreements'. Wien: Ludwig Boltzmann Institute Human Rights.

Marceau, Gabrielle. 2009. 'Trade and Labour'. In *The Oxford Handbook of International Trade Law*, edited by Daniel Bethlehem, Donald McRae, Rodney Neufeld, and Isabelle Van Damme. OUP Oxford.

Maskus, Keith. n.d. 'Should Labor Standards Be Imposed Through International Trade Policy'. Colorado: World Bank.

Oehri, Myriam. 2015. 'Comparing US and EU Labour Governance "near and Far" – Hierarchy vs Network?' *Journal of European Public Policy* 22 (5): 731–49. doi:10.1080/13501763.2014.966743.

Orbie, Jan. 2011. 'Promoting Labour Standards Through Trade: Normative Power or Regulatory State Europe?' In *Normative Power Europe*, edited by Richard G. Whitman, 161–84. Palgrave Studies in European Union Politics. Palgrave Macmillan UK. http://link.springer.com/chapter/10.1057/9780230305601_9.

Polaski, Sandra. 2003. 'Trade and Labor Standards: A Strategy for Developing Countries'. Trade, Equity and Development Project. Carnegie Endowment for International Peace.

Scherrer, Christoph. 2014. 'Introduction: The Challenge of TTIP'. In *The Transatlantic Trade and Investment Partnership (TTIP): Implications for Labor*, edited by Christoph Scherrer. Vol. 5. Labor and Globalization. München: Rainer Hampp Verlag.

Scherrer, Christoph, and Stefan Beck. 2016. 'Trade Regulations and Global Production Networks'. No. 43. Working Paper. Germany: Global Labour University.

Schillinger, Hubert Rene. 2016. 'In Need of Rethinking: Trade Policies in Times of De-Globalisation'. Dialogue on Globalization. Friedrich Ebert Stiftung.

Schmieg, Evita. 2014. 'Human Rights and Sustainability in Free Trade Agreements: Can the Cariforum-EU Economic Partnership Agreement Serve as a Model?' 24. SWP Comments. Stiftung Wissenschaft und Politik. https://www.swp-berlin.org/fileadmin/contents/products/comments/2014C24_scm.pdf.

———. 2015. 'Trade and Investment Agreements for Sustainable Development? Lessons from the EU's Economic Partnerhsip Agreement with the Caribbean'. 6. SWP Research Paper. Berlin: Stiftung Wissenschaft und Politik. https://www.swp-berlin.org/fileadmin/contents/products/research_papers/2015_RP06_scm.pdf.

Sengenberger, Werner. 2005. 'Gloablization and Social Progress: The Role and Impact of International Labour Standards'. Global Trade Union Program. Bonn: Friedrich Ebert Stiftung.

Singh, Ajit, and Ann Zammit. 2000. 'The Global Labour Standards Controversy: Critical Issues for Developing Countries'. South Perspectives. The South Centre.

Van den Putte, Lore. 2015a. 'Divided We Stand: The European Parliament's Position on Social Trade in the Post-Lisbon Era : Global Governance of Labour Rights Assessing the Effectiveness of Transnational Public and Private Policy Initiatives'. In *Global Governance of Labour Rights Assessing the Effectiveness of Transnational Public and Private Policy Initiatives*, edited by A Marx, J Wouters, G Rayp, and L Beke, 63–82. Cheltenham, UK: Edward Elgar Publishing. https://www.elgaronline.com/view/9781784711450.00010.xml.

———. 2015b. 'Involving Civil Society in Social Clauses and the Decent Work Agenda'. *GLOBAL LABOUR JOURNAL* 6 (2): 221–35.

———. 2016. 'The European Union's Trade-Labour Linkage Beyond the "Soft" Approach'. Doctor of Philosophy, Netherlands: Ghent University.

Van den Putte, and Jan Orbie. 2015. 'EU Bilateral Trade Agreements and the Surprising Rise of Labour Provisions'. *International Journal of Comparative Labour Law and Industrial Relations* 31 (3): 263–83.

Van den Putte, Lore, Jan Orbie, and Fabienne Bossuyt. unpub. 'The US and EU's Trade-Labour Linkage in Peru and Colombia: What Does It Mean for Domestic Stakeholders?'

6. Corporate Due Diligence: A Contribution to the Enforcement of Human Rights?[1]

Christian Scheper

In recent years demands for the political regulation of corporations have increasingly had recourse to international human rights. This includes not only issues such as forced labour, discrimination and child labour, but also demands for fair wages, union rights, protection of health and safety in the workplace, and limitations on environmental damage. Increasingly we can see that not only the actions of states but also the activities of private companies are scrutinised with regard to respect for human rights. This trend harbours opportunities for formulating comprehensive expectations with regard to social and environmental conditions of globalisation based on international law, but it also raises new political questions with regard to the regulation and political authority of companies.

One core question, which has been debated for a long time in legal and political terms, is which specific obligations arise for companies from intergovernmental human rights treaties (Bilchitz and Deva, 2013; Ratner, 2001; Weissbrodt and Kruger, 2003). The most recent institutional turn in this regard has been introduced by the UN Guiding Principles on Business and Human Rights, which have been endorsed by the Human Rights Council in June 2011. The Guidelines have introduced a distinct *corporate responsibility to respect* human rights. The key concept for defining the scope and reach of this responsibility is the concept of *due diligence*. This concept is now being mainstreamed in international institutions and guidelines on various policy levels, such as the OECD Guiding Principles for Multinational Enterprises (OECD, 2011) or the "Social and Environmental Performance Standards" of the International Finance Corporation (IFC, 2012, p. 6)[2]. The concept has also been included in the EU policy on Corporate Social Responsibility (CSR, see European Commission, 2015) and it is currently taken up by National Action Plans to implement the UN Guiding Principles.[3] Thus, in a period in which international soft law instruments[4] have

---

[1] This chapter is a modified and updated version of Part I of the study "Corporate Obligations With Regard to Human Rights Due Diligence", published by the Friedrich-Ebert-Stiftung in 2015 (Grabosch and Scheper, 2015).

[2] Within the World Bank group the IFC is responsible for cooperation with private companies. As part of the IFC's »Sustainability Framework« the Performance Standards represent the main guidelines for social and environmental criteria to be applied to project funding.

[3] At the time of writing (March 2017) 13 states have adopted a National Action Plan on business and human rights and another 22 are currently developing such a plan. In another eight countries efforts are being made by civil society or national human rights institutions to start a comparable process (OHCHR 2017b).

become a prominent political instrument, the still relatively freely interpretable notion of a corporate human rights due diligence seems to become a key concept. On first glance it seems to bring together conflicting political positions: While UN Guiding Principles are a response to wide-spread calls for a legal clarification of transnational corporate duties with regard to human rights, at the same time they seem to offer a high level of flexibility, which satisfies those who hold reservations towards any form of binding market regulation. Above all the notion attempts to do justice to the high context dependency of corporate activities and the demand for flexibility in the provisions and measures to be applied. In principle, the concept of a due diligence for companies is not new: as a legal concept it is well established in many areas, for example, in administrative, criminal and regulatory offences law, as well as in competition law, but especially in tort law. Also, as a management concept due diligence is very familiar. Its transposition to the area of human rights, however, is a remarkable novelty. Here its precise meaning, scope and the consequences of non-compliance have hitherto remained largely open. The UN Guiding Principles, too, provide only general answers.[5] Furthermore, the concept is by no means uncontroversial. The role of companies in human rights protection and the path embarked on by the Guiding Principles with regard to the approach to corporate responsibility are the subject of heated discussion.

This chapter provides a critical introduction to the concept of human rights due diligence and the current state of play of including it as a policy instrument for enforcing human rights. I discuss the meaning and political significance of the concept as well as important reservations and criticisms in the current discourse. I argue that the concept of due diligence risks substituting the legal character of human rights with its focus on individual entitlements for a strongly management-oriented concept. This rather serves management interests as long as it is not properly embedded in accompanying policy measures. Therefore, given the current national, European and international processes for implementing the UN Guiding Principles[6] – but also in a broader sense of a global governance culture that is increasingly geared towards soft law and corporate responsibility – tackling the question of companies' human rights due diligence seems imperative for a better enforcement of human rights and the

---

[4] Various forms of non-(directly) binding guidelines and standards are characterised as »soft law«, as frequently found especially at international level. It is »soft« because it is primarily based on self-commitments, incentives and general social norms and in the event of non-compliance there are no »hard« sanctions in accordance with established judicial procedures.

[5] See also De Schutter et al. (2012), who discuss how different states have already integrated the due diligence approach in their policies.

[6] Besides the abovementioned EU strategy and the working out National Action Plans this effort also became discernible in the G7 agreements of 2015 (G7 2015: 6).

future path of the human rights system more generally. In the last section I shed light on discussions about key policy areas in which the concept could be refined.

Corporate Due Diligence as an Element of the Human Rights System

Since the end of the Second World War the international human rights regime has developed primarily as a system of international law. It is oriented in the first instance towards the state and its relations with the individual. Human rights impinge on transnational companies only via an indirect third-party effect. That means that for companies there are no direct international law obligations and corresponding international options for sanctions in the event of corporate misconduct. It is rather the state that is obliged to ensure that human rights are also protected and safeguarded in the context of corporate activities. In the wake of economic globalisation, however, the political role of private companies has become more visible and the 'traditional' international law approach of the human rights regime has come under pressure. On the one hand, many states – for a wide variety of reasons – do not protect human rights adequately or even bluntly violate them. On the other hand, companies, given largely unconstrained capital mobility, in many instances act transnationally, while state authority is largely territorially confined. Above all, the issue of the extraterritorial scope of state obligations to protect human rights is now the object of intense international law discussion and controversy (see Bernstorff, 2011). All in all, there is a high agreement today that we are facing a situation of inadequate human rights enforcement in the global economy (OHCHR, 2008, para 3).

Since the 1990s, with the so-called "UN norms"[7] an international effort had been under way to subject companies to international regulations with regard to respect for fundamental human rights.[8] This attempt met with stiff political opposition, however, and ultimately foundered as an instrument of international law in 2004, when the UN Commission on Human Rights stepped back from making the UN Norms binding under international law (see Weissbrodt and Kruger, 2003). After this the so-called "Ruggie Process" began, named after John G. Ruggie, who had already co-designed the UN Global Compact under Kofi Annan and from 2005 to 2011 was twice Special Representative for

---

[7] Officially: "Norms on the Responsibilities of Transnational Corporations and Other Business Enterprises with regard to Human Rights".

[8] There were earlier attempts at international regulation, in particular in the 1970s, when the first international code of conduct (Sagafi-Nejad and Dunning (2008), p. 63) and the first version of the OECD Guidelines for Multinational Enterprises were adopted. At that time, however, human rights were not being discussed in relation to companies, see Cragg *et al.* (2012, p. 1).

business and human rights.[9] From the outset he rejected the course set by the UN Norms and instead tried to develop a political framework for human rights protection supported by a broad consensus between governments, civil society organisations and transnational companies. It was published in 2008 under the title "Protect, Respect and Remedy" (OHCHR, 2008) and resulted in the UN Guiding Principles on Business and Human Rights in 2011.

Corporate Obligations in the UN Guiding Principles on Business and Human Rights

The UN Guiding Principles do not impose any international law obligations on companies, but rather represent a mesh of existing international law and general "social expectations" (OHCHR, 2008, para 54) in relation to companies. In this sense they conceptualise human rights protection in the context of the global economy on the basis of three normative pillars: (i) the states' duty to protect human rights under international law ('protect'), (ii) the corporate responsibility to respect human rights ('respect') and (iii) making available judicial and extrajudicial complaints procedures, including procedures on compensation for victims of human rights violations ('remedy').

The three pillars are supposed to be mutually reinforcing and interlocking in order to represent a 'smart mix' of different public and private regulatory mechanisms. The UN Special Representative emphasised that his approach should be understood as 'principled pragmatism': "an unflinching commitment to the principle of strengthening the promotion and protection of human rights as it relates to business, coupled with a pragmatic attachment to what works best in creating change where it matters most – in the daily lives of people" (OHCHR 2006: para. 81).

The fundamental principles arise from the International Bill of Human Rights, comprising the Universal Declaration of Human Rights of 1948, the International Covenant on Economic, Social and Cultural Rights (ICESCR), the International Covenant on Civil and Political Rights (ICCPR) as well as the ILO core labour standards.[10] However, the UN Guiding Principles emphasise that in particular cases other international agreements can be relevant to company activities. According to the UN Special Representative, a pragmatic approach was necessary in the interests of victims because rapid minimisation of human rights violations should be achieved without having to resort to long-drawn-out negotiations on international treaties. The UN Guiding Principles thus do not call for any revolutionary changes, but rather specify the current state of affairs with regard to international law. The state duty to protect, corporate obligations

---

[9] Officially: "Special Representative of the Secretary-General on the issue of human rights and transnational corporations and other business enterprises".

[10] Core labour standards in accordance with the International Labour Organization's Declaration of Fundamental Principles and Rights at Work of 1998.

to respect human rights and also the need for access to remedy could, in principle, have been derived from the international human rights system even before the Guiding Principles (Lopez 2013; Deva 2013). With its formulation and specification with regard to transnational companies, however, the political framework has acquired broad international support. The notion of a 'smart mix' of state regulation and corporate self-responsibility is today the dominant approach in the debate on business and human rights.[11]

In the next section we will look more closely at the aspect of corporate responsibility to respect human rights within this framework and specify the concept of human rights due diligence.

Corporate Responsibility to Respect Human Rights and the Concept of Due Diligence

The corporate responsibility to respect human rights encompasses three aspects:

1. the company must commit itself to human rights in a declaration of principle and promulgate it both internally and externally (policy statement);
2. it must proactively implement corresponding measures and management procedures to fulfil its *human rights due diligence* in all its business activities; and
3. it must establish recourse options for instances of human rights violations.

The UN Guiding Principles, first of all, distinguish the notion of responsibility from state obligations under international law. Although they assign companies an obligation to respect human rights, this does not derive directly from international law but from "social expectations" and moral considerations (OHCHR, 2006, para 70). The concept of responsibility as it pertains to companies has already been taken up in the extensive debate on corporate social responsibility (CSR). The UN Guiding Principles thus link the CSR debate[12] – which usually underlines a strong notion of voluntary commitment beyond the law – with the human rights regime. Although it is suggested that this responsibility is not to be understood as a voluntary commitment, the Guiding

---

[11] For an overview of the debate see, for example, Cragg *et al.* (2012); Deva and Bilchitz (2013).

[12] We can also discern a corresponding shift in the political debate on CSR. Representative in this respect are the European Commission's CSR definitions. Originally, the Commission defined CSR "as a concept whereby companies integrate social and environmental concerns in their business operations and in their interaction with their stakeholders on a voluntary basis". Since 2011 it defines CSR more extensively, as "the responsibility of enterprises for their impacts on society" (European Commission 2011). The Commission recognises that companies, in many respects, have obligations that are not confined to the laws of the country in which they are operating.

Principles refrain from a clear assertion of legal consequences in the event of non-compliance:

> *"The responsibility of business enterprises to respect human rights is distinct from issues of legal liability and enforcement, which remain defined largely by national law provisions in relevant jurisdictions." (OHCHR, 2011, para 12, Commentary).*

Depending on the specific instance, responsibility thus could also have a legal justification, but this further depends on national legislation. The extent to which obligations arise for transnational companies on the basis of international law in the absence of effective legal protection at national level remains a core controversy in the debate on business and human rights, which the definition of corporate responsibility in the UN Guiding Principles does not resolve. This conflict had already led to a political standstill in the preceding process concerning the UN Norms. The Special Representative presumably wanted specifically to avoid this issue in order to be able to reach a broad consensus on the framework. Instead of designating a particular set of human rights obligations the Guiding Principles leave this question open and focus on the due diligence concept, with a view to coming up with feasible procedures for companies. As the above mentioned three aspects of the responsibility to respect already show, due diligence expressly requires active measures from companies. The specific scope of these measures, however, remains strongly dependent on the context, which leaves a high discretionary power to company management.

The Guiding Principles introduce the nature of due diligence in a general form by means of basic *principles* regarding the coverage, variability and long-term character of assessment procedures. Measures to comply with the due diligence obligation should:

(1.) address adverse human rights impacts that the company causes, contributes to or is linked to through its business activities, its goods or services;

(2.) vary in their complexity, depending on the size of the enterprise, the risk of serious human rights violations and the nature and context of the activity;

(3.) be considered as a long-term and regular obligation because human rights risks can change over time (cf. OHCHR, 2011, para 17).

Furthermore, the Guiding Principles go into more detail about a number of *substantive and procedural components* on complying with the due diligence obligation. Due diligence, accordingly, must at least encompass the following:

(1.) Measures to ascertain the potential and actual human rights impacts of a company's own activities and commercial relationships. These measures can involve internal or external experts and must include meaningful consultations with (potentially) affected stakeholder groups (cf. OHCHR, 2011, para 18).

(2.) Measures to deal effectively with the findings of risk assessments and impact assessments;[13] from these findings must follow the attribution of responsibility to the relevant management level and the apportionment of decision-making authority, budgets and supervisory functions, so that, as a result, human rights risks are effectively minimised and negative impacts can be prevented (see OHCHR, 2011, para 19). Requirements with regard to measures to be taken vary in accordance with whether the company itself directly causes the (potential) human rights impacts, indirectly contributes or is linked to them through its operations, products or services. They also vary in accordance with the company's leverage on the situation or risks.

(3.) Measures to assess the effectiveness of steps taken to prevent or eliminate negative human rights impacts; these should be based on appropriate quantitative and qualitative indicators and here too internal and external stakeholders should be involved (OHCHR, 2011, pp. para 20).

(4.) Public communication of human rights risks and corresponding company measures to tackle them (OHCHR, 2011, para 21).

With these requirements the Guiding Principles provide a basis for further refinement at the national level and in various sectors. Given the rather general formulations in the Guiding Principles it is useful to underline a number of key characteristics of human rights due diligence: first, companies have to assess human rights risks in all their business activities. This includes possible indirect linkages to human rights impacts, such as those of business partners or the use of purchased products.[14] If there is a risk that human rights might be affected by business operations (directly or indirectly) companies must take further steps. They must assess the actual impacts of their activities on human rights (ex ante and ex post) and take corresponding measures to minimise risks or prevent negative impacts. What measures are to be regarded as adequate in this respect depends on the company, the activity and the context, and on the company's leverage over the situation. If, for example, a clothing brand finds out that its short-notice orders for T-shirts at the same purchase price leads to unpaid overtime for sewers in supplier factories, the company must use its influence to prevent this negative impact. The specific measures that the company should take – for example, refraining from short-notice orders or renegotiating unit

---

[13] The definition of human rights impact assessments (HRIA) and how they differ from human rights risk assessments was much discussed in the context of developing the Guiding Principles. There is no consensus on which procedures can be recognised as HRIA. For a detailed discussion see Harrison 2013. In any case the company should first carry out an assessment of human rights *risks*. The outcome of a risk assessment may require that further procedures are implemented for a deeper impact assessment.

[14] On product use and consumer protection as elements of due diligence see Schutter et al. (2012, Chapter 7).

prices with the supplier that contain an appropriate premium for overtime – are left open by the due diligence concept.

Second, in compliance with the third pillar of the Guiding Principles it can be added that companies must establish procedures for the event of negative impacts that allow those affected to raise a complaint. The procedures through which these complaints are addressed must be effective; in other words, they must in fact constitute an adequate means of avoiding the human rights abuse and compensating damages.[15]

The provisions of the Guiding Principles leave a number of important issues open; as a result, there has been heated debate in recent years concerning the political significance, the scope and reach, as well as the opportunities and risks to which the corporate due diligence approach has given rise. I will discuss some key critical aspects in what follows.

Due Diligence as an Instrument to Foster Human Rights? Criticisms and Controversies

With the UN Guiding Principles the discourse on international human rights in the context of the global economy has shifted in the direction of a corporate management and global governance discourse (Dhooge, 2008; Scheper, 2015). This shift emphasises the perspective of management and governance more strongly than the perspective of bearers of human rights; questions of compliance and shared interests in a regulatory framework have come into focus, rather than questions of establishing legal procedures, addressing conflicts of interest and disputes arising from transnational business activities. The ideals of defining entitlements to rights that would balance situations of corporate domination, and of specifying moments of rights violations that could be charged and sanctioned, are increasingly replaced by a more open, process-oriented ideal of defining and measuring attributable impacts of corporate activities that can be assessed and whose negative elements can be minimised as far as possible (cf. Deva, 2013, pp. 96f). Thus, the Guiding Principles, and especially the concept of due diligence, deviate from the rights-based language of the human rights system, which used to be oriented towards obligations and entitlements. Instead, the concept of due diligence emphasises a standard of conduct and requirements for corporate performance. This semantic shift is significant because the human rights system as an international law regime is built on a precise linguistic scaffolding. If this is changed, so critics claim, there is a risk that the binding entitlement to human rights may be diluted (see Deva, 2013, pp. 92f).

---

[15] On the criteria of effectiveness with regard to private, extrajudicial complaints mechanisms, see OHCHR 2011, para 31.

In the following, I will further specify and complement this general criticism by bringing forward three reservations against the current due diligence concept as an instrument for fostering human rights: 1.) a lack of clarification of corporate obligations and of legal consequences; 2.) an increase in private corporate authority to define standards based on human rights; 3.) a lack of motivation and contradictory incentives to act with due diligence in cases of conflicting business interests; and 4.) a tendency to bracket structural supply chain conditions.

First, despite the shift from rights holders to the perspective of management and governance, specific obligations with regard to human rights-related corporate conduct remain obscure. The Guiding Principles offer no detailed interpretation in this regard (see Deva, 2013, p. 88). Instead, they point directly towards international human rights treaties and emphasise that companies in principle must respect *all* human rights (OHCHR, 2011, para. 12, commentary). Clarification thus remains necessary because a mere transposition of intergovernmental human rights agreements to private companies throws up many issues concerning responsibility or imputability and thus material duty of care. Since the UN Guiding Principles cannot say much about legal infringements, their focus is on the risks and impacts of corporate activities, which, in order to remain feasible, have been limited from the outset by adding the precondition of *severity* of impacts (OHCHR, 2011; Tromp, 2016). If companies assess or assume severity of impacts they must seek to prevent them and, as the case may be, arrange for reparations. It is a context-dependent question of defining severity, and assessments will vary widely in practice. On a case by case basis, therefore, this gives rise to great legal uncertainty concerning the point at which the company is responsible for a rights violation. The Guiding Principles leave this grey area open and declare that companies in the first instance have moral obligations, but for the time being no legal obligations on an international level. Accordingly, the consequences of non-compliance are to be tried primarily before "the court of public opinion":

Failure to meet this responsibility can subject companies to the court of public opinion – comprising employees, communities, consumers, civil society, as well as investors – and occasionally to charges in actual courts.(OHCHR, 2008, para. 54)

Deva (2013, p. 98) elucidates the problem of the lack of precision of the concept of impact in comparison with the 'legal violation approach' by means of a (hypothetical) example: if the company Walmart opened a branch in India this would have a major impact on the lives of many people in the vicinity, for example, consumers, farmers, retailers and suppliers. If, for example, small shop owners in the vicinity had to close their stores the company would incontrovertibly have a considerable negative impact on their possibilities to enjoy their social and economic rights. Deva emphasises, however, that he would not consider this to be a legal *violation*. It would be more clear-cut if the staff at the Walmart branch were treated in a degrading manner (for example, through the suppression of freedom of association or unpaid overtime). In both cases the company's actions would have severe negative human rights impacts, but only in the second case would there be a clear legal claim on the part of employees (see Deva 2013: 98). At the same time, the opening of the branch would presumably also have positive consequences, for example, if regular jobs were created. Even if Walmart might, as part of their due diligence procedure, decide to compensate shop owners who lost their income, the problem remains that the definition of rights and violations is shifted towards a discretionary management decision. Elsewhere, Deva (2012: 103 f.) cites the example of the right to the highest attainable standard of physical and mental health. Would companies be violating this right if they provided no health insurance for their employees or if the wages were too low to enable employees to avail themselves of medical care? When is a human rights impact relevant, when is it severe (see also Tromp, 2016)? According to what criteria will this be decided? How far must the company go in its response to such impacts? The examples indicate that the Guiding Principles leave open many fundamental questions about corporate obligations. This might be the price of a strategy based on broad consensus, in which controversial issues have either been left aside (Nolan 2013: 161) or a largely defensive position has been taken in controversial fields.[16]

Moreover, it remains open what the legal consequences in case of a violation of the due diligence obligation would be (Michalowski, 2013, pp. see). According to critics we can expect that only a few companies will make sufficient efforts to assume responsibility when there are no clear legal consequences attached (see already Addo, 1999, p. 11; Nolan, 2013, p. 161). Many would do so only to the extent that specific measures were also in the company's own interest or at least as long as no fundamental business interest stand *against* it. For a policy framework, however, it would be important to establish guidelines especially for cases in which there is *no* vested company interest to conform to human rights. The debate on responsibility on the basis of a social 'license to operate'[17] at

---

[16] An example for a defensive position is the Guiding Principles' position on extraterritorial state obligations under international law, as explained by Augenstein and Kinley (2013).

[17] This concept usually refers to the public assent required for corporate activities. It is independent of the law and other legal provisions. The UN Special Representative, too, has used this expression in his paraphrasing of social expectations with regard to companies: »the broader scope of the responsibility to respect is defined by social expectations – as part of what is sometimes called a company's social licence to operate« (OHCHR 2008, para. 54).

international level thus remains vague for as long as it avoids the discussion of specific obligations and the legal consequences of corporate misconduct.

Second, drawing on due diligence as a governance approach depends strongly on self-responsibility. In the field of human rights, especially social and economic rights, this suffers from a problem with regard to companies' motivation because it is above all self-interest – for example, in minimising reputational risks – and social expectations that are supposed to lead to consistent compliance with the due diligence obligation. The quality of the process implemented to safeguard human rights due diligence depends on the functioning of the "court of public opinion", which not least would require comprehensive transparency along the global value chain. Far-reaching incentive mechanisms are lacking that would encourage self-interest in comprehensive due diligence processes, in particular when, in individual cases, they run counter to other corporate interests. Indeed, often it is very much in the company's own interest to identify and avoid human rights risks, but that is not always the case, far from it. For example, many companies are not visible to consumers in such a way that their reputations might be at risk, which means that they have little incentive to bear the higher cost of implementing human rights due diligence. This applies, for example, to many small and medium-sized enterprises (SMEs), which, as suppliers of large brand name companies, do not themselves serve the markets for end-consumers. However, this is also the case in parts of the electronics industry, where powerful manufacturers largely remain invisible to consumers (Lüthje, 2002). Moreover, in all branches with complex supply chains, such as the garment industry, even committed brand companies at best reach only the first or second tier in the chain with their monitoring efforts. Large parts of production are not reached, especially areas in which informal labour is widespread.[18] In addition, many consumers still take relatively little interest in social and environmental considerations when it comes to purchasing decisions.

More generally, we can say that given the existence of global production networks incentives based on public opinion are fairly constricted because there is insufficient transparency or inducement. Public opinion is also generally dependent on elaborate civil society campaigns to bring abuses to light. However, civil organisations have only limited resources and general monitoring of companies' human rights impact can hardly be expected from them. Public opinion thus does not represent a proper basis for human rights protection. A further problem with a strongly company-driven approach in the area of human rights protection is that there is a certain prioritisation of rights in accordance with the public interest and reputational risk. This leads to more avoidance of certain risks in the company's self-interest (for example,

---

[18] On the increase in informal and precarious employment forms see ILO (2015).

minimisation of child labour in their supply chain – which is a particular threat to a company's reputation), while other human rights risks are less heeded (for example, trade union rights). The same applies to the measures to be implemented for assessing risks. We can conclude from this that companies' obligations with regard to transparency and disclosure must be extended and corresponding policy design approaches are needed, if the due diligence concept is to contribute to human rights protection in the global economy as a basic principle.

This leads to the third problem: due diligence, as a general principle of action, needs to leave open what is required in a specific case. By shifting the context-specific decision over to private management, however, the concept confers considerable authority on companies, if the general assertions of the Guiding Principles are not further refined, for instance, by national law. This authority comprises the interpretation of human rights in specific contexts and is increased by the fact that risk and impact assessments largely draw on practices of corporate knowledge about the situation in the supply chain. Corporate monitoring, auditing and reporting practices – although their flaws and weaknesses are widely known – become a key cornerstone of human rights policies and often they are the only knowledge base against which the due diligence obligations can be measured. Until today no comparable 'labour-based' information systems or public practices of knowledge production about the supply chain have evolved that would form a counter-weight to the increasing role of management-based knowledge and its effects on how human rights conditions are being assessed.

Fourth, by assigning responsibility to companies according to their leverage, the approach of the Guiding Principles and the concept of due diligence tend to overemphasise an individualistic conception of causes and effects in the global economy and underestimate structural conditions (see, e.g., Hoover, 2012). For instance, if a company is responsible to act with due diligence with regard to the right to equal treatment of men and women, it might attempt to avoid instances of discrimination, but it is questionable whether it will be able (or required to) address a general situation of unequal treatment of women along the supply chain.

Based on these four reservations we can assume that the openness of the concept of due diligence suggested by the UN Guiding Principles might be inadequate as an instrument for effective human rights protection. The Guiding Principles must be seen in light of a corporate-based CSR approach that is sceptical about or hostile to regulation (López, 2013). Ultimately, this also represents a more general problem for the human rights approach: as a broadly encompassing concept it enjoys almost universal assent. In specific instances, however, its implementation involves fundamental conflicts of interest. These require the institutionalised empowerment for rights holders to make claims against the authority of corporate management. Otherwise, rights would be no more than consensual corporate minimum standards of conduct. Interpretation of rights can scarcely be standardised top-down by company management. The 'correct' standard – that is, the threshold at which impacts of corporate activities would be considered as rights violations – is rarely self-evident and determinable top down. It is important to recall that human rights and their potential violation have to be negotiated in individual cases. Where there are no adequate legal remedies or no rule-of-law institutions, or when impacts have to be evaluated, the interpretation of human rights in the relevant context as part of the corporate due diligence concept cannot satisfactorily be performed by the company itself. Precisely this, however, is necessary according to the approach of the Guiding Principles, as long as these are not specified by corresponding national or other policies. The policy design of the human rights due diligence approach must, on the one hand, further refine minimum standards, but on the other hand, it must remain open to further legal possibilities for dispute resolution and legal remedies, so that in specific instances rights holders are able to claim their rights and bring cases to a court.

Consequently, there is a need for further specification of the concept of due diligence in specific contexts and policy fields. To some extent a process in this direction has already started. For instance, at the international level this has been done within a UN working group on business and human rights[19] and also the OECD is further trying to specify due diligence (e.g. OECD, 2017). Remaining challenges in relation to the necessary specification of the concept comprise, for example, labour law obligations in the supply chain, including obligations for companies that arise from trade union rights. The latter represent key human rights issues with regard to the global economy,[20] but are largely excluded from the UN Guiding Principles.[21]

Embedding Corporate Due Diligence in Policy Approaches

After the successful adoption of the UN Guiding Principles many countries, both within and outside the OECD, are currently engaged in defining national policy steps for their implementation. This involves a further specification of how due diligence is supposed to be understood and how it is linked to the other

---

[19] Officially: »Working Group on the issue of human rights and transnational corporations and other business enterprises«, see OHCHR (2017c).

[20] see also OHCHR 2008, para. 52.

[21] In the Guiding Principles the key role of trade unions is first mentioned in the context of the need for complaints mechanisms (OHCHR 2011, para. 29f), not in the context of due diligence. Overall, rights at work, which in the ICESCR go far beyond the ILO Core Labour Standards, are not given much emphasis.

pillars of the Guiding Principles. For example, states can provide companies with incentives and conditions to implement their due diligence processes and they can define both minimum standards as well as legal 'safe harbours' for companies. This seems necessary if a 'smart' regulatory mix is to emerge from the Guiding Principles and existing 'governance gaps' be closed up.

In this sense a holistic view of the due diligence concept is needed as part of the more comprehensive approach of the three pillars of the Guiding Principles ('protect, respect and remedy'). The key requirements for fulfilling the *corporate responsibility to respect* human rights could be supported and strengthened by national governments: 1.) The demand for a *policy statement* – an explicit commitment to human rights and adequate communication at all levels of the company – can be supported by more clearly defining what is to be legally expected from companies; 2.) at the level of *measures to implement due diligence processes* state governments together with international organisations, especially the ILO, could develop minimum standards and support the involvement of both company and labour through tripartite consultations – in particular with regard to risk and impact assessments, as well as appropriate follow-up measures, and the specification of legal thresholds and consequences in cases of non-compliance. This should take place in relation to specific sectors and human rights issues. 3.) The same applies with regard to the third requirement, *the provision of judicial and non-judicial complaints mechanisms*. Here, too, the state can formulate expectations and criteria for appropriate procedures for grievance mechanisms on a company level.

More importantly, however, states need to make available its own judicial and non-judicial court and arbitration mechanisms for those who are affected by corporate activities, both domestically and abroad, and eliminating existing obstacles (for civil society demands in Germany see Heydenreich *et al.*, 2014: Chapter 6). This also entails the scrutiny and reform of existing extrajudicial proceedings, such as the National Contact Points (NCP) for the OECD Guidelines with regard to their compliance with the effectiveness criteria formulated by the UN Guiding Principles (see OHCHR, 2011, para. 31).

The following will summarise further key areas in which a comprehensive policy integration of the due diligence concept could lead to a better enforcement of human rights.

Providing Public Information on Human Rights Conditions

The provision and organisation of information on issues relevant to human rights becomes an important area of state policies, if non-state actors are supposed to act based on considerations about human rights risks and impacts. This includes, first, the development of country-specific know-how; second, the compilation of sector-specific information, for example, on human rights risks and options for dealing with these risks; and third, the development of guidance on specific human rights issues and how abuses are expected to be handled, with reference to relevant international frameworks and guidelines. Many issues require clarification in this respect beyond existing international standards, such as the UN Guiding Principles and the OECD Guidelines. The development of a comprehensive public information base would be important for balancing the above-mentioned increasing tendency towards 'corporate-led' knowledge about supply chains, generated by corporate auditing firms and the like.

Promoting Networks

The establishment and promotion of networks for companies, trade unions, employees and civil society actors could play a key role in the generation and exchange of relevant knowledge, in particular if it strengthens solidarity and participation among employees along the supply chain. Besides corporate membership-based networks, such as the Global Compact Networks and CSR circles, networks need to engage better with employees and trade unions. Regional or state-organised forums might be suitable for this purpose, as well as efforts to link up with trade union federations or civil society networks in production countries in Europe and abroad. Central to all this must be the establishment of new forms of social dialogue between companies and labour representatives along the supply chain, as well as the provision of effective participation and complaints options for bearers of human rights. Due diligence understood as one element in a transnational context of improved company-labour dialogue could strengthen the enforcement of human rights.

Promoting 'Good' Competitive Conditions

Whereas companies' regularly demand a 'level' playing field – equal competitive conditions – it seems necessary to include due diligence requirements in defining the social *quality* of this playing field. This would require governments to provide conditions and incentives through which failure to comply with human rights due diligence obligations would lead to a competitive disadvantage, or consistent compliance with due diligence obligations could bring competitive advantages. The aim should be to ensure that the competitiveness of companies that properly comply with their due diligence obligations does not suffer, for example, because competitors are able to charge lower prices based on violations of fundamental rights in production sites. In order to promote such good and progressive competitive conditions internationally, governments (and the EU) can work strategically to ensure that social, environmental and human rights provisions are included in multi- and bilateral trade agreements and investment protection treaties. Such opportunities have been the subject of controversy for many years now (see Scherrer *et al.*,

1998; Jacob, 2010).[22] The UN Working Group on Business and Human Rights for this purpose proposes more intensive coordination of the implementation of the UN Guiding Principles between trade, investment and financial institutions in the international system (UNHRC 2015: §§ 15–17). This proposal seems a necessary step in order to embed the concept of corporate due diligence in wider policy solutions for promoting human rights.

A further step towards creating good competitive conditions would be to enhance the requirements on the corporate disclosure of non-financial affairs. Reporting about measures for compliance with human rights would be an important precondition for due diligence as an element of political regulation. Although many – especially large – companies already report on their CSR activities this has hitherto not been done in accordance with set criteria, and nor have human rights issues been systematically dealt with. To date, as a rule not all essential human rights risks, impacts and concrete measures have been evident in company reports. Legal definition of certain material reporting obligations, graduated in accordance with company size, could strengthen compliance with the human rights due diligence obligation. However, as the above discussion about the politics of corporate-led knowledge and transparency shows, a one-sided policy reliance on increased corporate transparency would be problematic from a human rights perspective.

At the international level a process towards further defining minimum standards with regard to corporate due diligence could be reached by the 'Intergovernmental working group transnational corporations and other business enterprises with respect to human rights', whose goal is to negotiate a binding treaty on the issue of business obligations in the field of human rights (OHCHR, 2017a).

Economic Incentives and Conditionality
Closely linked to the promotion of good competitive conditions at national and international level is the creation of consistent incentives and conditions for companies. There are key policy fields in which effective support for due diligence obligations are possible by attaching legal conditions on business conduct to economic policies: a.) public procurement, b.) foreign trade promotion and c.) development cooperation.

    a. Public procurement falls primarily in the area of the state's duty to protect (see OHCHR, 2011, para 5, 6). It can be used to create economic incentives for companies to comply with their human rights due diligence obligation by taking it into consideration as a requirement when awarding

---

[22] Recently, civil society initiatives seem to increasingly take up this path again, see http://www.fes-europe.eu/news-list/e/core-labour-standards-plus-linking-trade-and-shared-prosperity-in-global-supply-chains-in-asia/ [accessed 24 March 2017].

contracts (for further information and demands in Germany see CorA-Netzwerk für Unternehmensverantwortung and Forum Menschenrechte, 2013).

b. In the granting of export credit guarantees and related public instruments of export promotion, compliance with the human rights due diligence obligation can be laid down as a fixed criterion for public support. Including consistent human rights criteria and active human rights consultancy capacities at the mandatory companies of foreign trade promotion could provide a strong incentive for export-oriented companies. Developments have already been initiated in this area in recent years on the level of the OECD framework of the international cooperation of export credit agencies, but so far no systematic human rights-oriented approach has been established. For the sake of continuous improvement in particular a complaints option would need to be created for people affected, for example, through an independent ombudsman for foreign trade promotion and foreign direct investment projects. It could play an intermediary role and serve as a contact for rights holders abroad, for instance in cases of large infrastructure projects.

c. To promote the due diligence obligation among companies, development policy could build up a human rights approach in the field of economic and social rights in close cooperation with companies and trade union federations. This includes the establishment and further development of expertise for human rights risk analyses, which could be applied on a country and sector-specific basis via the development agencies' offices. The promotion of tripartite forms of dialogue alongside supply chains would also constitute a key task that so far has played only a minor role for most development agencies. Furthermore, partner countries could be advised and supported in working out their own national action plans for implementing the UN Guiding Principles.

The Role of Trade Unions for Strengthening the Contribution of Corporate Due Diligence

As the discussion so far has shown, trade unions, with their national and international federations, could play a much more active role in promoting and demanding corporate human rights due diligence obligations. In this context they can take up company commitments to human rights systematically and demand that they be met along the supply chain. To date, only a few trade union federations have been active in the debate on the corporate human rights due diligence concept. International engagement has been confined so far largely to International Framework Agreements (IFAs) or Global Framework Agreements (GFAs). GFAs represent innovative agreements between international trade union federations and top managements on global minimum standards. They can make an important contribution to strengthening due diligence because they can disseminate the agreed standards through company and works councils structures throughout the supply chain. However, the top-down approach of GFAs is also controversial. Agreements can, on the one hand, strengthen the transnational capabilities of trade unions and the role of international trade union federations, but on the other hand, they run the risk of reproducing existing hierarchies in company structures and restricting trade union capabilities in production networks, if they pass on the pressure and responsibility for implementing minimum standards "from above to below" in the supply chain (see Fichter *et al.*, 2011). The real contribution of GFAs in the implementation of rights at work in production countries must, therefore, be examined more closely. The goal should be primarily to empower the workforce to organise along global supply chains. Also, within the framework of multi-stakeholder initiatives, trade unions can contribute to the development of appropriate standards for employee participation along the supply chain, demand that attention be given to labour issues and promote transnational networking between employee representatives along the supply chain. International trade union federations or networks along the supply chain must play an increasingly important role in the ongoing negotiation of fundamental rights at work.

Conclusions

Corporate human rights due diligence is taking on an important position in the international human rights regime since the adoption of the UN Guiding Principles. Achieving the declared goal of closing 'governance gaps', however, has so far suffered from the failure to specify the concrete obligations that need to go hand in hand with this concept. Furthermore, for many companies there have so far been only inadequate economic incentives for comprehensive implementation of due diligence, including the obligations to disclose risks, measures taken and their impacts. Similarly, there are no clear sanctions if companies fail to meet their due diligence obligations. Overall, the engagement with these issues shows that the quality and functionality of the concept of human rights due diligence depends strongly on specific policy arrangements: if it is adequately specified and accompanied by legal conditions, it might make a decisive contribution to human rights protection. As a stand-alone policy solution, however, it threatens to remain a weak instrument that contributes to the legitimation of transnational companies and increase their political authority in the field of human rights interpretation, rather than strengthening rights in the context of global production and trade relations. The current process of working out national action plans for business and human rights can thus constitute an important moment in the further development of the human rights regime.

A further key challenge is the fact that a human rights policy that draws on corporate due diligence increasingly depends on corporate forms of knowledge generation about human rights conditions in transnational production networks. Transparency and the development of information about labour and human rights conditions is a key presupposition for meaningful due diligence obligations. Therefore, the demand for transparency also involves the need to strengthen labour-led forms of knowledge politics that go beyond existing regimes of corporate-led auditing and verification schemes.

The interpretation and policy design of the concept of a due diligence obligation can go a long way towards setting a course in the currently dominant trend of soft law as an approach to international human rights politics. The concept must, therefore, be shaped in such a way that the "soft" approach, despite the lack of binding force under international law, can be effective – through legal foundations in national law and international coherence – by gradually bringing about genuine human rights conditionality to the global economy and extending the range of options for rights holders to claim their internationally agreed rights.

References

Addo, M.K. (1999), Human rights standards and the responsibility of transnational corporations, Kluwer Law International, The Hague, Boston.

Augenstein, D. and Kinley, D. (2013), "When human rights 'responsibilities' become 'duties': the extra-territorial obligations of states that bind corporation", in Deva, S. and Bilchitz, D. (Eds.), Human rights obligations of business: Beyond the corporate responsibility to respect?, Cambridge University Press, New York, pp. 271–294.

Bernstorff, J. von (2011), "Extraterritoriale menschenrechtliche Staatenpflichten und Corporate Social Responsibility", Archiv des Völkerrechts, Vol. 49 No. 1, pp. 34–63.

Bilchitz, D. and Deva, S. (2013), "The human rights obligations of business. a critical framework for the future", in Deva, S. and Bilchitz, D. (Eds.), Human rights obligations of business: Beyond the corporate responsibility to respect?, Cambridge University Press, New York, pp. 1–26.

CorA-Netzwerk für Unternehmensverantwortung and Forum Menschenrechte (2013), "Position Paper on Business and Human Rights - Expectations of a German Action Plan", available at: https://germanwatch.org/de/download/7793.pdf.

Cragg, W., Arnold, D.G. and Muchlinski, P. (2012), "Human Rights and Business", Business Ethics Quarterly, Vol. 22 No. 1, pp. 1–7.

Deva, S. (2013), "Treating human rights lightly. a critique of the consensus rhetoric and the language employed by the Guiding Principles", in Deva, S. and Bilchitz, D. (Eds.), Human rights obligations of business: Beyond the corporate responsibility to respect?, Cambridge University Press, New York, pp. 78–104.

Deva, S. and Bilchitz, D. (Eds.) (2013), Human rights obligations of business: Beyond the corporate responsibility to respect?, Cambridge University Press, New York.

Dhooge, L.J. (2008), "Due Diligence As A Defense To Corporate Liability Pursuant to the Alien Tort Statute", Emory International Law Review, Vol. 22 No. 2, pp. 455–498.

European Commission (2015), "Commission Staff Working Document on Implementing the UN Guiding Principles on Business and Human Rights - State of Play", available at: http://ec.europa.eu/DocsRoom/documents/11621/attachments/ (accessed 24 March 2017).

Fichter, M., Helfen, M. and Sydow, J. (2011), "Regulating Labor Relations in Global Production Networks. Insights on International Framework Agreements", Internationale Politik und Gesellschaft, Vol. 2, pp. 69–86.

Grabosch, R. and Scheper, C. (2015), Corporate obligations with regard to human rights due diligence: Policy and legal approaches, Study / Friedrich-Ebert-Stiftung, Friedrich-Ebert-Stiftung, Global Policy and Development, Berlin.

Harrison, J. (2013), "Establishing a meaningful human rights due diligence process for corporations. Learning from experience of human rights impact assessment", Impact Assessment and Project Appraisal, Vol. 31 No. 2, pp. 107–117.

Heydenreich, C., Paasch, A. and Kusch, J. (2014), Globales Wirtschaften und Menschenrechte: Deutschland auf dem Prüfstand; Bericht 2014, Germanwatch, Berlin, Bonn.

Hoover, J. (2012), "Reconstructing responsibility and moral agency in world politics", International Theory, Vol. 4 No. 02, pp. 233–268.

IFC (2012), "IFC Performance Standards on Environmental and Social Sustainability", available at: http://www.ifc.org/wps/wcm/connect/c8f524004a73daeca09afdf998895a12/IFC_Performance_Standards.pdf?MOD=AJPERES (accessed 24 March 2017).

ILO (2015), "World Employment and Social Outlook", available at: http://www.ilo.org/wcmsp5/groups/public/---dgreports/---dcomm/---publ/documents/publication/wcms_337069.pdf (accessed 24 March 2017).

Jacob, M. (2010), International investment agreements and human rights, INEF Research Paper Series on Human Rights, Corporate Responsibility and Sustainable Development, Vol. 03, INEF, Duisburg.

López, C. (2013), "The 'Ruggie process'. from legal obligations to corporate social responsibility?", in Deva, S. and Bilchitz, D. (Eds.), Human rights obligations of business: Beyond the corporate responsibility to respect?, Cambridge University Press, New York, pp. 58–77.

Lüthje, B. (2002), Contract manufacturing: Transnationale Produktion und Industriearbeit in der IT-Branche, Studienreihe des Instituts für Sozialforschung Frankfurt am Main, Campus, Frankfurt.

Michalowski, S. (2013), "Due diligence and complicity. a relationship in need of clarification", in Deva, S. and Bilchitz, D. (Eds.), Human rights obligations of business: Beyond the corporate responsibility to respect?, Cambridge University Press, New York, pp. 218–242.

Nolan, J. (2013), "Responsibility to respect. Soft law or no law?", in Deva, S. and Bilchitz, D. (Eds.), Human rights obligations of business: Beyond the corporate responsibility to respect?, Cambridge University Press, New York, pp. 138–161.

OECD (2011), OECD Guidelines for Multinational Enterprises, 2011 Edition, 2011st ed., OECD Publishing, Paris.

OECD (2017), "OECD Due Diligence Guidance For Responsible Supply Chains in the Garment and Footwear Sector", available at: http://mneguidelines.oecd.org/OECD-Due-Diligence-Guidance-Garment-Footwear.pdf (accessed 24 March 2017).

OHCHR (2006), "Interim report of the Special Representative of the Secretary-General on the issue of human rights and transnational corporations and other business enterprises".

OHCHR (2008), "Protect, Respect and Remedy. a Framework for Business and Human Rights Report of the Special Representative of the Secretary General on the issue of human rights and transnational corporations and other business enterprises, John Ruggie".

OHCHR (2011), "Guiding Principles on Business and Human Rights. Implementing the United Nations "Protect, Respect and Remedy" Framework", available at: http://www.ohchr.org/Documents/Publications/GuidingPrinciplesBusinessHR_EN.pdf.

OHCHR (2017a), "Open-ended intergovernmental working group on transnational corporations and other business enterprises with respect to human rights", available at: http://www.ohchr.org/EN/HRBodies/HRC/WGTransCorp/Pages/IGWGOnTNC.aspx (accessed 24 March 2017).

OHCHR (2017b), "State national action plans", available at: http://www.ohchr.org/EN/Issues/Business/Pages/NationalActionPlans.aspx (accessed 24 March 2017).

OHCHR (2017c), "Working Group on the issue of human rights and transnational corporations and other business enterprises", available at: http://www.ohchr.org/EN/Issues/Business/Pages/WGHRandtransnationalcorporationsandotherbusiness.aspx (accessed 24 March 2017).

Ratner, S.R. (2001), "Corporations and Human Rights. A Theory of Legal Responsibility", The Yale Law Journal, Vol. 111 No. 3, pp. 443–545.

Sagafi-nejad, T. and Dunning, J.H. (2008), The UN and transnational corporations: From code of conduct to global compact, Indiana University Press, Bloomington.

Scheper, C. (2015), "'From naming and shaming to knowing and showing'. human rights and the power of corporate practice", The International Journal of Human Rights, Vol. 19 No. 6, pp. 737–756.

Scherrer, C., Greven, T. and Frank, V. (1998), Sozialklauseln: Arbeiterrechte im Welthandel, Schriftenreihe / Hans Böckler-Stiftung, 1. Aufl., Westfälisches Dampfboot, Münster.

Schutter, O.d., Eide, A., Khalfan, A., Orellana, M., Salomon, M. and Seiderman, I. (2012), "Commentary to the Maastricht Principles on Extraterritorial Obligations of States in the Area of Economic, Social and Cultural Rights", Human rights quarterly, Vol. 34 No. 4, pp. 1084–1169.

Tromp, D. (2016), Assessing Business-Related Impacts on Human Rights: Indicators and Benchmarks in Standards and Practice, INEF Report, Vol. 110, Institute for Development and Peace, University of Duisburg-Essen, Duisburg.

United Nations Human Rights Council (2011), Report of the Special Representative of the Secretary-General on the issue of human rights and transnational corporations and other business enterprises, John Ruggie: Guiding Principles on Business and Human Rights: Implementing the United Nations "Protect, Respect and Remedy" Framework, Geneva.

Weissbrodt, D.S. and Kruger, M. (2003), "Norms on the responsibilities of transnational corporations and other business enterprises with regard to human rights", American Journal of International Law, Vol. 97 No. 4, pp. 901–922.

Labor and Globalization
Edited by Christoph Scherrer

Donna McGuire:
Re-Framing Trade. Union Mobilisation against the General Agreement on Trade in Services (GATS)
Volume 1, ISBN 978-3-86618-392-6, Rainer Hampp Verlag, München, Mering 2013, 237 S., € 27.80

Christoph Scherrer, Debdulal Saha (Eds.):
The Food Crisis. Implications for Labor
Volume 2, ISBN 978-3-86618-393-3, Rainer Hampp Verlag, München, Mering 2013, 225 S., € 19.80

Sarah Elisabeth Schmelzer-Roldán:
The Impact of Electricity Sector Privatisation on Employees in Argentina and Brazil. A Comparative Institutional Analysis
Volume 3, ISBN 978-3-86618-394-0, Rainer Hampp Verlag, München, Mering 2014, 249 S., € 27.80

Akua O Britwum and Sue Ledwith (Eds.):
Visibility and Voice for Union Women: Country case studies from Global Labour University researchers
Volume 4, ISBN 978-3-86618-395-7, Rainer Hampp Verlag, München, Mering 2014, 229 S., € 24.80

Christoph Scherrer (Ed.):
The Transatlantic Trade and Investment Partnership (TTIP): Implications for Labor
Volume 5, ISBN 978-3-86618-396-4, Rainer Hampp Verlag, München, Mering 2014, 209 S., € 24.80

Veerashekharappa, Meenakshi Rajeev, Soumitra Pramanik:
Reforming Cooperative Credit Structure in India for Financial Inclusion
Volume 6, ISBN 978-3-86618-397-1, Rainer Hampp Verlag, München, Mering 2014, 98 S., € 19.80

Luciana Hachmann:
Pursuing a Developmental State Trade Agenda in a Neo-Liberal Context: Brazil and South Africa in Comparison
Volume 7, ISBN 978-3-86618-398-8, Rainer Hampp Verlag, München, Mering 2014, 214 S., € 24.80

Oksana Balashova, Ismail Doga Karatepe, Aishah Namukasa (Eds.):
Where have all the classes gone? A critical perspective on struggles and collective action
Volume 8, ISBN 978-3-86618-893-8, Rainer Hampp Verlag, Augsburg, München 2017, 300 S., € 29.80

Christoph Scherrer (Ed.):
Enforcement Instruments for Social Human Rights along Supply Chains
Volume 9, ISBN 978-3-86618-894-5, Rainer Hampp Verlag, Augsburg, München 2017, 215 S., € 24.80